Please Excuse
MY BOUNDARIES

Kristy Jean

ALSO BY KRISTY JEAN

Decision Permission:
Five States of Support for Every Level of Decision Making

Please Excuse My Boundaries
Copyrighted © 2025 by Kristy Jean
SC ISBN: 9781645385899
Please Excuse My Boundaries
By Kristy Jean

Cover design by Dana Breunig

All Rights Reserved. Written permission must be secured from the publisher to use or reproduce any part of this book, except for brief quotations in critical reviews or articles.

For information, please contact:

Ten16 Press, an imprint of Orange Hat Publishing
www.orangehatpublishing.com
Wauwatosa, WI

This book is a work of personal reflection and memory. All descriptions in the work are from the author's recollection and point of view. The author has made every attempt to convey facts accurately. In some cases, names, places, details, and other information has been changed to protect privacy of individuals and to further narrative flow.

For those who have honored my boundaries,
you have been my foundation.

For those who have tested my boundaries,
you have been my lesson.

…but mostly per la mia famiglia.

Contents

Preface   I

PLEASE

"Puttana" Means *Whore* in Italian	1
Divorce Theater	11
Popcorn and Air Jordans	14
Tradition, Dammit	19
Teachers are Fucking Amazing	23
Smile for Jesus!	28
Only Dicks Allowed	34
"C" is for Christian	43
Dookie	47
Bros before Hos	52
Most Vulnerable Player	63
Cinderella and the Glass Ceiling	70
Souvenirs of Womanhood	77
Taunting Richard	85
This is a Man's World	91
Working Girl	103
Catholic Kids for Sale!	106
Oh, Mickey, You're So Fine	109
Dear Asshole	112
Bigger and Better Things	118

EXCUSE

Shit Sitting	125
Buzzed Betty	131
Badass Brains	139
I'm Not Your Mommy	147
Be Still, Dammit	160

Delayed Departure	163
Get Your Ass Moving	168
You Have a Pattern	175
God's Vision Statement	180
Labor Pains	195
Baby Mama	201
A Million Reasons	208
A New Adventure	216
When the World Shut Down	220
Blending	223

MY BOUNDARIES

Dear Diary	229
Dear Christian	235
Dear Professional	237
Dear Friend	244
Dear Daughter	250
Dear Mama/KJ/Kristy Jean	256
Dear Wife	265
Dear Femininity	271
Dear Self	278
Acknowledgments	292
About the Author	296

Preface

The Giving Tree, written by Shel Silverstein, is a story cherished by many all over the world. And I, too, adored this book for over three decades of my life. I adored it right up until the point when I had survived enough therapy, meditation, and journaling to realize that my warped interpretation of this book—*the book that captured my heart for so long*—had literally captured *me*, urging along my naïve pursuit of a life I never truly wanted.

And a little less than a decade ago, at a time when I was still blissfully ignorant to this future revelation, I tattooed its most repeated phrase in one of the least discreet places on my body—my forearm. And like a "good" mother, I even requested that my sons' birthstones of diamond and emerald symbolically shade the Silverstein-esque, whimsical leaves that created the "dot-dot-dot" ellipsis *I* added for dramatic effect. That little ellipsis of leaves led right up to those five little words that make up the book's most notorious and, what I now consider to be, its most *damning* phrase:

"...And the tree was happy."

For anyone whose childhood wasn't influenced by this brilliant book, *The Giving Tree* is a classic piece of children's literature. Like all great children's books, *The Giving Tree* has transfixed audiences of all ages with its layers of symbolism and theme. It has grown in popularity since its publishing in 1964, and, more often than not, *women* have proudly visualized themselves as the *tree* in the story. In summary, it goes something like this:

- The narrator begins, "Once there was a tree, and she loved a little boy."
- The boy loves the tree.
- The boy communicates need after need... *after need after need.*
- The tree literally gives her body for him—*her apples, her shade, her limbs*—and asks for nothing in return.
- Says the narrator, "And the tree was happy."
- As the boy grows, he wants more in life, so he comes and goes, but only after taking from the tree. The tree tells the boy to chop her down so that he can build a boat, skip town, and leave her again.
- Narrator adds, "And the tree was happy... *but not really.*"
- The boy returns in his final years of old age, hoping for a place to sit, and, you guessed it, she offers him her rotting, decaying stump so that he can take a load off after his *strenuous* life of adventurous experiences.
- "And the tree was happy."
- The end.

Did this to-the-point summary ruin the interpretation you lovingly remember? In the words of Demi Lovato, *"Sorry, not sorry,"* for re-interpreting *The Giving Tree* for you too. Because if anyone should feel frustrated, it's me. I'm the one who proudly tattooed that freaking phrase **boldly** onto my forearm for the world to see. Fuck. Me.

I was so incredibly eager to become the sacrificial tree as a woman, daughter, wife, and mom, that I had this phrase *permanently etched* into my skin, similarly to the tree who allowed the boy to scar *her* with a heart and the initials of his new girlfriend. Apparently, I wanted to proudly display my *own* commitment to gradually bleeding myself dry so that I, too, could one day become a withered, rotting remnant of what I once was! And that's the exact path I *was* paving for myself. But not anymore, and never again.

Later in life, as I re-examined the interactions between the tree and the boy, my romanticized view of their relationship began to fade away, and something more *sinister* became apparent. One of the first requests that the boy makes is to ask the tree for money so that he can buy things and have fun (*my words, not Shel's*). The tree, heartbroken to disappoint him with the truth that she has no money, offers apples from her limbs so that he might sell them in the city to earn money. Then, in our budding little narcissist's teen years, he begins a romantic relationship. We infer this based on the illustration of two people snuggled up at the base of the tree next to the narrator's words: "And the boy grew older." This is when we learn that the boy has carved a heart and the new couple's initials into the tree's trunk, just above the place where he *originally* carved his love for the tree herself. He permanently scarred her with two truths: 1. She has lost priority placement with the boy, and 2. She permitted him to put *his* wants before *her* needs—just as I etched that same truth about myself, and what I was willing to allow others to take from me, into my own arm.

Silverstein is known for his minimalist but symbolic illustrations. That's why I think it's important to know that throughout this entire text, the tree is illustrated from the lower portion of the trunk, never possessing a face. We can't read her facial expressions to know how she's actually feeling, so all we have to go off of are the words of the narrator telling us that she's always happy. I do find it interesting, though, that the boy is *always* illustrated with a face throughout the book, and other than those few pages of his childhood, no matter how much he takes and no matter how many adventures he goes on to get away, his face always displays the same, disappointed *grimace*. Two beings in a relationship, only one with a face; one with a lack of fulfillment always drawn on his and the other whose faceless feelings are always expressed by someone else (*narrator*). I can't help but read *way* into that artistic decision in his drawings.

These illustrations require the reader to give more attention to Silverstein's selection of *words*. I've found this approach challenges me to also read more deeply into the words he selects and the punctuation he chooses. Like that constant phrase the narrator repeats, "And the tree was happy." It's written with no exclamation point at the end, which leads me to believe that she *wasn't* actually happy. She wasn't happy, but she sure as hell felt like she had to *pretend* to be happy. And then, I can't help but read into that singular moment when the narrator communicated a *new* feeling that the tree had. This feeling contradicted the toxic positivity we were spoon-fed over and over. This time, the narrator tells us, "And the tree was happy... but not really..."

"*...but not really.*" I've been there before. It's like those moments when you have what society lovingly refers to as "Resting Bitch Face," and someone naïvely assumes you're pissed off. But all you can think is,

"Listen, jackass. Life is not always sunshine and rainbows, and I'm carrying more than my fair share in this world. So forgive me for taking a moment to *not* give two shits what people think of me OR my face right now. You don't like my face? Look away."

But what do we do instead when we sense disapproval of our RBF (*especially as women*)? We plaster on a fake smile, bring our voice up an octave, assuring everyone,

"I'm fine! Everything is fine! And oops—sorry you had to see me existing in my most natural state; I'll go back to pretending so that I can make this situation more comfortable for *you*."

We use exclamation points and a fake smile—*both of which Silverstein never even allotted the tree*. Like our moments of RBF, the tree *wasn't* happy. She, too, was feeding into a patriarchal society, staying in her "place," giving all of her support and listening, *always listening*, to figure out how she could *fix* the boy's problems for him. Sound familiar?

While we're on the topic, I find it interesting that we call a woman at *rest*... a *bitch*. Apparently, in those rare moments when she isn't running around, giving to everyone with a smile on her face, then she must be a bitch, right? What if we just cut that demeaning word out and just called it her "Resting Face?" Or better yet, WAR—*"Woman At Rest."* Because society needs to realize, it's better to experience a woman with a *resting* bitch face than a woman with a *fighting* bitch face (or a *Mama Bear* bitch face), because then you will have an actual <u>WAR</u> on your hands!

The boy gradually grew into a man, communicating that now he wanted a house, a wife, children, and (*years later*) a boat to help him sail far away to continue fulfilling his own desires in his final years of life. Never asking how she's doing or what she wants, and never showing even the slightest sign of gratitude by sharing stories of his adventures. He remained ignorant to the truth that he was living the life of his dreams *because* of her sacrifices. He was living his own version of freedom while she was rooted to the ground, never able to explore a life of her own.

Finally, after gallivanting around the globe, the "boy" makes his last return, now in his final years of old age, and what does our stump of a tree (*who has quite literally given every part of her existence*) say to this greedy little shit? The first statement out of her mouth, before he can even make another request of her to make himself happy, is an *apology*:

"'I am sorry, Boy... but I have nothing left to give you...'"

She continues with this apologetic tone as she lists all of the ways she once helped him but no longer can—apples, branches, trunk—all gone now (because of *him*). And yet her apologies continue:

"'I am sorry,' sighed the tree."

"'I wish that I could give you something... but I have nothing left. I am just an old stump. I am sorry...'"

That's right. He has actually cut her down limb by limb and she's *still* exhausting herself as she desperately tries to serve *him* with the cold, decaying remnants of what she once was (*and could have been*) if she hadn't willingly sacrificed everything for the "Boy who Cried *Entitled*."

Predictably, by this point in the story, he has only returned because he "needs" something, so of course he asks for more as he makes his final request—*a seat to rest upon*—surely *exhausted* from a lifetime of indulgence. He takes from her one last time, as he rests his bony, elderly, self-righteous ass on her rotting, regretful, barren stump.

I highlight these highly patriarchal examples NOT because I hate Shel Silverstein—I'm actually in love with his poetry, still in love with this book, and I value the infamously positive impact he continues to have on readers and writers alike, including my own interest in writing.

Only recently have I realized, though, just how much *our* popular interpretation of *his* story sucked the life out of any progress we've made as women. As a matter of fact, I didn't realize it until I began writing this book, uncovering the truths of my past *(and present)* that I was oblivious to. I will clarify here that though the tree is referred to as "she," after I conducted a little *(very little... one Google search, in fact)* research, I came to find that in 1978, when interviewed by The New York Times, Silverstein himself clarified that he had no specific intention or symbolic roles in mind when he wrote the text the way he did, other than to say, "It's just a relationship between two people; one *gives* and the other *takes*."

Just as we read into Rod Serling's episodes of *The Twilight Zone*, taking note of his not-so-subtle statements about our society in each allegory he carefully crafted, we absorb *The Giving Tree* in much the same way. However, Silverstein didn't spend the final page of his book sharing a synopsis with direct opinions and forewarnings about the issues of our society as Serling so ominously provided at the close of his episodes. Instead, Silverstein left it to us, the readers, to make connections to our own relationships, life, and humanity in general based on this *seemingly* simple, personified story he penned for us.

    I don't hate *The Giving Tree* anymore, because I've come to understand why I *initially* was so desperate to hate it. As I engaged in my own wellness work, I realized that I actually hate the way we as women naïvely, *and a wee bit masochistically,* presume that the character taking the literal beating in sacrifice for another is always, ALWAYS presumed to be the model of a virtuous *woman*. And even more specifically, based on her interactions with the boy, we presume she represents the pinnacle of martyrdom—*a mother.* We can blame society and the patriarchy all we want—and let's do that for a moment... Ah, that feels good... *I have visions of comfy sweats, pitchforks and torches, and waterproof mascara...* But then, let's remember that what we permit we *promote*, and it's up to us to use our voices to break down those stereotypes and generalizations. And yet, what do we as women continue to hone in on? We focus on the sacrificial lamb in this literary relationship, so by the time we read the final, "And the tree was happy," with tears in our eyes, we have unknowingly determined that the *tree* is the character we aspire to be! *(or, minimally, aspire others to perceive us to be...)*

    Let's be real. The simplicity of the storyline and the romantic essence of it all are the exact reasons why EVERY woman who sees my tattoo gets those gushy eyes and says, "I **LOVE** that book!" *(Just like I did when I requested that the 22-year-old, aspiring gym teacher/current tattoo artist brand it onto my arm.)* Just like everything from *The Little Mermaid* to *Fifty Shades of Gray* makes us, as women, fall in love with the idea of giving so much of ourselves to a person *(voice... virginity... you decide which movie is which...)* that there is no longer a "me" and a "you"—there is only "*us*." What. A Crock. Of. Shit.

Maybe it's the juxtaposition of the two characters—we simply don't see ourselves as the boy since he was referred to as "boy" throughout the story, so we choose the tree by default? If that's the case, what would happen if we imagined the tree with *male* pronouns? Following this same sequence of symbolism, what if the tree was a *father*? Can we even imagine it? Is it too far a cry for us to believe that the father would willingly sacrifice every apple, limb, and his very life for the boy? Or is it that we are just so damn eager to see *ourselves* that way that we don't want to hold space for the dad to step into that role?

When were we sold this idea of happiness? What made us believe that completely sacrificing our lives for others *(our significant others, our parents, our friends, our children, complete strangers, a company's bottom line...)* was such a noble cause that our own needs should just *poof* vanish? The generic answer always lies in pointing to childhood—we were given baby dolls instead of building blocks or Easy Bake Ovens instead of Etch-A-Sketches. And there's a lot of research to back up that idea, but I wasn't exactly your typical "girly girl" growing up. I was bucking the superficial stereotypes of bonnets and bows as soon as I could talk. My boundaries were *instinctual* at that time in my life, and it's only now that I realize how pure and priceless those instincts were.

So then I guess I have to blame it on my teens, twenties, and a good portion of my thirties. Decades of life I spent 100% brainwashed on the idea that not only should I *want* to be the tree, but that there was something wrong with me if I *didn't* want to be the tree. I don't believe this lie anymore, but I sure as hell was sold down that river for a large portion of my life.

I think a large part of envisioning ourselves as the tree connects with the sense of *selflessness* that the tree embodies. Each of us wants to be known as someone who is giving, caring, and supportive even to the point that she is willing to tell the person she loves *(friend, family, spouse, child...)* to *please* cut her down so that she can give *them* happiness by fully giving up her own. It's the story of self-sacrifice to the worst degree, and yet rather than interpreting it as an *abusive* relationship, we *applaud* the tree for giving away every ounce of her energy to one singular goal—fixing things for a man.

For argument's sake, let's imagine that she *is* a mom, and the boy *is* her son. Though I agree that the decision to have children requires that parents set healthy boundaries so that the child does not feel responsibility to care for, emotionally regulate, nor be their parent's best friend, I do expect that children learn respect and appreciation for others, especially their elders. I expect my own children to be mindful of others, aware that life is not your self-serving opportunity to *take, take, take*. A quality life is one lived in consideration of, and care for, fellow human beings. So even if the tree is a mom, by not setting healthy boundaries that enable *her* to live a fulfilled life nor setting boundaries so that her *son* doesn't turn into a complete asshole, this is still a damaged, unhealthy relationship that every parent should avoid mimicking.

I see that truth now, but my definition of parenting was quite opposite when my children were young. I distinctly remember my mindset when I decided to tattoo that loaded phrase onto my arm. I wanted it to be a daily, symbolic reminder that all I needed in life was my two sons. I wanted to be the mom who lived *for* her kids—a mom who quite literally *bled* to prove that her kids were the *only* priority in her life. I can see now that I was undoubtedly a shell of my most authentic self, able to believe the maternal lie that society spoon-fed me. I was so blinded by the need to prove myself as a mom that I completely ignored that there was a *"me"* before I ever became a *"mom."* And since I was gradually losing her even *before* having kids, she didn't stand a chance of surviving *after* I had kids. I've found this in so much of my work and engagement with fellow moms. We have our own version of the Biblical BC and AD—*Before Children* and *After Delivery*. And once that AD hits, forget about it. We experience a sort of amnesia, forgetting the truth that the original, truest version of ourselves was the one who inspired this whole "having children" idea in the first place! I didn't just let her go in my *parenting*, though. My patterns gradually revealed themselves, as I came to realize that I left "me" out of the majority of my relationships. I gladly molded myself to the boundaries of others, never identifying, *let alone voicing*, boundaries of my own.

I look around, and I see so many women I admire. Women who have left emotionally and/or physically abusive relationships or spoken back to injustice and discrimination. Women who have decided to put their foot down with their own kids when those brats, I mean *children*, start acting like the world revolves around *them*. Women who have clearly communicated boundaries that were once deemed taboo or unacceptable for a woman to establish in the past. Boundaries like:

"No, I don't want to have kids."

"I've decided that I'm going to start my *own* business."

"I don't want to have sex tonight, *and* I love you."

The times have changed, and this classic text can come right with them.

I've found my way back to loving that book again—just in a much different way for a much different reason. I'm grateful for Shel's insightful challenge to us as readers to make sense of these relationship dynamics for ourselves. And so, inspired by the author, I've considered a few revisions to the original telling. I would begin by taking *back* the tree *before* she completely loses her sense of self. I would let the story unfold as it does, *as life does*. She would lose her apples, a few limbs, and even let the boy carve into her, scarring her trunk. I'm on board with the tree learning that life's lessons are often hard-earned through a healthy mix of well-intentioned effort, sitting in the challenging aftermath of your decisions, and, eventually, reflecting on your needs. Those experiences track with the way we as humans learn our own lessons too.

But then, I would pump the brakes around three-quarters of the way through the book when, for the first and *only* time, the narrator follows up "And the tree was happy" with that standout phrase: "*...but not really.*"

This is that turning point moment many of us only see in hindsight in our own lives. That moment when we had the choice to listen to our own inner voice and set a boundary *or* ignore her completely and go all in on living *for* someone else. For the tree, that added phrase tells me that this is *her* moment—right then, she has become aware that this *isn't* the life she was meant to live. She has this glimmer of realization that makes us hope that she'll change course and listen to her own voice. But instead, as is so often the case for many of us, she dismisses her instinct the very next time she sees the boy (*now a man*) as he steps back into her life because, once again, he wants more from her. It's at that moment when I would write an alternative ending *before* she sacrifices her entire life for that greedy little bastard.

My first rewrite? The tree wouldn't dismiss her moment of opportunity. Instead, she would make use of all that quiet time while his ass was traveling the world. She would ponder her current reality, realizing her penchant for enabling others. And then, she'd prepare to face the fear, guilt, shame, doubt, and any other self-destructive emotion that was keeping her from living her most authentic tree-life so that when he returned, she'd be ready.

She'd begin by using her *own* branches to erect a fence, *a boundary if you will,* around herself with a gate that only *she* could control from the inside. And when that ungrateful little asshole came back asking for more, she would greet him at the gate, confirm for herself that, once again, he was only there to ask for more, and then finally say "No" to his bogus request, *literally* letting the front gate hit him in the ass on his way out.

But before we imagine all the ways we could reclaim *The Giving Tree* into a more modern, female-empowered interpretation—*still not sure how "bra burning" would translate for a tree, seems like a fire hazard*—I must be clear about the rationale for my desire to give her an *authentic*, emotional makeover. Though I'm still waiting for Jesus to ride down on a cloud from Heaven and tell me my *exact* purpose on this Earth, I do know for *damn sure* that he did not intend for me, or anyone else, to give our entire God-given life in complete sacrifice for other human beings, void of our own needs. For God's sake (*literally*), He let Jesus spend 33 years on this Earth questioning, teaching, and challenging authority before He made *His* ultimate sacrifice... on a tree... coincidence?

My drastically brief summary of the New Testament in The Bible would go something like this:

Jesus sacrificed himself so that *we* wouldn't have to. Treat others the way you want to be treated, stop settling for less and guilt-tripping yourself—Jesus took all of that shit away on the cross. Now go tell people about it, and eat tasty food.

Okay, I took my license as an author a little too far on the food part, but there were fish and loaves and wine... and I'm a foodie—so kill me! *Just not like that tree...*

Suffice it to say, Jesus was the sacrifice, not us. So if God didn't make me in His image to *be* the sacrifice, then why do I still innately pursue a life lived like that damn, boundary-less tree? Maybe she didn't have any tree friends around to tell her that she was being taken advantage of. Maybe her roots kept her so deeply anchored in the ground that it felt like she was stuck and didn't have a choice. Or maybe she was raised, as a young sapling, to believe that she was *worthless* and that if someone found her lonely ass worthy, she'd better give up all that she has and run with it, grateful that *someone* wants her. Regardless of the *why* behind her actions, her story is a reminder that we all have a choice. As I shared in my book, *Decision Permission: Five States of Support for Every Level of Decision Making*, "No choice is still a choice." So, *unlike* the tree, how can we give ourselves permission to say "No" when our boundaries have been crossed? How can we identify struggles in our past, change course, and then establish boundaries that enable us to live lives that are truly our own?

THAT is why I wrote this book. I write, as the irreplaceable Joan Didion once said, "to remember what it is to be me" and to encourage you to remember, or uncover, what it is to be *you*. To remember what it is to be me is to revisit my past to understand where, when, and how I grew to believe that sacrificing the first few decades of my life by pleasing and fixing everything for others, *especially men*, was the best use of this blessing of life that God gave me. Because then, and only then, can I question my present and better understand who I am, what I need, and where *my* boundaries lie. Sure, those five little words, "*...And the tree was happy,*" are still visible every day of my life, but I have decided to redefine what those five little words mean to me. I no longer interpret that phrase to mean that, like the tree, I should happily sacrifice every part of myself, leaving nothing left to fulfill my own purpose in life. Instead, I see them as an ironic statement. Let's be real, if the tree was *actually* happy, would Silverstein have needed to state it over and over again? I used to hear that phrase, "And the tree was happy," as the echoing of a lovely sentiment of genuine care for someone you love, but now I hear it as a cold, robotic reply:

"And the tree was happy."

"And the tree was happy."

In other words:

"*She's fine.*"

"*She's fine.*"

I took these emotions that the narrator told us *about* the tree for face value since Silverstein never gave her the opportunity to share them *herself.* But I think Shel actually meant for that character to be a self-deprecating, self-loathing person who felt her only purpose in life rested in giving others what they wanted. A person who sacrificed everything so that *others* could live a fulfilling life. A life she never knew she, too, innately had the freedom to live. Just because we aren't sure *who* we are and *what* we need, that does NOT mean, then, that we should settle by feeding others' perceptions of who *they* are and what *they* need. This keeps us from uncovering our own dreams, and if we defer them too long, we're in danger of forgetting the value of our very existence. The tree is not a symbol to emulate; the tree is a **wake-up call**.

Maybe you're a sacrificing grandma, mom, daughter, sister, aunt, girlfriend, wife, and/or friend who gives until it hurts, never communicating your own needs. Maybe you're a man who experiences life in the same ways or wants to understand the experiences of the women in your life. Maybe you find yourself in relationships that never feel fully reciprocated. Or maybe you can actually remember deep down when there was a time in your life that you just *knew* what you wanted, but her voice has become so small that it feels like she's nearly disappeared at this point.

I hear you. I've been you. And I'm still doing the work to ensure that my roots never settle in so deeply that I allow myself to believe that I don't have the power to change my words, my situation, and my life ever again. So now, I am my own version of *The Giving Tree*. I'm living my life to honor her sacrifice by doing everything in my power to ensure that my daughter, fellow women, and I feel empowered to make ourselves a priority and live life on our own terms that we confidently communicate with those we love. Because I don't know about you, but I have a *wealth* of kind and caring men in my life who are simply looking for me to communicate my needs, and that's taken a long time for me to fully understand. It's *my* responsibility to clarify *my* boundaries for them so that they understand what support looks like, sounds like, and feels like for *me*. And I can only hope that showing up in this way empowers my sons, husband, and the other wonderful men in my life to feel just as confident in communicating their *own* boundaries along the way.

One day, when I'm long gone, I confidently believe that people will say, *"...And she was happy!"* And they'll mean it.

Not because I tried to *prove it* to anyone and not because I tried to fix anything *for* anyone. They'll mean it because it will be impossible *not* to believe that it's true when they hear my words and see my actions. My hope for you, and myself, is that the people closest to us respect *and* bear witness to the boundaries we've set as we pursue the lives we were always meant to live.

With a few extra pages to the story, I'd like to imagine the narrator telling us this was all a *dream*—that the tree awoke just after letting the boy carve the initials of his budding relationship into her, suddenly aware of the path her life was taking. The narrator would share,

"The tree awoke to realize that, though she wasn't *really* happy, she did have the *choice* to be happy. At that moment, she fully understood her role. She wouldn't be known as *The Giving Tree* because she gave to a little boy until she had nothing left to give. She would be known as *The Giving Tree* because she *redefined* what it meant to give. She would prove to the boy, herself, and the world that giving to others is only a part of the story, because you can't live a truly fulfilled life until you finally learn how to give to *yourself*."

Please

"Puttana" Means *Whore* in Italian

I am the product of two parents whose intentions were to raise me in the exact *opposite* way that their stern, German parents raised them. My dad's WWII veteran father and mother were first-generation Americans fighting against the Nazis, ironically, the country their family had recently emigrated *from*. So I'm sure it comes as no surprise that my grandfather expected his son to suffer before he could ever hope to earn Daddy's love. My dad has a collection of passive-aggressive parental statements in his core memories, but the most prominent one was, "I will only attend your football games if you make varsity." His dad never attended a single game. And now I know why my own father never *missed* a single one of mine.

My mom's mother, a second-generation American of the same origin country as my paternal grandparents, was best known for what she *didn't* say. "I love you" and "I'm proud of you" weren't in her vocabulary—not for her own children, nor her children's children. Sure, it was implied, baked into the hours she spent on cakes, cookies, and meals that she provided for you, but it was up to *you* to read between the lines. These three of my four grandparents were, also, a product of their own upbringing, so I sometimes wonder if they shared that same perspective that *they* raised *their* children in the exact *opposite* way of their *own* parents...

Fast-forward through my dad *voluntarily* signing up for his tour of duty during the Vietnam War. Yes, voluntarily. Apparently, when given the choice between turning 18 and staying at home with his parents, the final of four to leave the nest, *or* voluntarily enlisting in a universally unpopular conflict that had been raging since the very year he was born, my dad felt that the latter held more hope. I've recently wondered if he felt that he was born into *two* wars in 1955— in one, he couldn't even save himself, and in the other, he could save the lives of others with the *hope* of saving himself. Did he really have a choice?

Fast-forward through my dad continuing to find ways to serve others by setting his eyes on the FBI. This began with a trip far south of his Midwestern roots to Texas for initial testing. Texas was a leap in the exact opposite direction of his birth-state of Wisconsin. They say, "You can never go home again" after you leave, but what do you call that same place if it never *felt* like home? The results of his testing were destined to become inconsequential, as it turns out. Though he eventually did end up pursuing a career in this same vein of public service as a police officer and security for the U.S. Marshals, he never ended up leaving Wisconsin, because he was about to meet his one and only reason to never have to run again. A person who would finally make the place he was born feel like home.

Fast-forward to my parents meeting at a party in 1983 when they were *supposed* to have been introduced to each other years before. Fast-forward to my mom learning who she was and what she needed, making sure this new man in her life knew that *she was doing fine on her own, thank you very much*, and if he wanted to join her in this journey, he would have to bring something to her life that she couldn't get on her own. *(Ex-boyfriends have a way of hardening your heart and diminishing your willingness to settle for less.)* Fast forward to the moment my dad will still replay in his mind and his stories even now, over forty years later: "At our first date, I saw how the candlelight was shining in her eyes, and I just knew..." Six weeks later, they were engaged. He was finally home. And *less* than nine months after they said, "I do," they brought *me* home.

They tell me that I was born a month early because my mom experienced toxemia in her pregnancy... I'd call bullshit except that my mom was raised Roman Catholic and had a deeply irrational fear that sperm could *jump* from toilet seats. Literally. One of the many irrational fears that her mother planted in her head and that *she* would eventually plant into *mine*. If jumping sperm wasn't enough to scare her into a youth of abstinence, then I'm sure sitting through mass, worrying that at any moment, oversized, Catholic Jesus might step down from that crucifix and chastise her was enough to keep her legs closed. Possibly the only thing more frightening than stigmata Jesus giving you a glare was the guilt trip one experienced at Sunday mass when looking into the eyes of the "holier-than-though" parishioners, staring judgmentally from the pews that their family had "paid for" for several generations now. I imagine my mom having nightmares of Jesus's face as he condemned her, "Puttana! Puttana! Puttana!" "Puttana" means *whore* in Italian. Laying on the Italian Catholic guilt (*and red sauce*) in thick layers was a blessing bestowed upon all of us from her father's Calabrese side of the family. Suffice it to say, that when she says she *didn't* get knocked up until her honeymoon, I believe her.

Somehow, in God's unique plan, three demanding German dictators and one complacent Italian, more devout to calling bingo than the call to worship, gave way to a couple who were embracing their beautiful marriage and the birth of their one and only baby girl. From the day I was born, it would always be the three of us. And when Dad was off fighting the bad guys, it was Mom and me. The only parenting style that my mom had in common with her mom was the fact that she stayed at home to raise me.

Every other aspect—*quality time, intentional teaching, and love*—seemed the polar opposite of my mom's account of her own childhood. Grandma spanked my mom with whatever kitchen utensil was handy when she was naughty; my mom barely gave me a time-out. Except that one time when I *lied*... nothing affirms that ninth Commandment more than Ivory soap gradually foaming and melting into your taste buds. I learned my lesson that day, and I'll be damned if lying isn't *still*, to this day, a major cardinal sin in my mind.

Grandma never told my mom that she loved her; my mom told me, showed me, and never gave me a reason to doubt her love for me. Grandma kept her distance (*literally and figuratively*) from my mom as her daughter grew older; my teen years were spent wondering if I could get a restraining order from my mother's smothering love. *Where are you going? Who will be there? How are you getting there? When will you be home?* As a mother myself, I can now look back and see that she was an engaged parent who didn't let me get away with shit, but back then, I filled my journals with the ways she pissed me off. To this day, we still have different definitions of how we like to receive and give love, but hours of individual (*and joint*) therapy, sharing our *real* feelings—*gloves off*—has made all the difference in learning how to love and respect each other.

In contrast to her relationship with her mom, my mom's father, my *Italian* papa, was the center of my mom's world. I don't know how she made room for my dad and me. We always came first, but she continues to have this awe for her father that seems so much bigger than the typical father-daughter bond. It's like there was a hole that her own mom should have filled in her life, so she invited her father's influence to grow two sizes bigger to fill *both* roles.

Right in step with my papa, my mom spoiled me like a princess. We have had some challenging talks around spoiling when it comes to my own kids (*her grandkids*), but it's also hard to set that boundary when I reflect on the sugar-coated glory I absorbed as a child of the 90s. As an only child, the spoiling showed up as endless praise and attention *(I walked on freaking water... with Jesus, of course.)*, but quite a bit of the spoiling also came in a very tangible form. Even with my dad working two to three jobs at a time, Mom taking on various jobs, and their many sacrifices to send me to Catholic school, my mom would find a way to get me the finer things in life—the things she never had growing up. Like those light-up Jordan high tops that we bought at JCPenney to prepare for another season of elementary, recreation league basketball. The high tops that, "Dad doesn't need to know about"—until I was running down the court with a big smile on my face and a "Thanks, Daddy!" after the game. The sport that instinctually became *my life*—you know, after that first game where I skipped the tip-off to run over and cower in my mom's lap.

Finances are quite a bit different now, but I still recognize the look he gives her when she's just purchased something that he knows isn't going to last. It's a blend of short-term frustration mixed with forty years' understanding that the benefits of this love far outweigh her retail-therapy tendencies. He's fought enough wars to know he doesn't stand a chance winning this one anyway! The greatest spoiling, though, the spoiling that would lay the foundation for who I would become, began in the way she was hell-bent to raise a strong, smart, independent young woman and then, later in life, *resent* me for it.

I grew up through the lens of a maternal matriarchy. My dad's parents had their own opinions about my mom, for whatever reason, and my mom about them, and so my dad chose the family he was collaboratively building rather than the one he was traumatically raised within. Maybe it was the way my dad's parents reminded my mom of her own mother in their cold, stereotypically German demeanor. Maybe it was the fact that no one was going to pull her away from her *own* father for the holidays. Or maybe it was the fact that at their wedding, my grandpa, father of the groom, was overheard in the bathroom remarking, "I give it three months." Yeah, maybe it was that last one...

Either way, their decision to step back from my dad's

side of the family directly influenced my childhood, as the foundation of my upbringing was solely developed within the traditions, customs, and values of my mom's side of the family. Though my maternal grandma was German with some family in the area, my Italian papa's side of the family dominated geographically—all living within one mile of each other—and vocally. (*Side note: I fully developed my family's knack for talking and gesturing with my hands so much so that, from a distance, you'd think I was signing the conversation for someone in need. If you're ever nearby when I get rolling, keep a safe distance. You've been warned.*)

In true family-comes-first style, when Papa married Grandma, his parents, *my great-grandparents*, moved out of the home where they raised their children, so that my papa could start his own family under the *same roof* that he was raised under. To bring mia familia even closer, Papa's sister, my auntie Dolly, moved in next door with *her* husband. And I'm not saying "next door" as in down the street. I mean literally—their front doors were no more than forty feet apart. And in the back, these siblings installed one of those old-school metal, cyclone fences between their backyards with a gate so that all of us cousins could easily come and go between homes. Italian household rules: You don't ring the doorbell—just walk in, mind the plastic on the furniture so that it doesn't get creased, and never, *ever* refuse food. Ever.

My cousins and I felt like we had it all when we were running between our grandparents' and our great-aunt and uncle's homes. We had complete freedom to play in one yard, run inside to the basement to look through the inventory of soda that was sure to be stocked, chug one that grabbed our eye, and then run across the yard to the *other* house's basement and find a different selection there! Personally, I was always on the hunt for RC Cola—a treat that was *never* going to be added to the grocery list in my own home. I'm telling you, a kitchen and second fridge in your basement is still an Italian sign that you've made it in this new world (*even if you never actually lived in the "old country"*).

The soda paled in comparison to the sweet treats my

grandma and great-aunt would notoriously stock. Grandma was a master baker, so you ran into her kitchen to steal a hot-out-of-the-oven cookie or still-warm muffin before she jokingly chased you out with a wooden spoon (the same spoon she *un*-jokingly spanked our parents with.) Auntie Dolly, on the other hand, was the one you went to for card playing and windmill cookies. I don't know if they still make these, but I keenly remember sitting at Auntie Dolly's table, munching away at those classic, store-bought windmill cookies after, unbeknownst to her, we had just slammed a Tab and Sun Drop in my grandma's basement. We knew no boundaries because we didn't need them—we had the safety of two homes, two yards, and a shit-ton of adults making sure we didn't run into the road. Back then, the only boundary we had from our adults was to make sure that if they yelled for us, we came running into sight immediately. But that's what cousins are for—listening for their own name *and* yours, because otherwise, you were both shit out of luck, and the fun was over. The adults didn't give a damn about sugar, because they knew we were running miles between those homes and around the block. Sitting on your ass was the enemy that our parents warned us against, not sugar.

I learned that being a part of this large, loud, Jesus-loving Italian family was a birthright that came with birth-*expectations*. First, be sure that you know that you're blessed—*always blessed*—to have this amazing family. Second, remember that Jesus blessed you with this family, oh, and also *DIED* for *you* so that *you* could have *this* family. Third, you had better always be there for your family, even in ways that sacrifice your own needs, because, well, that's the definition of *"family."* Fourth, you'd better get your ass to Grandma's house *(It was Grandma and Papa's, but we knew who ruled the roost.)* every Sunday for dinner, every holiday's eve, holiday itself, and, *especially* in comfy clothes on the day *after* said holiday to make sure that Grandma's leftovers are eaten up because *food* equals *love*. Just in case you forgot, no, you're not taking a to-go bag away from the holiday gathering—What are you, capatosta?! This was the time before Tupperware and

Ziploc were readily available, but even if they *were* around, there was no way Grandma was letting you walk out that door with the food she just *gave her life* to make for you. You wanted her food? Then you ate her leftovers right there in her home where she could watch you enjoy it—all while sitting at the head of the table, chain-smoking Marlboros and drinking a full pot of coffee before *Price is Right* came on, of course. Grandma needed *your* hunger to drive *you* back to *her* home, because, remember, food equals love, God dammit.

It truly was a blessing to be raised in this matriarchy on my mom's side, no matter how well it would have played on a reality show before reality shows were a thing. I can't tell you how hard I laugh with complete understanding every time I watch *My Big Fat Greek Wedding*, and no similarity rang more true than the moment when the mom instructs her daughter in the inner workings of marriage,

"Toula, the man is the *head* [of the household], but the woman is the *neck*, and she can *turn* the head any direction she wants.'"

That might be true in Greek families, but in my big, extended Italian family, the women were the head, neck, and *strong arm* of their households. Sure, there were some stereotypically traditional roles at play, don't get me wrong. Most of the women stayed home to raise their kids, and they were the first to do dishes at family holiday gatherings, but beyond those two, that's where mainstream America ended in our homes.

Grandma was a former JCPenney employee who spent her retirement pulling Marlboro 100s out of her cigarette purse (*envision an oversized coin purse*), solving crossword puzzles with incredible accuracy, crocheting, frequenting local bingo halls and cooking homemade meals that were so delicious that Papa would often comment, "Why would I go out to a restaurant when the food is so much better here?!" I was blessed to find a deeper connection with my grandma many years later when, in my twenties, I was able to visit on my own and just have personal time with the two of them. She was at a slower place in her life, and I was growing in my awareness of how precious it is to have your grandparents alive and *in* your life. We would later play cards, and I would hear her fantastic laugh, genuinely enjoying quality time together. I will always wonder why she didn't feel capable of being that version of herself much younger in her own life, but I am grateful that she raised women who imparted that lesson to me in my own youth.

While Grandma had several retirement activities, it seemed that the one she engaged with daily, often multiple times a day, was yelling at Papa for something she just *knew* he was doing wrong... two rooms away. Though her family was German, she was infamous for Italian cooking and yelling Italian expletives—"Stutacete, Gene!"

The meals and desserts Grandma prepared were nothing short of delicious, and since I grew up before the world went to hell and kids developed every allergy you can (*and can't*) imagine, my cousins and I benefited from her *homemade* birthday treats that we proudly brought to school for our classmates.

My papa was an Assistant Fire Chief with a fifth-grade education who spent his retirement much as he did on the fire department—connecting with as many people in the community as he could. Papa could always reassure himself of his notoriety throughout the city by frequenting Dunkin' Donuts and diners. After he stepped one foot in the door, he (*and our family*) came to expect that same welcome that he got everywhere he went: "Geno!!" Imagine that everywhere, and I mean *everywhere*, you went in your hometown, you were absolutely certain that someone would joyfully shout your name, so damn happy just to see your face. Papa ate that energy up, but he also dished it out. I saw how he looked people in the eye, shook their hand, and made time to listen—*better than he ever listened to Grandma at home!* He heard their stories, and he was the master of showing compassion even when he didn't know who the Hell they were or where he knew them from. He left people feeling seen and heard, and all it cost him was his time and patience. Come to think of it, I can see how I'm becoming a little more like him as I grow older—I can't remember shit, but I can talk my way into *and out of* most situations.

Papa gave a lot of his life to the Roma Lodge, our local Italian-American club, where he called bingo and notoriously uttered, "Uh-oh!" before dramatically calling the ball "N-35." This, alone, made him recognizable to most of the community. In this same vein of sketch comedy, Papa couldn't just take us grandkids to McDonald's for a traditional and "nutritional" Happy Meal; he had to inject some pageantry. Infamous as he was in bingo calling, he was even more infamous for his drive-thru orders where, to this day I can't comprehend why, he would inflect his voice and toss in a stutter here and there as he ordered, "W..w...w... one...H...h...h...aaaaaa....pppp....yyy... Mmmmm....meal." Needless to say, our fast food became incredibly *slow* food, and we would roll our eyes, shouting, "Papa! Stop!" Because no matter how hilarious we actually thought it was, we knew that we would soon slink down in our seats out of embarrassment when he pulled around and came face-to-face with the worker at window one who *always* had a confused look on their face. Papa didn't give a shit, though. He flashed his *uniquely* friendly smile, passed off the money, and closed his sketch comedy with a, "Th...th...thaaaaa...nnn...kkk..... Y...y...yooooou!!" He would drive away laughing his ass off as we slid back to an upright position, quickly reaching to see what toy was at the bottom of that red, cardboard box. Without ever cursing in front of me, I can now see that he lived his life with a "fuck it" approach, infusing joy into even the smallest moments that most people breeze right by.

Divorce Theater

Grandma and Papa's driveway was always meticulously clean, freshly hosed by Papa, in traditional old Italian man way... even when he *hadn't* just cut the grass. Walking up this driveway, your eyes would catch the seemingly impossible sheen on the concrete, but your ears would shift that attention to the bay window above your head as Grandma's volume and blood pressure were rising in response to something Papa did or didn't do. The panes on that bay window were always cranked open as far as they could go, and I've come to believe that this was for two reasons:

1. To release the billowing cigarette smoke

2. To ensure anyone who arrived could hear Grandma's yelling to gauge what level of pissed off she was in today

This was such a predictable experience that I remember imagining that going to Grandma and Papa's was like going to the *theater*. I envisioned both of them sitting around, casually drinking coffee, and enjoying conversation when, suddenly, they saw our family vehicles pulling up as we parked at the end of their pristine driveway where their cars were parked bumper to bumper, the keys undoubtedly sitting in the ignition. It would be at that moment, I envisioned, that they would spring into action, participating in all of the preparations of professional stage performers. Grandma would gargle salt water to ensure she enunciated her scream of "GEEEENEE!" just right, and Papa would grab a rag and oversized can of Pledge to set the scene that he was getting yelled at for (*once again*) abusing the oily product by not only polishing the wooden trim on the couches, but yellowing the white walls *behind them* in the process. I thought these two were a comedy duo, but in hindsight, I can see that they were two people who were raised with very different definitions of how to love and who, somehow, genuinely *needed* each other.

So this stern German woman and this goofy Italian man, both children of immigrants, somehow found one another, fell in love (which is *still* hard for me to believe based on the pageantry from my childhood), and were married. Papa proposed in his Buick on the graveled shoulder of the road, adjacent to the local rock quarry—now the lack of romance begins to make sense. As he would recount, their surprise engagement party was scheduled for that very evening, and now that he had delayed long enough, he had to get the proposal out as soon as possible. Because when Italians throw a party in your honor, you'd better be there on time (*10 minutes early*), and you'd better have a smile on your face, God dammit.

And when you're attending an Italian's party, you'd better make damn sure you make it there *with* a dish to pass; a dish that will be privately critiqued for having too much mayo or being too basic—*Really, just salt and pepper? Don't you know that Italians have our own salt and pepper?! They're called "basil" and "oregano"... such a disappointment.* And Heaven forbid you *don't* attend! They *will* notice, fiercely judge you behind your back, and passive-aggressively expect that you bring an *additional* antipasto (*with basil and oregano*) to the next gathering to atone for your sins. Unless they find out you were in an accident or the hospital, God forbid. Then they'll make the sign of the cross, prophesize that they "saw a sign today and knew something horrible was going to happen," and send over a homemade meal (partially just to teach you how food *should* taste).

It's so interesting to imagine what your grandparents were like when they were younger. It's nearly impossible for me to think about my grandparents being a young couple so in love that they wanted to get married, but it was *their* reality at that time in their lives and at that time in society. Maybe before their kids and grandkids came along, neither of them learned how to love themselves from within, let alone impart this wisdom to their offspring. Maybe that's why each of them sought and shared love in uniquely *external* ways—Grandma through cooking for her family and seeking the rush of a win at bingo, and Papa through his attention-seeking hobbies like calling bingo, greeting his adoring fans at every local diner, and faking a stutter at a fast-food drive-thru just to get a laugh out of his grandkids. They were raised long before phrases like "self-care" and "mindful parenting," so I like to imagine that they did the best with what they had—not knowing that it's through healing our *past* that we give our best to our *present*. It seems that's the gift that *my* generation has only begun to unwrap.

Popcorn and
Air Jordans

My grandparents went on to have four children—three girls and one boy. And each of them could not, to this day, be more different, which, I believe, was the most beautiful aspect of this matriarchy I was raised within. I learned very different and equally important lessons about personal identity at a young age by watching my mom, my aunts, and my uncle:
- Each person is going to have his/her own view on life. You can love it or hate it, but don't expect to change it.
- Women are strong, and when they have their minds set, that's that.
- Family comes first. Even if you're struggling. Even if you don't want to. Even if you're mad as hell at one or more of them, family comes first.
- When a war is brewing between siblings, throw a "20" in the machine and split the winnings.

Wisconsinites read that sentence and knew EXACTLY what I meant, but let me translate for everyone else—a "20" is a $20 bill, and a "machine" is one of those digital slot machines often found at casinos. Except *this* machine is still only a stone's throw away in any direction, because every bar on every corner has a minimum of three. Gambling is to my family (*with the exception of my frugal ass*) like board games are to others—they laugh, they become competitive, and when they win, *everyone* in the entire family is going to hear about it.

My mom, my aunts, and my uncle all have very different views on *who* my grandma and papa were and *why* they behaved the way that they did. I think this is true of all families when you lose a loved one "too soon," and I've realized that we each have different memories because each of us experienced a *very different* version of my grandparents. As a mom, I can now see why my grandma would have been very different in temperament and self-awareness as a stay-at-home mom who raised her *first* child versus her *last* child and then, to some extent, her *grandchildren*. Toward the end of her life, irony struck in a cruel way as her once delicious cooking became *salty*, but, with me, anyway, she became very *sweet*.

Papa was the exact opposite of my grandma in every way, but *wow*, did he love her fiercely. She could scream at him about the way he parked the car, and he would still turn on that Sinatra smile and move closer in an attempt to peck her cheek with a loving kiss (*and titty grab*) that she, as captured in many candid photos, would inevitably fight away from. He was a hopeless romantic who was at his happiest when his family filled his home, and he was obsessed with us, his grandkids—his legacy. He loved us so much that he took it in stride when we stole and snapped each of the cigarettes in his pack—our health-conscious, Millennial attempt to force him toward a healthier lifestyle after his first heart attack in his forties. Lacking even the slightest strict bone in his body, he responded by tousling our hair and sending us on our way. He loved us so much, in fact, that he quit smoking shortly thereafter, leading us to believe that our expensive shenanigans *were* effective.

This matriarchy that raised me, through my young lens,

was dominated by my grandma, my mom, and my aunt Terri. My mom and aunt Terri aren't too far apart in age, which offered the greatest blessing of my childhood as an only child—two cousins who were in every way, except legally, my brother and sister. Jimmy, Steph, and I were a trio. We were passed between our moms when we were young, as they both stayed at home and supported each other with childcare and everything else a family needs. My dad and my uncle Jim *(Terri's husband)* were equally my dad and second dad as much as my mom and aunt Terri were my mom and second mom. Both my dad and uncle Jim always held a minimum of two to three jobs at the same time. They were always on the lookout for side gigs and extra cash, and it always seemed that they were proud to do this kind of work, because they were keenly aware that their wives were doing equal (*if not more important*) work at home, raising us kids. My dad and uncle Jim are both strong, loyal, do-anything-for-their-family men. Those traits and many more have led them to willingly follow the leading ladies of this matriarchal family. Watching their contentment led me to understand that a happy marriage was one of balance—each person putting in effort and taking a step back according to the needs of the bigger picture. Later in life, I got engaged under the assumption that I was marrying someone like my dad and uncle Jim. Little did I know that I was actually entering the marriage not as the *female* in this scenario, but in the role of my dad and uncle Jim. And on top of that, I came to the unfortunate realization that, unlike the marriages I saw, my own efforts wouldn't be reciprocated, and my sacrifices would nearly swallow me whole.

    As I watch old family videos—now converted from VHS to DVD—I can't help but notice a family of strong, opinionated women supported by strong, loving men. Sometimes I feel like I grew up in a bubble, far from the patriarchy of stereotypes around the feebleness of women and their "place" in society. Sure, my mom stayed home to raise me until I was in kindergarten, but she was also active in her own interests—bowling leagues, drawing, puffy-painting sweatshirts (*all the rage in the 90s*), and once, only once, crafting the *ugliest* homemade wreaths out of tied yarn and wire hangers with Aunt Terri. They stuck to bowling after that.

I also watched Aunt Terri play softball and run around the yard playing with us. I saw my aunt Di (*Diane*), the youngest sister, crimping and curling her hair to go out with her friends for the night. She introduced me to the latest 90s hit songs, and she gave me the first perspective of what it meant to be cool. These women set the tone for who I wanted to be. Whether they realized it or not, back then, they were showing me that I had the right to learn about anything and everything in this life and that I, and only I, had the power to set boundaries around who and what I welcomed into my life. I can see that in hindsight now, but it would take me nearly four decades to truly *earn* those lessons for myself.

And like any kid with a great childhood, the bill for all of this spoiling has come later in life in hearing (*over and over again*) my mom's own version of the "up hills, both ways" story, but instead of being about her own childhood, hers is the story of raising me:

"And do you remember what we ate just to get by and send you to parochial school? There was one night your dad came home from working his third job of the day, and he found me eating popcorn for dinner. Popcorn! But that's all we had, and we made do so that you could have a great education. *(..and Jordans)* And your aunt Terri and I used to take the three of you kids (*my cousins and me*) to the Racine Zoo—back when it was *free*—and you know what we'd have for lunch? A Happy Meal. ONE Happy Meal. And then we'd split it between the three of you, because that's all we could afford at that time, and Aunt Terri and I just wouldn't eat."

As I reflect on stories, I've come to understand that the sacrifices we make as parents *for* our kids are a result of what *we* determine they need. Our chosen sacrifices aren't something we should hold over their heads as though they were responsible for those choices. I know this, and yet, I find myself following right in step as I, too, have my own version of that generational story. Maybe it's a right of passage—sure, I'll live with that excuse for today.

I am grateful for stories like these, though, because they provide an essential reminder of the connection between sacrifice and success. Ultimately, our parents could have treated us like shit and made the excuse that they also had a shitty childhood, passively allowing us to experience an existence we didn't ask for. Instead, our parents raised us in *spite* of what they experienced, wanting better and doing better for us. Each generation should be better off than the last, and I think only within my generation have we begun to view the American Dream as more complex—beyond financial wealth, and, instead, focused on *mental* health and happiness.

Kristy Jean

Tradition, Dammit

My grandma would direct us that "Christmas Eve dinner is at my house starting after church"—a church that she never went to because she was "busy preparing all of the food"... *52 Sundays out of the year*. When she set the time, it was final. There were no negotiations or compromises in an attempt to help the in-laws' side of the family "fit in." That didn't exist in this matriarchy. The time was final, and the guest list was final. My mom and her siblings all followed suit, which meant those of us who were born into *or married into* the family *also* followed suit. In our homes, beyond Grandma and Papa, my mom and aunt Terri also led the way. When they chose a date and time for all of us to make our traditional fall visit to Jerry Smith's Pumpkin Farm or where and when to get on the Fourth of July Parade route (*sidewalk in front of the jail, west side of the street, 4 a.m. to be exact*), our dads never questioned it.

That word "tradition" was always HUGE in my family and has since become a word that Mom and I say with a tinge of sarcasm in our voice, well aware that my blended family with four kids, three schools, two exes, and a partridge in a pair tree leave little room for the predictability of tradition that we once experienced. But even though there were so many of us, and I'm still not sure how we all fit into my grandparents' small basement with a drop ceiling that only the short, full-blooded Italians could clear without ducking, traditions seemed to make impossible things *possible*. I'm sure it had a lot to do with Italian superstition, Grandma's expectations, and/or everyone's eagerness to drink brandy slushes on Christmas Day, but no matter the rationale behind it, traditions kept us coming back, never ever questioning *why*.

We were all raised with a system of unspoken values that were only evident when you looked at the rules that the adults held us to. I'm sure every generation experiences this, but it's confusing as hell when you're a kid! As a kid, you don't realize that your grandparents are spoiling you rotten, but they didn't give *shit* to your parents when they were little. You think, "Wow, they must have been the coolest parents—letting us stay up late for sleepovers, giving us candy, and surprising us with gifts all the time!" Nope. Wrong. SO wrong. Those grandparents only went soft because they didn't have the incessant sound of whining and complaining around them anymore, *and* they can send those sugared-up grandkids back to their actual homes whenever they damn well please!

The best example of this unwritten code of rules was the way my cousins and I were expected to ask politely for anything we wanted at Grandma and Papa's. It was like we were in on that play that I assumed was happening around me, but now we were written in as characters, given our own script to follow, trying to get "off book" quickly to avoid that side-eyed glance from our moms. See, it was hammered into *our* parents as kids that they'd better have manners around *their* grandparents, and so *our* parents hammered it into us. But the hilarious contrast is that the grandparents always feigned *surprise* when the grandchildren show them this respect—confusing the grandchildren even more. Here's what I mean:

Step 1: You realize you want something at your grandparents' home.

Step 2: Ask politely—"Could I please have a glass of milk?"

Step 3: Grandparent replies, "Of course!"

Step 4: Be sure to ask one *more* time to show that you're being extra polite: "Are you sure?"

Step 5: Grandparents adamantly reassure you, "Yes! You *never* have to ask—just take what you want!"

Step 6: NEVER believe what they said in Step 5. It's a trap, because the minute you *don't* ask, your parents are going to hear something passive-aggressive like, "We raised you better than that, so I don't know why your children don't have those same manners," and then *you're* going to have to pay for *their* shitty childhood. Trust me—always ask!

Step 7: Before taking, say, "Thank you."

Return to Step 1 and repeat in all scenarios where you want to ask for something from your grandparents. *Except money.* Money requests require a script all their own:

Step 1: NEVER ask.

That's it! *Never* ask for the money that your grandparents earned working harder than you'll ever have to work. However, if money is offered *to* you, be prepared with this response:

Step 1: When it's offered, say, "No, thank you. You keep it."

Step 2: When it's offered a second time, say, "Are you sure?"

Step 3: When it's offered a third time, accept it saying, "Okay, thank you. I will use this to help pay for (*insert something rational that sounds like it will help you achieve something one day*)."

Step 4: Don't spend the money on crap; be sure it's a smart purchase like a calculator or a toothbrush. Better yet, put it in your *bank*—old people love to hear you saving for retirement at eight years old. Follow up in 48 hours or less, or, reminder, your parents *will* hear about it, to communicate *how* you used it and how amazingly helpful it was. Be specific. If it's your First Communion, graduation, or any other significant life event, this must be in writing, on a card, *mailed* to their home. (*Even if you plan to see them within those 48 hours.*)

This also works for non-monetary gifts as well, just substitute in the phrase "You really shouldn't have!" within Steps 1 and 2.

No family is perfect, and I'm grateful that mine never tried to hide that. We're still a group of misfits laughing at inappropriate times and ready to pour a fresh pair of "cement shoes" for anyone who pisses off someone in the family—even if we were pissed off first. We can be pissed at each other, but you have no right to cross MY (*fill in the family member's relationship to you*). I was blessed to have a childhood built around a sense of pride for self and family. I was given this wonderful foundation, so *how* did I fuck it up?

Teachers are Fucking Amazing

Some of my earliest and most vivid memories of my childhood are those of the public library. My mom would take me as often as I asked, and we would leave with the most impossible stack of books that she and I carefully picked from the shelves together. I left with a minimum of twenty picture books and/or VHS tapes (*90s child*) that piqued my interest, and my mom would check out her Danielle Steel and Mary Higgins Clark novels that she could rip through in 3-4 hours tops. I keenly remember that about my mom—she was a *reader*, and I wanted to be like her.

So there I was gobbling up the pictures in my book when, one day, the *words* began to leap from the pages in a way they hadn't before. I don't remember the first book I read or the first words I mastered, but I remember the *power* that I felt when I realized that I could read. Reading felt so personal, like I was given a license to access all of those amazing books in the library and nothing was off-limits. It was my first young sense of freedom, and I made the quick connection that all of my hard work learning words with my mom had now paid off in the form of this ability to read. My first young value was set: working hard pays off, if you're patient and persistent.

I attended two years of faith-based preschool before transitioning to a Catholic elementary school to attend kindergarten. Why *two* years of preschool, you ask? Oh, because I was an only child who sucked at playing with others, so my parents gave me an extra dose of social exposure to make sure I didn't turn into *that* kid when I started legitimate schooling.

It was in kindergarten that I first experienced my first adrenaline rush from speaking in front of others. Contrary to popular belief, I started life as a shy kid—the most you would get out of me in public was a whiny noise while I stared at my toes, waiting for the adults to move on with their conversations. So when I started kindergarten and my teacher gave me the opportunity to read in front of the class, I didn't know how the hell I was going to respond. But I did know that I was a confident reader, and with that skill in my pocket, it gave me the motivation to give this public speaking (*reading*) thing a try.

My teacher situated all of my classmates on the carpet, sharing that we would have a special reader today. When they realized it was their own classmate, I could see the surprise on their faces as I walked to the front of the classroom with *Amelia Bedelia* in hand. Then my teacher did something that all teachers know is a very powerful act of trust and support—she let me sit in *her* seat. And then I began, holding the book in a similar fashion to the way I had seen my teachers hold it before, trying to help my classmates see the pictures while I read the words. I'm not quite sure if I picked up on all of the comical puns that the *Amelia Bedelia* series is known for, but who the hell cared—I was *reading*, for my kindergarten class! That was a core memory in the making for a five-year-old who didn't know that she was building her own identity.

Now, while this was all sunshine and rainbows, I do have to admit that it simultaneously fed my overly competitive nature. That excitement to just plain read was also born out of my realization that I was the first student to be able to read to our class and that others weren't at the same place in their reading journeys as I was in mine. I was the only one in the teacher's chair, doing what only the *teacher* could do. I realized that the world had a boundary that I had just crossed, and it was not only okay with the adults and classmates around me, it was *celebrated*! I had the power to step into a role that was, up until this point in my life, only reserved for adults, and I was instantly hooked on a single focus—what *other* boundaries could I positively cross that would keep all of this positive praise coming?

In first and second grade, I continued on this path in reading by being one of a small group of students who earned the right to use the "reading kit" on the counter. I can't remember what criteria we had to meet to earn this privilege, but what I do remember is my sense of pride. Being part of this group meant that I could freely get up from my seat when *I* was ready, walk over to the reading kit, and select the next color of text and questions that *I* determined *I* was ready for.

It was at this time that I also began my love for sports—even though I only saw two seconds of game time on the court in my first basketball game before I ran to my mom and cried in her lap for the remaining 44 minutes and 58 seconds... For someone who was gaining confidence to speak in front of others, this visceral response was a huge WTF moment for my young brain. I walked on the court confidently, but as soon as I realized that the crowd had been watching me try something new (something I couldn't *talk* my way out of), I froze. Until I *fled*, of course, right into my mom's lap. Something within me—a voice, a feeling, my realization that I was nearly a foot shorter than some of my opponents—gave up on people-pleasing and responded by seeking my comfort zone. In that moment, I didn't give a shit what anyone thought—I needed my mom, and I needed her now. I was sent into survival mode by something my brain processed, and I was suddenly aware of fears I didn't know I had.

This situation does make me wonder why we're so quick to talk kids *out* of their fears, since their fears are so often *communication* about what they *need*. If we sugarcoat their fears or, worse, completely protect them *from* their fears, then they never have the opportunity to face them. And if they never face their fears, they never get the necessary opportunity to listen closely to what the fear is saying. That struggle, that challenge to look fear in the face and listen to it is the *only* way I've learned to realize why the voice behind it sounds so familiar. It's because the voice of fear is *your own*. When that reality hits, it hits hard. But that adversity is what helps kids realize that if their inner voices are going to talk shit, then they can use that same inner voice to talk right back to the fear and shut it down.

Eventually, I finally found my comfort zone on the court, but by then it was spring, and the change in seasons brought on another new sport—softball! And this time, I felt ready because my parents challenged me to face that fear with basketball. They didn't play this game of bullshit parenting like we see nowadays, where parents are trying to remove every obstacle from their kids' path and then act *so* surprised when their kids turn out to be assholes, entitled pricks, and/or depressed narcissists who feel like the world is always out to get them. Nope, not my parents. They supported me *through* the fear, and *that* is what instills intrinsic motivation and pride. *That* is what made me know, from within, that I was ready to take on a new sport.

Until I broke my pinky finger while playing this new sport, that is. In hindsight, it was a foreshadowing of many more injuries to come as my aggressive and competitive natures blended haphazardly with my natural clumsiness, creating a cluster fuck of athletic experiences. I'm not sure if the medical field would treat my injury the same way that my doctor did in 1994, but I had a cast that started at the very tips of all *five* of my fingers and ran all the way down to my elbow. To add insult to injury (*pun intended*), the pinky I broke was on my *left* hand. Have I mentioned that I'm *left*-handed? There I was, a lefty (*already outcast when it came to the universality of right-handed scissors*) with a giant cast on my left arm, making it impossible for me to have any dexterity at a developmental age when writing and penmanship are *essential* skills to practice. It sucked for so many reasons, but most of all because I was *good* at school, and now I worried how I could please my teacher when I couldn't even complete my work.

To my surprise, this second-grade teacher who was just getting to know me must have seen my disappointment, because she responded to my injury by deciding that *she (of all people)* would write *for* me. I have tears in my eyes recounting this beautiful moment when a teacher stepped in and stepped up in a powerful way to show me that I was seen and valued, even before she truly knew me. Thirty-three years later, and that seemingly small choice that she made still hits me to the core. It was a profoundly compassionate moment that I have carried with me all these years. Teachers are fucking amazing.

This was the 90s and Catholic school, so though she wrote for me, there was no way in H-E-double-hockey-sticks she was going to do the *thinking* for me. I shared *my* ideas and *my* thought process, but this kind-hearted woman made time to write for me *and* find other peers who would help as well. In this singular act, she communicated to me that what I had to say was so important that it was worth having my peers, or even my teacher herself, sit down to collect *my* thoughts.

Beyond that realization in the classroom, the idea was reinforced for me on the court and on the field that getting injuries while playing sports was just part of the deal when you're active. Sports taught me that there is no such thing as "perfect," and if you struggle or fail, that just means you need to reflect and keep practicing. My teachers and coaches helped me find ways to honor *both* parts of myself—the academic and the athlete. Again, I was shown that I could follow my own path and that there could be a balance between pleasing others and making myself happy.

Smile for Jesus!

If you are, or have ever been, Catholic, there's no surprise what BIG event takes place in every little Catholic boy and girl's second-grade year. I'm, of course, talking about my first, memorable indoctrination into Catholicism: First Communion. It's like a girl or boy's first taste of his/her eventual (*and expected*) wedding day. As a girl, there were months spent shopping for the perfect, overpriced white dress with matching veil. Invitations were carefully selected by proud mothers who thought aloud, to no one in particular, as they selected invitations that were just right:

"Which one says 'I love Jesus' more? The one with the cross *alone*, or the one with the traditionally Catholic crucifix with Jesus' body hanging on the cross?"

Spoiler alert—she's going to go with the cross because it's a tad less morbid. However, she will make sure the traditional gift of a sterling silver necklace is a *crucifix*, because every good little Communicant needs a crucifix swinging close to their hearts. Besides, the crucifix reassures everyone who sees it that you, too, are signing up to carry your own cross—*Catholic guilt.*

The miniature brides and grooms experience several other similarities to their future nuptials, the most prominent being the big church ceremony with your priest, family, and close friends there to witness and support this life-altering sacrament.

On my first of *two* wedding days, decades later, I had something old, something new, something borrowed, and something blue. As an only child making my First Communion, I was a "one-and-done." I didn't have hand-me-downs to receive, and there would be no one to pass them along to, so there was no *old (or blue for that matter)*, but there was a *lot* of new—lacy white gloves, a shiny crucifix necklace, white patent leather shoes, and a crisp, gilded Bible (unlikely to be opened—*I was Catholic, after all*).

And just like your future wedding day, there is always an extravagant reception held after your Holy Communion. Ironically, the opulent Italian lodge where my papa was a member would not only be the venue for my First Communion reception, it would also be the exact same location as my *wedding* reception. Because nothing says big Italian family like supporting the lodge where your papa is already paying dues—in both money *and* bingo calling. Not to mention, their food is freaking phenomenal, so even across decades, there really wasn't a choice to be made.

Prior to gorging ourselves on food crafted by nonnas and papas tucked away in the kitchen, still forming Italian gnocchi with their old-country recipes and old-country hands, I had to endure the same expectation as I did on my wedding day—smile for a LOT of staged photos. Smiling for photos like these is proof. Not proof for *you*; they are proof for your family that they:

A. Properly raised God-fearing children,

B. Spent a ton of money on *you* when they didn't even "have a pot to piss in," and

C. That you, the child, looked grateful for all of the efforts they put into this day for you, *God dammit.*

I can still remember walking into Roma Lodge. My feathered 90s bangs and oversized buckteeth were only overshadowed by the sheen on the puffy shoulders adorning my polyester dress, my laced white gloves (*worn post-Madonna's "Like a Virgin" performance—coincidence?*), and the iridescent glow from my veiled tiara. But a "Material Girl" I was not and still am not. (*To this day, I'm so cheap that my mom says that I probably still haven't spent my First Communion money...*) So while I recall the formality of the clothes I was expected to wear, true to my "tomboy" nature, I'm sure all my running around and playing resulted in scuffing the crap out of those white patent-leather shoes and creating several runs in my thick, opaque, white tights—the ones I kept twisting with the impossible hope of making them feel comfortable. All this to say that nothing would get in the way of those passive-aggressive photos that were *going* to happen, come hell or high water.

My cousin and I made our First Communion together, as we were in the same grade level. (*Thanks to my Mom and aunt deciding it was best to keep us together by keeping me back a year—Lord knows I needed all the social support I could get.*) Jimmy was in his groom-esque suit, and I in my bride-to-be dress. With our small stature and quintessential bridal outfits, we could have made literal wedding cake toppers that day. Jimmy was a notoriously awesome kid and people-pleaser, so he took cues from everyone around him and smiled like a good little future groom. (*Who would later marry a groom of his own, mind you. Thanks for the inspiration, Catholic Church!*) And then there was me, the stubborn ass. I was headstrong and obstinate. I made inaudible noises when I didn't want to listen, and I gave looks that only come from spoiled little brats who still haven't learned how to be grateful for what they have.

Your First Communion is a sacrament that you are supposed to enter into as a seven-year-old who now understands that the sacrament of Holy Communion is not just a stale wafer that comes in a Girl Scout cookie look-alike tube. You're supposed to understand now that that wafer represents Jesus' body, because he *died* for you... lest you forget. And not only that, but you should also have the awareness that that stale carbohydrate is actually *turned into* Jesus' body after the priest says some words and makes the sign of the cross over them with his hands. It's called transubstantiation. It's a real thing. Google it. In Catholicism, you're taught to believe that those bought-in-bulk tubes of wafers *literally* become Jesus's body when you receive them... Yup. Creepy, I know. But cannibalistic visions aside, all of this pomp and circumstance *should* be so official and ornate that even as a child you "get it" that you need to be on your best behavior on this day... But not me.

No, I chose to waste the wedding photographer's, I mean *First Communion* photographer's, time by giving my sassiest, most I-don't-give-a-shit face in every photo I was asked to pose for. There's my cousin Jimmy, three months my junior (*we were always considered "the twins"*), smiling until it hurts, because he always understood how to listen to adults and do as he was told. And then there was me—you couldn't see those buckteeth because of my clenched lips, nor could you see my furrowed brow through my Aquanet-starched feathered bangs, but you *could* see the devil in my eyes, as I communicated with a most selfish look that I wanted nothing to do with these photos nor the miniature bride getup I was expected to wear.

Now, maybe my lack of enthusiasm was a result of the same issues on my *first* wedding day—I hadn't eaten much that morning, sat through a long-ass ceremony, and on top of that, I had to sit up straight and wear clothes that were meant for tradition, *not* comfort. Maybe I simply couldn't hide the exhaustion I kept at bay all freaking morning. It's somewhat alarming just how similar this scene on my wedding day was to that day decades before when I made my First Communion. Same small town. Same church. Same reception hall. All two decades later. Were the choices on my wedding day actual *choices*, or were they made in hopes of pleasing my family and the traditions I was bound by? In the moment, I would have said they were *my* choices based on *my* decisions, but in hindsight, I can't help but imagine a very blurry line where my childhood transitioned into adulthood.

To recap: gowns, veils, suits, formal shoes, invitations, church ceremony, photographs, reception hall. And lest you forget, *good Catholic guest,* at this—the First Communion of Kristy Jean, *(just as you will two decades from now at her wedding—)* it's assumed that you will bring a padded envelope which both card and cash should reside within. At both events, be sure to drop this generous gift into the hand-crafted card box *before* you find your seat and indulge in your meal. For those of you who were not raised Catholic (*or Italian... or Jewish, for that matter*), I challenge you to look in the card aisle the next time you're at Walgreens or, *let's be real,* The Dollar Tree, and specifically look through the "First Communion"/ "Bar/Bat Mitzvah" section. Sure you'll find the unicorn of all First Communion cards—*the full-sized version*—but I would bet you my First Communion money (which I *still* have, don't tell my mom) that the majority of those cards are similar in size to a travel brochure. And on the inside, they have a not-so-hidden printed direction that guides the gift-giver to, "Insert Money Here." As a Catholic, the fact that so many different themes of this same style of card existed taught me to presume that we always give to others, *financially*, when they experience a milestone in their faith. But as an Italian? It taught me that unless you're around your own grandma's table, if you want to eat, you pay in cash.

I genuinely value my Catholic upbringing, because I know it gave me a foundation that I would eventually grow into a personal relationship with God and my faith, but WOW, are there some alarming trends in *all* structured religions that have me concerned. My biggest takeaway from this milestone, though, was that even though I went along with 80% of this over-the-top formal day, there was still a good 20% of me that decided *not* to smile—20% that was no longer willing to please anyone, and it's that little badass that I continue working to reconnect with to this day. Because, sure, she was out of line and ungrateful, but I'll be damned if she wasn't setting some nonverbal boundaries of her own until she was old enough to find the words to express them properly.

Only Dicks Allowed

Fourth grade was the pinnacle of pre-teen experiences: There were Pogs (*the 90s version of shooting marbles*), new friends, and a *repeat* essay writing contest win for a trip to our state capitol. The trip to our capitol of Madison, WI, was a big deal in my little parochial school. They weren't about to haul all of our uniformed asses that far with those transportation expenses, but in third (*and then fourth*) grade, if you *wrote an essay*, you stood a chance to be one of the only *two* students at each grade level who would receive that honor. The honor, of course, being the opportunity to endure a two-and-a-half-hour ride on a standard yellow school bus with no air conditioning, experiencing the traffic jams of interstate vehicles and construction, and facing potential heatstroke as the sweltering Wisconsin sun in those late spring months blasted onto your gray, cracked vinyl seats. Victory would be mine! And it was—*twice*! Apparently, my twice-winning classmate Becky and I were both gluttons for punishment when anything competitive was involved. Did anyone else even *enter?* Now I have questions... We both also became teachers, *surprised?*

Outside of those adventures, until I wrote about my

childhood, I never realized how much emotion I still carry around a single, brief event in my fourth-grade year when I had my first male teacher. As an educator for nearly two decades now, let me be clear—I know we all make mistakes, especially when emotions are running high and teachers are trying to support the multitudes of students while balancing so many expectations. However, when it comes to *shaming* our students, the only grace I'll give is for those who apologize in the same manner in which they shamed. When adults in positions of power act like gods who have all of the answers, like flawless beings who never make mistakes, they do irreparable damage to the kids who innately trust them.

I'm not going to pretend that this teacher's one phrase and his one action changed the course of my life, but... *what if it did?* At nearly forty years old, I still get a little misty-eyed remembering that brave, boisterous girl and recalling how after that day, she lost an enormous piece of that inner strength. Sure, she showed up as though she was wholly there, and she even *thought* she was, but in hindsight, it was the first sign that I was losing myself because society (*and the system*) was telling me not to trust her anymore. I was about to forget who I was becoming and who I was affirmed to be—and it was the first time in my young life when I started wondering how to live *in* the world rather than expecting the world to live *around* me.

Every student in the early 1990s at Holy Name Catholic School would come after me if I didn't acknowledge another drastic shift that happened in our school around the same time I was stepping into fourth grade—our beloved principal was retiring. Ms. K was THE BEST principal. Her bright white, signature, feathered-bob haircut was second only to the genuine smile she shared every time she was around her students. So when she retired, both kids *and* parents were devastated. We loved her so much. When the next principal arrived, we were hopeful and relied on Jesus to send us someone who would love the children just like He and Ms. K. did. Unfortunately, Jesus must have been extra busy up in Heaven on the day of the interviews, because the woman who they selected was every bit of Professor Umbridge from the *Harry Potter* series—sweet as pie on the outside but mean as hell on the inside. She was cold, and she REALLY needed Jesus.

Many years after she left, when I was far beyond the days of elementary school, I learned that our parents, who knew each other better than their own *siblings* at this point in their children's nearly five years of shared schooling experiences, had an alternative name for her behind her back. Her name already ended in "wich," so that would have been an easy nickname to shorten it too, but she caused so much trouble for our tuition-paying, several-job-working parents that they couldn't help but swap that "w" for a "b." You can't believe that a well-intentioned group of Catholic families would sink down to the depths of adult name- calling? Oh, don't worry. With the penance of a few "Hail Marys" and an "Our Father," Catholic Jesus would forgive all of us again… and again… and again…

This change in command had a crucial impact on my fourth-grade year because Ms. *****bitch* stepped into power the very same year I was about to have a significant altercation with my teacher. With her quickly earned, shitty reputation, you can assume that even this straight-A-earning, twice Madison trip-winning student didn't stand a chance to be heard.

There was always a lot of bustling about in my fourth-grade classroom. It had much more of a laid-back vibe than the rigor of my previous years. There was no academic challenge as I'd previously experienced. Nothing like reading to my class in kindergarten, exploring next levels of text in first and second grade, nor the plethora of enjoyable contests and enrichment opportunities that my third-grade teacher offered. I felt a bit lost, but I could tell the boys were obsessed with the chance to finally have a male teacher. On top of this, we had a male *student* teacher, and so, for me, it was very foreign territory. I looked to my mainstays to anchor me—I still ordered from Scholastic Book Orders *(one of the few students still doing so at this point in our elementary careers)*, and

I joined a group of mostly boys before school to play Pogs in the classroom.

On that day that still lingers with me, the classroom was even busier than usual. The chaos of that classroom was very challenging for my undiagnosed (*future self-diagnosed*) ADHD. It was a sensory overload that I struggled to process, but it was the norm, so I learned to adapt. Students were shuffling about the room, gathering resources for their work, passing back papers, or completely goofing off. Being the overachiever and perfectionist that I was (*and somewhat still am*), I reviewed the work that was passed back to me and noticed that I received a lower grade on one of my assignments. I read and re-read the directions and my work, confused about the resulting score at the top of my paper.

I looked to the front of the room where the teacher and his desk were always firmly in place. As had become a frequent occurrence, many of the boys were chuckling with the student teacher and our lead teacher around his desk. It was as though they were in a huddle for the meeting of a private club that only dicks were allowed to join—*both definitions suit the example in this case.*

Intent to get some work done in this shit-show of a classroom, I nudged my way into their testosterone party, armed with the belief that I had the right to ask questions. After all, all of my female teachers had empowered me with that belief. Once the guys realized that I wasn't there to join in with their fart jokes, I posed my question and received a very curt response from the teacher. For a student who was always encouraged to think deeper and question further, his crappy response just wasn't good enough. Also, as a student with a very linear, black-and-white sense of right and wrong, my brain *needed* clarity. In my past years, I was taught to speak up, share my thoughts, and challenge myself to learn more, so I mustered all of that positive reinforcement and reluctantly asked once again for further explanation.

Apparently, my attempts to *learn* at school were in vain, because I saw the frustration grow across both the furrowed brow of my teacher and the confused looks from the student teacher and his adoring fans. My teacher responded in a way I had never heard a trusted adult speak *at* me at any point in my life:

"Shut up, and sit down! Stop being a crybaby, and go back to your seat."

My world was shaken. *What just happened?* I looked around through the onset of my blurring vision, realizing that all of the boys around the teacher's desk were now looking directly at me. The looks on their faces seemed to carry the same weight and expectations as their fearless leader—*He's right. You're obsessing over something stupid. Let it go.* Those next moments felt like I was mentally and physically trudging through mud. I gradually made it back to my desk, let my head fall down for the first time *ever* at school, and the tears rolled down my cheeks, droplets falling to my plaid uniform skirt and even further down to my fidgeting feet in their dingy-white Keds.

I tried to process the situation in my mind, wondering what I did wrong, but my thoughts were interrupted by another roar of laughter from the pulpit where I was, only moments before, publicly shamed. I couldn't comprehend the overwhelming noise, the feeling of alienation, and the casual way that my teacher could move on with his jokes after what he did, so I just *cried.*

This was the first time an adult told me, very vehemently, to "shut up." It was the first time I felt like an outsider in a moment when I was vulnerably being myself. And it was the first time my eyes were opened to the striking separation between the boys/men and the girls/women in my life.

When my mom picked me up in the parking lot after school, my tears flowed once again. Emotions have their own sense of timing when you're in the safety of a space that only you and your mom share. I recounted the experience to her, and she shared compassion and the next predictable step—let's sit down as a family and discuss what happened.

When my dad returned home from work, my mom shared my experience with my dad, and they decided it was best to discuss the situation with the teacher and principal so that we could all be on the same page. This gave me hope. This was how I was raised to function in the world—distance yourself so that you can process, and then work together to find a solution. My family functioned in the same way that my teachers and school community functioned up until *this* moment and *this* year. I had always felt reaffirmed that it's worth *facing* your fears, because speaking up *does* make a difference. In the comfort of my home, talking through the situation with my parents, I felt maybe, just maybe, my world could be realigned and fixed so that it was back to the way it was before this crazy incident.

Until the teacher denied it. His whole posse around him when he snapped back at me, and yet, he had the balls to *deny* it. I couldn't believe what I was hearing until the *appropriately nicknamed* principal chimed in to leave no doubt that she trusted his word over mine. And then I lost all hope.

My parents gave their trust to this parochial school, principal, and the teachers that they respected and supported. A school that listened to its students and challenged their faith, academics, and social skills. Because of this, my parents were adamant, *as I still am today*, that you question your *child* first before you ever question or throw accusations at the *teacher*. Developmentally, children will test limits and make statements that they know aren't true, and it's not because they're bad kids. It's because they're still learning how to communicate their feelings and needs, and so their survival instincts to get attention (*any kind of attention*) will kick in. Children don't have boundaries, which can be a beautiful thing when it comes to creativity and curiosity, but it's fucked up when the adults think that parenting equals zero boundaries and never saying "No." All this to say that my parents provided healthy boundaries and never assumed their princess was perfect. And in that same breath, they also empowered me to have a voice—to be listened to *and* not always get my way, but to know that I would be heard and that my voice had value.

My parents listened, helped me reflect, and made sure I had space to be heard. But this was long before the days of investigating further or pulling camera evidence (*of which there were none*), long before the procedures of asking for student witness statements, weighing all of the information, and drawing evidence-based conclusions. Not back in 1995, and not in Catholic school. This teacher, *this man*, said that it didn't happen, so that was that. *See you back in class on Monday!*

After that incident, I'm sure my mom used the principal's nickname a *lot* more frequently with the other parents who worked together at the Lenten fish fries, but in this case, my experience didn't matter to a group of people I had always trusted to have my best interests at heart. I had no closure, and with only *one* fourth-grade teacher in the school, I had to return to *his* classroom days after he berated me in front of my peers.

As a mom and educator today, I reimagine that day as though my fourth-grade teacher had the social-emotional wherewithal that *I* have gained after decades of training and experience. I don't envision a perfect world where he didn't make the mistake at all, because we are *all* human. Instead, I reimagine that moment as though he attended some form of training on restorative practices—strategies we use in education and counseling to genuinely listen to students and ensure there is understanding, a sense of closure, and support moving forward. With these tools confidently in his professional toolkit, in my mind, the scenario would play out something like this:

Me: *Questioning my teacher about my grade.*

Teacher: "Shut up, and sit down! Stop being a crybaby, and go back to your seat."

Me: *Gasp. Blurred vision, judgmental stares, crying onto my Keds.*

Teacher: *Inner thought*—Oh. I let my emotions get the best of me, and I went too far.

Me: *Head down, still crying.*

During a transition to lunch...

Teacher: "Kristy, could I please speak with you in the hallway before you go to lunch?"

Me: *Nods "Yes" through sobs.*

Teacher: *(When all students are gone)* "I want to apologize for calling you a 'crybaby' and for being so short-tempered with you. I realize now that I was in the red zone (*see: Zones of Regulation*), and instead of using my own strategies, I blurted out and called you a name. I should have offered a separate time when we could discuss your work, because I know you take your work very seriously. Can you forgive me?"

Me: "Mm-hmm." *(I would have been equally shocked that he apologized and eager to move forward from this situation.)*

Teacher: "I appreciate it. Would you like me to address the class, since I said it in front of everyone, or would you rather we move forward?"

Me: "Move forward."

Teacher: "Okay. Thank you for accepting my apology, and let me know if you want to talk about this later."

I have used nearly identical phrasing and conversation framing in my own career as an educator as I have made my own mistakes in working with students. I haven't had to apologize for *name-calling* my students, but I *have* apologized for being short-tempered, not listening, or not restoring our relationship after my students experienced consequences for their actions. If my fourth-grade teacher would have embraced a similar course of response, my parents never would have had to be involved (*mostly because my undiagnosed*

ADHD makes me super forgetful unless it's tied to unresolved emotions), and the witchy principal would have held on to our community's shared sliver of hope that she was actually going to make a positive impact on our school. Spoiler alert: she didn't. She actually dug herself further into controversy with the families in similar situations where she didn't have the strongest ethical code of conduct. And when families are *paying* for a quality education where *Jesus* is at the forefront, trust that they will simultaneously pray *for* you while fighting *against* you, as they encourage the school board to ensure that you lose your job. And she did. Not because of this isolated incident, but because many other situations occurred where she showed just as little character in them as she did in mine.

My teacher didn't respond—except to lie when he was confronted with my accusation, and the principal didn't truly listen to me or my parents. She blindly trusted the teacher rather than absorbing everyone's statements and determining the best next steps with all of the information in front of her. That truth, right there, is why fourth grade was a turning point for my relationship with boundaries. The truths I had come to embrace about the value of self-esteem, pride, and speaking up for yourself unraveled in an instant, and I was left questioning whether what *I* wanted and *needed* actually made any damn difference in the face of power.

Is there a connection between this teacher being my first *male* teacher and the way I internalized his words and blatant lie? Maybe. Maybe not. All I know is that years of therapy have taught me how to mine my past and invite my emotions to come to the surface—no matter how uncomfortable or impractical they may seem at first. At that point in my young life, there was no other man, *or woman, or child for that matter*, who broke my trust like my fourth-grade teacher did that day.

"C" is for Christian

When you enroll in a Catholic school, it's assumed that the entire school will attend Mass together once a week. This plan ensures a few things. First, the elderly members of the church who attend early morning, weekday Mass with the school—*those who tithe the shit out of their pensions and Social Security checks*—can see that their money is supporting the next generation of good little Catholics. Second, it's a great way to show parents who enroll their children that their kid is getting *more* God than kids who *don't* attend a church-based school. And third, it was a free ticket for families like mine *not* to attend Mass—because apparently *my* presence at Mass on Tuesday counted for *all* of us for that week.

It is funny how Catholics' 4 p.m. Mass on Saturdays is always a packed house compared to the minimal crowd at the traditional Sunday Mass. I guess we took that "...And on the seventh day, God rested..." note in Genesis *very* seriously. Later in life, I found that going to 4 p.m. Saturday mass was like taking a B-vitamin before you plan on drinking a shit-ton of alcohol—we all ingested God's absolution for the sins we were *about to make* as we partied the weekend away, hoping that we wouldn't feel too hungover (*in both cases*) in the morning. It was like an unwritten belief that Mass had a 24-hour window of coverage. Like you were Cinderella, and as long as you got home before the sun was up (*and you were in full hangover recovery by 4 p.m. on Sunday*), all was forgiven.

Initially, those weekly Masses put me to sleep. Don't get me wrong, from kindergarten-fourth grade, I loved our priest and his fun stories during the Homily, and it was always great to get an hour-long field trip across the parking lot every week. But those old people liked it *hot* in that church, and since they were keeping the lights on (*thanks to their efforts working 9-5 their entire lives*), that church was kept toasty warm.

I clearly remember one winter Mass, because I kept my coat on even after we began singing the first hymn. I wore my jacket because I tend to run cold, and this was the period of time just prior to the *new age thinking* of allowing girls to wear *pants* as a part of their uniforms—needless to say, romper, blouse, and tights were my only option. Well, the heat mixed with the meditative singing, which mixed with the kneeling, standing, sitting, kneeling, standing, sitting all stirred together to make my knees wobbly, as I was on the verge of passing out. I definitely would have had a concussion when my head hit that solid oak pew in front of me, if not for my middle school teacher's quick action behind me. She must have seen me swaying, because just as I was about to knock out, I felt her strong grip grab the back of my coat and pull me gently to my seat. I'll never forget the way she guided me outside to the front steps of the church, helped me remove my coat, and ensured that the fresh air was bringing some color back to my ghostly pale cheeks. I thought I was in serious trouble. Sure, Pentecostals are known for passing out in response to the Lord's influence (*and speaking in tongues among other things*), but all of that was far from the norm in comparison with Catholic Mass. There were several unspoken expectations when attending Catholic Mass, two of which were: 1. Sit upright on impossibly uncomfortable, wooden pews that will surely incur a future trip to the chiropractor, and 2. Speak only when it's time to say our secretly memorized phrases. With those two norms in mind and hearing historic tales of boys receiving a whack of the teacher's hand to the back of their head when they began to nod off in church, I worried that my episode would also appear as though I was succumbing to the devil's temptation to sleep through Mass. She was so supportive, though, and as a precaution, I still take my coat off as soon as I find my seat at Sunday service.

By the time I was in fifth grade, though, I began to notice the rhythm to the Mass, the routine and repetition that allowed everyone to let their thoughts fade away and lose themselves in the predictable call and response and order of things. I think back to the sights and sounds of church in my childhood—elders saying rosaries aloud in groups, touring the Stations of the Cross as a class (*literally walking with Jesus through the journey to his crucifixion*), and that time when Jimmy and I pursued Confirmation, attending the mandatory *five* Masses in *three* days. Somewhere between Masses four and five, we were required to engage in the washing of people's feet, just as the Bible recounted Jesus washing feet to serve others. At the time, through the lens of my immaturity, this all looked like a lot of unnecessary pageantry (and by all means, holy *shit* is the Vatican *still* gilded in gold...), but I also realized that there is a peace in losing yourself in faithful practice and routine. Like all forms of meditation, it's not about doing it "right"—it's about quieting the voices around you so that you can find your *own* rhythm and build your *own* connection with God.

Later in life, I learned to set my own boundaries around my faith as I downshifted from the BIG "C" for Catholic to a simpler "C" for Christian. While I agree that Jesus died for us, He *didn't* prophesize that a bunch of old white guys would come later with their own jacked up rules that we needed to follow (*P.S., the disciples weren't white guys*). I could have easily become a jaded and judgmental former Catholic, condemning the pageantry and the sometimes sleep-inducing, rhythmic pace. Instead, though, I chose to look deeper to understand this religion I was born and raised within, because it obviously spoke to many, and I just wasn't one of them. I became curious instead of criticizing, as I dug beneath the surface to understand why others would feel called to this version of their faith, and I was surprised by what I found. I gained a newfound respect and understanding where I once only held confusion and slight contempt. I realized that my experiences with religion and faith-based education gave me many opportunities to reflect on my own needs—what I "liked" and what I didn't "like"—on the road to understanding my relationship with God. I was gradually coming to the realization that faith wasn't a "one size fits all" situation like I always believed it to be. I didn't have to please others in how I practiced my faith, only *God*.

I gained the gradual awareness that being myself was not only *acceptable* by God but *pleasing* to Him. Now *that* was a profound moment no priest, pastor, or rabbi could give *to* me—it was something I became keenly aware could only be discovered *within*. I wondered if there were other areas of life that I could challenge myself within, learning to define *my* needs apart from the world around me. That curiosity was short-lived, as fear of the opinions of others encouraged me to tuck it back to the far corners of my mind. It may have lain dormant then, but I would call on it decades later when I was brave enough to say, "Fuck fear," and live life the way I was always intended to live it.

Kristy Jean

Dookie

Thankfully, my middle school years were inviting and engaging again in large part due to teachers who trusted their students with choices. One such teacher had recently moved to our area from the South. She ended up having a profound influence on my passion for reading and writing because she took notice of the curiosity I coyly hid behind my middle school self-doubt and desire not to ruffle feathers. I remember her comfy reading carpet filled with pillows and bean bag chairs where I would curl up with a good R.L. Stein Goosebumps book because they were easy reads, and *everyone* else was reading that series. That carpet was my first taste of her challenge, though, as she made time to ask me more about what I was reading and would I like to try (*insert all kinds of great recommendations*). Gradually, as she stocked her library based on our interests, those of Mary Higgins Clark and John Grisham—both authors of fiction whose books, unbeknownst to me, typically had a readership of adults twice my age. In that classroom, it felt like I had a license to be myself—I didn't care what anyone else was reading because we were empowered to trust our own instincts and celebrate our differences.

This challenge to our typically peer-pressured minds likely had varying degrees of acceptance by my classmates, but I was here for it. My fondest memories in her class were those around her lessons in writing. These weren't your traditional sit and get lessons about the different forms and structures of writing—this was a brief mini lesson and then *explore!* I'll never forget her lesson on "perspective," because I remember sharing it with my *own* students many years later as a middle school English teacher myself. She showed us image after image (*on paper—again, pre-internet, and it was a Catholic school—Jesus did not have money for Promethean Boards even if they were around!*), posing the question, "What do you see?" In one of the photos was an intricately woven spider's web with dew drops glistening in the sunlight behind it.

"Ewwww!!!" one of my classmates shouted.

"Spiders are creepy!!" another added.

"What do you see, Kristy?" she questioned.

"It's beautiful," I replied.

Instantly, my face flushed with wonder, wondering where the hell I just went in my imagination that I had the balls to say that shit in front of my class of peers that I was typically trying to fit within. Social suicide for sure.

Before my peers could respond, though, she energetically stepped into that silent space, shouting, "Yes!!" with hands clasped and the biggest smile across her face. "Tell us why you see it as beautiful—*I do too*—but I'd love to know what *you* think." That's the freaking magic of teaching, folks. She single-handedly created a safe space for being yourself while engaging us in a lesson that would eventually help us develop a sense of perspective as readers, reinforcing that each of us was welcome to have our own interpretation of a story or poem. For me, she was single-handedly helping me trust the classroom space once again. She re-opened the door of academic and creative possibility, patiently waiting for me to walk *back* through it, consistently using her words and actions to create a classroom that became known, by all of us, as a space to test your limits.

And she didn't reserve these life lessons for reading alone. She gradually helped us develop our voices through writing, which is no small task when you're working with pre-teens who cared more about orchestrating a common time for our moms to drop us off at the mall that weekend than we did about creative writing. I still don't know how she did it, but when you looked around the classroom, *everyone*, was writing. We wrote draft after draft, never worrying about perfection, because her energy and excitement for what we were doing led us to believe that the *journey* truly was more valuable than the *destination*.

Sure, we all wrote argumentative essays around the same time, but she gave us permission to give our writing authentic purpose. That was a game-changer for me, as I had obviously regained my voice when I tackled an essay titled: "Reasons I Deserve my Green Day 'Dookie' Album Returned from my Parents."

A little back-story—I played that album on loop repeatedly. To this day, it still stands up as a kick-ass album about the angst, emotions, and stupidity of your youth. I had it blaring on my CD boombox in my room one day when my mom walked in. She paused for a minute, picked up the acrylic case, and, in what seemed to be slow motion, slid the album booklet from the case. Every 90s child knows where this is going, but for all the others, the album booklet included all of the *lyrics* to the songs on the album. It was a dream for a pre-teen trying to learn the latest songs, but it meant *death* to your music idols as soon as your parents read some of the explicit language in the songs. This was also *before* the EXPLICIT warning slapped on the front of albums thanks to the FCC and Tipper Gore.

Now, Green Day is still known for very selectively chosen curse words—*for art's sake*—but that rationale wasn't going to work for my mom. Also, the excuse, "I don't know the lyrics; I just like the music!" wasn't going to get past the brilliance of a parent who knew that her kid needed boundaries.

Needless to say, the album was gone. Even worse than losing Billy Joe Armstrong's voice in my life was that I had purchased the CD with my *own* money! Back in the 90s there was a company by the name of Columbia House. They regularly filled our mailboxes full of flyers that marketed all of the latest CDs for a ridiculously low price of ninety-nine cents. Their gimmick, while filled with hidden costs, worked, as the idea of owning so many CDs at once must have thrilled many others around the country as it did for me. This was, again, back before the internet, so if you wanted in on their fantastic deals that were far cheaper (*at first glance*) than those you bought at your local Best Buy or Record Town, you had to follow the standard 90s order form approach:

1. Use a black or blue pen to check off your album choices on the flyer.
2. Detach the perforated order form.
3. Find an envelope to handwrite the shipping address in the center, your return address in the top left corner, and place a stamp in the top right corner.
4. Include a check for payment—because credit cards were rarely used at that time, and anyone who *did* have one would *never* have trusted putting those digits out to the world!
5. Wait patiently (6-8 *weeks*) for your order to arrive in the mail. (*Amazon was only a glimmer in Jeff Bezos' eye as they were just beginning to package orders in his garage in this decade.*)

My parents trusted me when I gave them the money for the CDs. They trusted me when they gave me a check to mail out for my order. And they trusted that when I peeled off the plastic of those CDs (*the removal of which could take 6-8 freaking weeks in and of itself!*), I was playing *appropriate* music. To be fair, listeners usually didn't even know the lyrics until they reviewed the included album booklet itself—so many songs sung incorrectly based on what we *thought* we heard on the radio! And man, if she had ever laid eyes on my TLC "Crazy Sexy Cool" album booklet, she wouldn't have let me out of the house ever again!

Long story long, CD gone, parents disappointed, and the only power I had left was at the end of my pen. My teacher liked my intention for this argumentative essay, and she coached me to approach it from a positive angle of the responsibility I had demonstrated up until that point. I dove into my claim, evidence, and reasoning—amazing how writing flows when you have an authentic purpose. I drafted, revised, peer-conferenced, and edited the shit out of that paper, because it was more than a grade in this class; it was my first attempt at asserting myself as a young adult. Because even with supportive parents who listened to me, I knew this was new territory. I wasn't asserting a *boundary* per se, because *their* house, *their* rules, but I *was* testing my own voice and perspective—unsure how they would respond.

I brought the published copy home to read to my parents. We regularly had sit-downs at the dining room table to talk about all kinds of things, so I knew that was the place to step into young adulthood. I read the paper aloud to my parents, and they listened attentively. I rationalized how I had always earned great grades in school, which showed I was responsible, and how I always respected their curfew, which showed that I knew how to honor authority. I argued that *listening* to swearing wasn't the same as *swearing* itself, and that I was fully capable of listening without repeating (*Ha! That's gone out the fucking window!*), but it was true back then. My jury deliberated, they debriefed me on my closing statements, and then a verdict was issued: Not guilty. WTF?! Did that actually work?!

My teacher encouraged me. My parents allowed me to advocate for myself and have a voice. And I learned not only the *power* of words but the *power* that comes from trusting your own voice, telling the fears and doubts in your head to, in the iconic words of my beloved band, "...fuck off and die."

Bros before Hos

While my teachers were offering opportunities in academia, and my extended family was making traditions and memories to remember, an unexpected *enemy* was lurking nearby. A Catholic school upbringing in your middle-adolescent years has a stark contrast to your public school peers. In public school, students are exposed to health lessons, learning the impact of unprotected sex. In contrast, Catholics were being told that *abstinence* is best—except we weren't exactly told *what* we were supposed to abstain *from*.

Being a "couple" at this age, in parochial school, meant that you secretly held hands on the playground and passed notes between classes—*very* seriously condemned and deterred by our teachers, likely for fear that we too would engage in the rampant unprotected sex apparently happening among our public school peers. Holding hands and passing heart-filled notes *was* a big deal to us, though, because we had been with the same damn kids since we were in kindergarten, so to begin seeing each other in a new light (*hormones*) was a very new world. It was also very strange to go from considering each other "family" for seven years to now engaging in a course called "family life"—causing all of us to begin looking at the opposite sex in a very confused way, often avoiding eye contact altogether.

My first recollection of the beginning of my "boy crazy" years began in sixth grade. One of my friends suddenly had a "boyfriend," and their relationship was the talk of the class. I suddenly found that my own Catholic school focus on Jesus and weekly mass was giving way to boys, passing notes, and gossip *about* boys. And since I had every intention of fitting in, it was, apparently, my turn to find a boyfriend in my class of twenty-six students, less than half of whom were boys.

Even in middle school, I continued to be the only girl playing quarterback in the boys' recess football game. My dad and I loved to watch football, and I can still throw a decent spiral—reminding my sons and my male students to *never* judge a book by its cover. It felt badass to be the only girl who was not only welcome to play football at recess but whom the boys wanted as an early pick on their teams, solely because they knew I was good at the game. Years later, I would play Powder Puff (*really, WTF?*) football in our senior-year high school football game. We won by one touchdown that I threw to a receiver! After that, we gave a fantastic show to the crowd with a touchdown celebration that was trending in the NFL... It was the one where the quarterback (*me*) uses the football like a weapon to "shoot" down each of the players in the end zone, watching each one drop to the ground before "shooting" herself and collapsing in the same way. As we engaged in this popular touchdown celebration, the eruption of cheers only increased as we hopped up and jumped into a giant huddle to celebrate. We thought we were bad-asses. *Talk about different times—shit you wouldn't even think about doing in this day and age...*

So there I was, still QB for this all-boys pickup game at recess, aware that I was obviously the only girl, but feeling badass because of it—I was welcomed into this "private" group. We were *bros*—we high-fived after a great game and headed to the cafeteria to recall the play-by-plays as we ate hot lunch. And then one day, *damn.* There's nothing more shocking to a pre-adolescent brain than the moment when, suddenly, that defensive lineman you've known *forever* blitzes out of nowhere, gives you the (*appropriate*) two-hand touch to mark that you're "down," and all you can think is…I wish he'd blitz *every* time… What was *happening* to me?!

From that day forward, I had totally new feelings about the game of football. In an instant, I shifted from the badass quarterback who naturally proved that girls could do anything that boys could do—*and better*—to a self-conscious preteen who was suddenly very aware of a million feelings all at once. Puberty was a dick, and he was only beginning to mess with my head.

That lineman became my first crush and then my first "boyfriend." I was in my first "real relationship," which entailed months of silent, parallel walking and frequent note passing. This new hormonal enemy was gradually taking over every ounce of my attention—the attention I once gave to friendships, sports, and academics. Being in a couple was the ideal identity I wanted for myself—*or so I thought.* We did all the things that typical "couples" of that age at a Catholic school did—caught each other's eye during class, walked *next to* each other at the annual school carnival, and wrote things like "Stay cool!" and "Have a sweet summer! I hope I get to see you!" with hearts under it in each other's yearbooks. This was also the first of *several* future relationships where I solidified an internal belief that truly caring for someone meant letting go of your own happiness, because *their* happiness is now *your* happiness. God knows where the fuck I got that idea, but I think I got such a dopamine hit when I saw *him* happy that dating was my gateway drug, and that's all I needed to become an addict. Devoting my time and energy to a boyfriend was my drug, and I wouldn't reach Step 1, *admitting I had a problem*, until fifteen years later when my first marriage was officially over.

I was constantly looking for ways to surprise that first middle school boyfriend—a CD single of Third Eye Blind's "Semi-Charmed Life" purchased from our local mall's Record Town, a thoughtful gift themed after his favorite baseball team and former hometown, and love letters to tell him just how much he meant to me. (*At least he broke up with me before I could give him the CD—it lasted far longer in my Walkman than the relationship did.*)

I didn't care how much work (*I assumed*) it took to be in a relationship. My friends had their own boyfriends, and I so desperately wanted to be a part of this "in" group. My two girlfriends and I each had a boyfriend. It felt so safe to have a tight-knit group to call, ready to roller skate at Skate Town or carpool in a mom's minivan to the local movie theater for a showing of the latest *Austin Powers* movie—well, we *purchased* tickets for *Toy Story 2* and then snuck *into* the R-rated movies—sorry, Mom and Dad. It must have been all of that explicit music that was a bad influence—damn you, rap music! In hindsight, I blame hormones for making all of us forget that we belonged to each other all along—hormones made us feel a sudden loneliness we were once so oblivious to, and that made us believe we *needed* a boyfriend to fill that void.

If you haven't thrown up just yet, let me tell you about the time I threw a fit during one of the high school-sponsored dances. Yes, back in those days the Catholic high schools sponsored the Catholic *middle school* dances. In other words, the Archdiocese laid the breadcrumbs to be sure parents knew how to direct their kids (*and tuition checks*) to Jesus from Baptism all the way to high school graduation.

So there we were, a gaggle of girlfriends primping and prepping for our first official dance. We had 1998 style perfected—butterfly clips adorned our twisted back hair, massive amounts of glitter caked into every crevice of our faces, Bath and Body Works nail polish haphazardly painted onto our fingers, and the exclusive charms collected *from* those nail polish bottles worn proudly on our dangling charm bracelets. I don't know which was worse for our pre-teen psyche, the hormonal draw to seem appealing or the fact that Bath & Body Works was our dealer.

We rehearsed our dance moves before it was time to pile into someone's mom's van. Our VHS copies of movies like *She's All That* were played until they wore out, especially because we had the amazing power to rewind and re-play the dance scene that we hoped to one day emulate. We so badly wanted to drop into one of these predictable, 90s rom-com scenes where an "unexpected" flash mob ensued, performing perfectly choreographed dance routines that were basically two eight-counts that repeated to the chorus of a quintessential 90s song.

But since that level of expertise and sex-tease had to be left to actors and sex workers, we just came up with our own, single 8-count of moves that tied directly to the lyrics in the chorus of the song. "I Just Wanna Fly" by Sugar Ray, for instance, looked like this:

"I"—Point to your own eye.

"Just want to..."—Cross your arms across your chest and hug yourself as though you love or want something.

"Fly"—Spread your arms wide and pretend to soar like the fucking eagle that you are.

I know. You're jealous. But please, please rest assured that you too can master the confidence of these moves after watching 90s TV shows and movies over and over until you make yourself believe that you could be a star too—*you just haven't had your big break yet.*

One of the moms dropped us off, and we walked in on a *mission.* A mission that was likely hormone-driven, but since we didn't know what those feelings were about (*abstinence means never asking "why?"*), we just knew we wanted to look cute and get a boy to look at us. And after endless conversations with my boyfriend via my Green Bay Packer football phone in the comfort of my bedroom—*luxury at its finest*—I knew that I was one of the lucky few who could brag endlessly that *her* boyfriend would be there to dance with *her*.

I thought I was a freaking princess walking in to find her prince, because that's what Disney sold me. Rocking my bushy eyebrows and more glitter than a Pride parade, I popped a strip of Wrigley's Spearmint gum and walked in like I *owned* the place and this was *my* night. Those damn "only children," I tell you...

I have to mention here that this was a time in my life long before I knew what it meant to be "gay." Being gay was like Voldemort—everyone must have believed that if you didn't say its *name*, then it would just stay *away*. This meant that I was also completely oblivious to the definite reality that several of my friends felt so alienated by our Catholic, heterosexual-because-homosexuality-is-an-abomination dances. I had no clue, but in hindsight conversations, I've learned that they *did* have clues, but in a Catholic school in the 90's, they were left without a single role model to reassure them (*besides Ru Paul, but I think his beauty confused the shit out of many people back then, so I wonder if the boys even knew...*)

So there I was playing pretty, pretty princess while so many closeted friends around me just wanted to get out of the event unscathed, without letting their hormones speak a truth they were too scared to share in those four walls, let alone their conservative hometown. It breaks my heart to see how naïve I was, unable to be there for them, but over time, I've realized that blind ignorance isn't a permanent ailment— you just have to remove your *own* hand from your *own* eyes and listen without judgment.

So there I was, a self-absorbed, glittery disco ball, expecting my boyfriend to take one look at me and propose future marriage right then and there. I mean, I had practiced *his* last name with *my* first name repeatedly during cursive writing practice in class. Disappointedly, I found him on the perimeter of the dance floor with his buddies, pushing each other around and snickering like Beavis and Butthead. Oh, my Prince Charming.

Like all young women, I was sold the romantic fairy tale story. I was brainwashed to believe that I would be swept off my feet, but then he barely spoke to me... *the entire night.* I can actually believe that women are from Venus and men are from Mars. The earliest signs of that truth are found in the way that pubescent girls step into their maturity with long-term visions at the same exact time that boys step into *less* maturity with *short-term* visions in the form of jokes about their balls and farting—*an endless vision, from what I've learned.* Girls are facing complex emotions, making attempts (*often in vain*) to please others and find a sense of belonging amongst fellow girls who wall off their group as soon as it's formed. Boys stick to surface-level emotional talk in the form of sports metaphors, and, except for the total douche bags, they're mostly open to any other guys who are hanging around. And somehow, many people could never understand why I had so many surface-level, male friendships most of my life...

But that night, at that dance, I put as much effort into my makeup as I did into my astronomical expectations for how *he* should engage with *me.* So I did what any self-absorbed drama queen would do—I ran to the bathroom with my friends in tow to show just how upset I was so that everyone began to feel badly for me, *which they did.* I cried about him not talking to me, which is girl code for "someone go tell one of his friends that I'm upset so that he comes and rescues me." Because nothing says solid relationship like *hiding* your true emotions from your boyfriend only to share them with the people you *do* trust, in subliminal hopes that they will relay the message back to the significant other you're too chicken shit to tell yourself.

Now that wheels were in motion, *I assumed*, and my tears had dried, I reapplied a bit more glitter lip gloss and gathered my girlfriends. It was time to fly right past the first few stages of grief, and dive into the stage they always seem to leave out—*Revenge Dancing.* I swallowed my emotions, grabbed a few girlfriends, and shook my ass to a censored-for-Catholic-School-dances version of "Mo Money, Mo Problems" *(Don't judge—a lot of our music idols fell from fame in the past decade)* like I didn't give a shit and was living my best life—all while side-eying him, of course. Fake it 'til you make it, right?

He remained distant for the majority of the night. Technically, the entire population of boys were *literally* distant that night. They wouldn't know what it meant to "make a move" any better than us girls would. Shit, even PG-

13 labels on movies were taken *very* seriously in our families. We were never exposed to *Dirty Dancing* or *Footloose*; instead, we gained greater confusion than clarity about interacting with the opposite sex from movies like *The Sandlot* where Squints fakes drowning in order to kiss the lifeguard and *My Girl* where Vada is hot for teacher and tries to make a move of her own.

When my revenge dancing proved unsuccessful, I walked to the refreshments table to swallow my pride and some unspiked punch when, suddenly, the first *slow* song came on. "This will be it!" I thought. This will be the song where he will find me, lead me by the hand, and stare longingly into my eyes as he realizes why I've been writing my name with his last name all over the cover of my notebooks—*he's in love with me!*

Just as this rationalization fully solidified, I walked back toward the dance floor, positioning myself so that he had a better chance of seeing me. But then, I turned around to see that he *was* dancing... with another girl. And not just any other girl—the friend whose house I was sleeping at *that night*. I stood and stared, not believing my eyes, and suddenly the boys woke from their trance, because they were also looking in my direction—even they were aware that this was fucked up. I ran back to the bathroom, glitter falling from my face like a breadcrumb trail for my friends to follow. Because that's what friends do—they step in when you're off your rocker about something, no matter what level of irrationality you're experiencing. And there I was, always taking those friendships *for granted*.

The dance was winding down, and our fairy tale carriage was going to turn back into a minivan in the next half hour— might as well make the best of it from the dance floor instead of the *bathroom* floor. I fully disconnected, finally soaking in the love from friendships I was beginning to see with new eyes—until he came *back* to me.

The backstabbing friend found me after that slow song because indirect communication travels fast, and it turned out that she was genuinely concerned for me. She clarified that *he* asked *her* to dance, and she thought we weren't together anymore—which by middle school standards was hard to detect anyway, and we were "on again, off again" quite frequently. She came right to the source, assured me that she had no interest in dancing with him again because of the impact it had on me, and that was that. She was a phenomenally kind friend who had *actual* struggles in her own life—she didn't have the luxury to give a shit about this insignificant situation that I was allowing *my* life to revolve around.

So when he walked up to me as the final slow song of the night cued up, my friends didn't know what to expect. I was too naïve to be a bitch and too needy to walk away, so I defaulted to the response that would define my future relationships—I settled. Through blurry eyes, I let him place his hands on my waist (*saving space for the Holy Spirit, of course*), and I placed my hands on his shoulders. Such a romantic dance form, don't you think? As we slow danced to LeAnn Rimes belting out "How Do I Live?" from the speakers of an upperclassman's DJ equipment, I rested my head on his shoulder and claimed "How do I Live?" to be *our* song... after I'd already claimed "For You I Will" by Monica from the Space Jams soundtrack as our *first* song... Once again, I began to plan our future because *he* chose *me* (*after some coercion...*).

At the sleepover, we did what all girls in that generation did—we ate snacks, MTV ran on the television playing music videos in the background, and we called boys on the landline. (*For my younger generations—this was before cell phones existed in the mainstream, so it was a phone that was connected to its base with a cord. Then the whole unit was connected to a phone line.*) My relationship struggles were the topic of conversation, thanks to my *humility*, and they all challenged me to call my boyfriend. I dragged the corded phone to the closet, closing the door in a way that allowed the cord to still slide under and keep the dial tone humming. Calling someone else's landline after 8 p.m. was like playing Russian Roulette, because you didn't know if the person you were calling would get to the phone after the first ring or, heaven forbid, their *parent* picked up instead, and you had to make the awkward request: "Is Steven there?" (*gulp*) or, more often than not, slam the phone down and hang up *(no Caller ID just yet, either)*.

Calling from the closet was partially to ensure that if his mom picked up, she wouldn't hear madness on my side of the line and partially because I wanted to speak with him alone. Because if you were a boy-crazy girl like me, rather than working out your struggles with the multitude of *friends* who were right there with you, you called the *boy* because boy attention is a drug, and you needed another hit. Or you believe that your only real happiness comes *from* him, so you stop all signs of fun with your girlfriends to be sure you can talk with *him* at the drop of a hat.

Through mumbles about the dance, he told me that he just didn't like me "like that" anymore. He said that now he had feelings for (*drum roll, please*) my sleepover-hostess friend. The friend who I'd bonded with ever since my first *true* heartbreak when my best friend, Amanda, moved away in the third grade. The loyal friend who was just a step more rebellious than me because she used to attend *public school.* The one who stayed up into the late hours, turning the TV on and quickly hitting the "mute" button so we could sneak and watch every parent's television nightmare, *Beavis and Butthead,* and who led me to the corner store that my parents would later lose their shit about me walking to. And by "lose their shit" I mean doing what only-child parents do—they had a safety talk with me about "stranger danger," and I don't remember ever going back to her house to play.

Eventually, I came out of the closet *(not that way, but maybe I should have...)* crying, with the hung-up phone in my hands, because nothing says slumber party like a sobbing bitch making it all about *her*... by making it all about some *guy*. It was awkward to say the least, but as it is with the magic of youth, all would be remedied with a bucket of popcorn and distraction. When the band Oasis came on MTV, we sang "Wonderwall" at the top of our lungs, forgetting the drama that had just unfolded.

It wasn't until later in this post-dance sleepover when another girlfriend whispered the truth to me. At the dance, my hostess proved that she was a genuinely great friend when she apparently told my "boyfriend" (*to his face, in front of the boys*) that she would never come between the two of us and that she would never date *him*. Damn. She stood up for the bond between girls, the bond between women, the unspoken code that says, "Thou shalt not even think about dating the ex of thy female friend." She got it—even at our young age. She understood that the value of friendship was always greater than a pseudo-relationship that would likely end through the passing of a note *(check "Yes" or "No")* in class or an untimely talk with his best friend, the go-to bad news messenger. And there *I* was ruining *her* sleepover, and, potentially, our friendship, over my obsession with a *boy*. Self-awareness would be a lagging life skill for me, if you haven't realized it yet.

In hindsight, I wish I could have seen two things back then:

1. How I was torturing myself and getting in the way of authentic friendships by doing whatever I could to gain the attention of a *boy*, and

2. How no matter what I was facing in life, it was my *friends* who would pick me up. I prioritized temporary relationships over (*what could have been*) permanent friendships.

I'm still figuring out how to balance various relationships in my life, but one thing is for sure, if I could go back, I would give more effort and energy to friendships when things were going *well* and spend less time only seeking out my friends when I was going through a *break-up*. It was a vicious cycle for me that I hate to admit. Undervaluing female friendships was one of the first signs that I had a single, target audience for my selfish sense of belonging: men. I trapped myself in the endless loop of pleasing their egos at the expense of my own. I would love them the way *they* wanted to be loved, no matter how little I received in return.

Kristy Jean

Most Vulnerable Player

    I keenly recall those middle school years solidly revolving around sports, boys, and friends—and in that order. I often lost myself in *who* boys wanted me to be and *what* coaches expected me to be. I was single-handedly keeping the patriarchy alive and well by ignorantly following the lead of men (*and boys*) who single-handedly possessed the one thing I wanted—*their approval*. Coaches had control over my fate from the first tryout all the way to game time. Boys had control from first impression to first kiss. I never realized that the approval I actually sought was never *theirs* to give. It was my *own* approval of *myself* that I was truly seeking all along.
    I allowed myself to believe that a sense of belonging was something that was given *to* you, not something that is actually found *within*. I would have to learn from several more relationships, including one marriage and the birth of two sons of my own, before I would finally ask myself what in God's name I believed *men* had that *I* so desperately needed. But beyond relationships, sports were another essential

element of my youth that taught me about so much more than the sport itself.

Central to all of the other sports I played, basketball epitomized my inner teenage conflict to fit in while simultaneously trying to stand out. Humility be damned, I was a *baller*. Yes, I said it—a *baller*. The basketball and court felt like second skin to me, and since I was struggling just to understand the skin God gave me, I went all in for this sport and the identity it gave me. Maybe it started way back with those light-up Nikes, because I just had to have the latest "drip" (*as the kids call it now*). I'm still learning how to use that word—is it a noun, like, "I have drip!" or "Check out my drip!"? Or maybe it's more of an adjective like, "Your outfit is *drip*." Come to think of it, it *could* be a verb! "I saw you *drip* when you walked in the room in those new kicks." Wow. Nerd alert. In the moment when I try to stay present with modern slang, I instantly lose myself in a language arts lesson of "drip" etymology. (*Thank you, well-served English degree!*)

Semantics aside, my aggressive *playing* was matched only by the aggressive *statement* made by my on-court style. Even in my first year playing for my middle school, we're talking all-white K-Swiss shoes with North Carolina Tar Heel Blue laces. My style evolved with my game as I traded teams from K-Swiss to all-white Nikes in the later years. Those were the years of Tar Heel Blue sweatbands, knee-high Tar Heel Blue Nike socks, and Tar Heel Blue *reversible* Nike shoe "wraps." Did I mention that I l-o-v-e-d Carolina blue? I wore this look far too long to call it a phase. It was a *faith* more than a phase.

There was no doubt that I had an athletic style all my own, for better or worse. Basketball gave me the opportunity to embrace the sides of myself that I just couldn't embrace on a daily basis. When you're a point guard on the court, you don't have time to overthink—you have to *act* and learn from your mistakes. Off-court, I lived for fitting in and people-pleasing, but on-court, you don't have time to weigh pros and cons; you trust your instinct. I embraced my alter ego because she had more confidence in her style and passion for this game than most people I knew, including my off-court self.

Those years playing basketball embody my first memories of feeling a sense of pride in embracing what it meant to be me, or that *version* of me, anyway. I dressed louder than most and played more aggressively than necessary—*see six broken fingers and one broken leg*—and I didn't give a damn what anyone thought. I didn't care what they thought because for once in my life I didn't *think*; I just *played*. That was a huge shift away from the norm for someone who checked everything she did, said, watched, and ate against what everyone *else* was doing. I had a natural talent, and I grew it because of my supportive coaches, my passionate teammates, and my drive to be the best version of myself *for* my team.

I embraced that confidence at every practice, when I laced up for a game, and even for a period of time after each game...*as long as we won*. Because another core trait that solidified around this age was my motivation (*obsession*) with competition—I wanted to *win*. I gave everything in me as I led my team in practices and in games for all four years of middle school. So when my eighth and final season began, naturally, I envisioned myself as a shoe-in for the coveted MVP award.

Our two coaches supported us in each of my fifth, sixth, seventh, and eighth grade seasons. They knew my abilities, but even more, they knew my heart and genuine love for the game. They also knew they could count on me. In our final Catholic school tournament, which was actually quite competitive, believe it or not, I started the game as usual, putting up points and running my ass off. The first quarter came and went, and I didn't need to look to the bench to know that I would continue fighting the good fight in the second quarter. At the half, my teammates and I rallied around each other, and I instinctively licked my hands and wiped the bottom of my shoes (*for traction, but gross, I know*), ready for the second half.

By the end of the third quarter, I was losing steam, but I was still in the fight. My coaches asked if I had a little more to give, as our opponent was closing in on our lead. I didn't hesitate to tell them that I did—*whether I had it in me or not*.

I would end up playing the entire game, all four quarters, and I wouldn't have wanted it any other way. Today, I can't remember whether or not we won that game, but I *do* vividly remember my polyester-blend uniform and Tar Heel blue headband both soaked in sweat after the game, as I stumbled down to the school cafeteria where my parents met me from the stands. I'd never been this exhausted in my life, so when I began hyperventilating, I wasn't sure what was going on. Someone rushed me a brown paper bag and coached me to breathe in and out, watching the bag expand and contract. Eventually, my breathing settled, and my mind returned, as always, to analyzing my part in the game—win or loss.

In a separate tournament in Milwaukee, less than an hour north of my hometown, a similar situation occurred. We were up against a completely new caliber of teams, and I remember my head coach telling me that he needed me to take the lead in the game. There was no way I was going to let him or my team down. I played nearly the entire game, helping us capture our 42-30 victory. I remember that game clearly, because of those 42 points, 21 were a product of my shooting with intermittent assists from my teammates. That's 50% of our total points. I'm not *nearly* that good anymore, which is probably why I speak with ZERO humility about my skills back then.

I share these stories partially to give context that I was beginning to find my identity in organized sports, and that I was, by most definitions, the leader on my team. But I also share these stories as clear examples of a character trait that would grow with me throughout my life: people-pleasing. I was an up-and-coming people-pleaser who was always willing to shoulder any necessary burdens to lead the team to victory. Sure, my competitive edge drove me to pursue this sport as a means for building my own self-esteem in a world that finally came so natural for me, but my endless drive was fueled by approval. Early signs of my issues with enabling? We'll unpack that later...

So when our end-of-eighth-grade ceremony took place in the basement of our parish church (*the common venue for bingo, fish fries, and wedding receptions)*, I sat up tall on my metal folding chair, assured by years of pats on the back and congratulations from peers and parents that my coaches were about to announce me as the MVP of our team. We'd never had an MVP, or any other award, in our fifth, sixth, and seventh grade years, so this was a big deal. We were only on the *cusp* of the participation trophy generation, but so we were the final few who would have to *earn* our accolades, or so I believed...

The MVP award was a once-in-a-middle-school-experience chance to be recognized for four consecutive years of cumulative effort. I kept looking back to my parents with the biggest smile on my face, soaking in this moment, reflecting on years of blood, sweat, tears, and broken bones that proved my allegiance. When my coach took to the podium, I mouthed back to my parents, "This is it!" He showed sincere emotion as he shared memories of all that we had accomplished as a team and how we had grown as individuals and teammates. He then commented that the person recognized as MVP was, "...a team leader who could always be counted on. A young woman who gave her all at practices and games, aware of not only her own needs but those of her teammates as well. A player who was an *essential* member of the team for all these years." I was truly humbled, as my efforts seemed to have an impact even beyond the court.

Then he surprised all of us when he stated that there were *two* MVPs, because he and the assistant coach couldn't choose just one. Huh? The "M" usually stands for "Most," as in *one*, but, okay, I can share the spotlight. I could see how my role as a point guard was only one of the *two* crucial positions on the team; maybe our center was sharing this with me. Yeah, that made sense. "Good for her!" I thought. And then he announced the two names...

MVP #1—Our center (the assistant coach's daughter). I was right! Awesome! (*See me clapping incessantly for her, my predicted partner in this award, and my excitement for what was coming next*). MVP #2—Here it comes... "I'm so proud to share that our second MVP is... *my daughter*!" His daughter. The *other* point guard.

What the f...ther, son, and Holy Ghost?!?! Tears filled my eyes as I settled back into my cold, metal folding chair, feeling like I was (*figuratively*) slapped in the face.

The past four years of intense, game-time interactions with my coaches flashed through my memory. All of those games where I was given the "big asks"—

"Kristy, we're going to need you on your game in this one..."

"Kristy, we're going to need you to take the in-bound and get that final shot..."

"Kristy, we need more from you because you're setting the tone for the rest of the team..."

He might as well have literally slapped me in the face, because their decision told me that on a team of less than ten players total, I was never going to be good *enough*. Their decision told me that trying my hardest and building up years of evidence that my impact made the difference would never be enough for these coaches—*my trusted coaches*—to make the right decision. I felt powerful on the court, but life dealt me a hard lesson that day—your power is nothing when someone has the ability to take it away. I was hit hard with the realization that even when you give your all, at the end of the day, no one owes you *anything*.

I had zero boundaries around my dedication to my team—missed events with friends to show up for practices and games, always responded with a "Yes" to my coaches even when I had nothing left in me, and played countless games with sprained or broken fingers, taping them together and playing through the pain. I believed that if I never set boundaries for *myself* that my selflessness would somehow prove my loyalty and maybe—just maybe—be rewarded. I had expectations. But right then and there, I learned that setting expectations is the worst lie we can build within ourselves—no matter how warranted our expectations seem in response to all that we sacrificed.

To this day, I still hurt for that fourteen-year-old girl and the life-altering rug pulled out from under her innocence in that moment. She had found her place in that sport, on that team, and she *trusted* her coaches. She didn't expect recognition, but when it was voluntarily given, she couldn't help but expect a certain outcome based on what she had always given so passionately for the team. It was more than just my competitive nature that caused me to feel such devastation in that moment. It was that for the second time in my young life, I did everything "right," and it didn't matter *enough* in the eyes of a trusted adult. I smiled my fake smile until I could walk out with my parents and finally ball my eyes out in the privacy of our car. The first of only two times I would allow this game and its leaders to take my tears. Fool me once, shame on *you*. Fool me twice, and now I'm truly losing hope. And yet, as with many hard-earned lessons in life, there was only more pain to come.

Cinderella and the Glass Ceiling

My competitive characteristic, it turned out, wasn't only reserved for sports. Naturally, it carried over into other areas of my life where it was less healthy—like with girls—what we wore, who we were friends with, and who we were dating. On the softball diamond, volleyball court, and basketball court, being competitive was a mark of dedication to your craft, but in the school hallways and at parties, being competitive with each other was an ignorant choice that society peer-pressured us into making. Except in this form of competition, there were no winners where self-esteem was concerned. And those who seemed to be "winning" on the outside fell into one of two stereotypes: babe or *bitch*.

As an only child who was, in hindsight, trying to find opportunities *not* to be alone, my severe bob haircut and athletic-inspired wardrobe kept me far from "babe," and being identified as a "bitch" was a scarlet letter that my people-pleasing self wanted to avoid at all costs. So, instead of attempting to navigate the polarizing world of girls, I simply decided to throw myself into the all-consuming, self-esteem-*depleting* world of boys.

As a rule-following, sheltered Catholic girl, the most *rebellious* things I did were:

1. Have my first kiss in my own backyard with friends nearby, tossing bonfire flaming marshmallows over our neighbor's fence (which one was a *greater* act of rebellion, I'm still unsure).

2. Found myself in trouble with my eighth-grade writing teacher for holding hands during a movie she was showing in class. (*When pre-teens are allowed to lie on the floor with pillows watching a movie in class, apparently even Catholic school isn't off-limits for meddling.*)

While these examples sound tame by today's standards, imagine what 1999 Jesus at a school called "Holy Name" would think of this. I was assuredly a "butana" in the making with choices like these!

I would love to blame my passionate nature on a fate that I had no hand in choosing. As a November baby, for instance, I have no control over the fact that I was born a Scorpio—the most passionate, most impulsive, and horniest sign in astrology. However, that very irrational but very effective myth that sperm could leap off toilet seats was alive and well thanks to generational fear, so at least there was an unhealthy balance to my inner Scorpio. We never talked about sex, but somehow the women in my family circumvented that conversation to get right to the point—we were a fertile clan.

Now, I can't comprehend why sperm would be in or around a toilet *(ew)*, but at that age, enrolled in Catholic school, I was simply taught to keep my legs closed and everything would be fine. So I peed with my knees locked together and found that toilet time was the best time to pray. Besides the scientific fact that our matriarchy was all "Fertile Myrtles," there was also God's Plan to consider. You made a promise to yourself and God that you would not have sex until marriage. And I'm proud to say that I kept that promise... *for a few years longer than my friends.*

Raging hormones, a rising moon in Jupiter, and Catholic guilt aside, I often wonder what it was that drove me to give so much of my attention to the boys around me. A big part of me assumes that it was a natural effect of being an only child. I had this subconscious fear, for many years, of being alone. I saw time and time again how my parents were there for each other, beyond being there for me as parents. Instead of making me hopeful for my own future, seeing their genuine love for one another made me worry that I would never find that kind of love for myself. I think I was eager to hurry up and find my *own* husband to be sure that I didn't miss him when God sent him into my life. Because even at that young age, I had picked up on society's (*false*) message that a life without checking the "married" box was no life at all.

I'm also a product of the Disney princess generation, so I fully blame that damn *mouse* for a portion of our brainwashing around patriarchal views. Every princess was waiting around, bored out of her wits or, worse, in a torturous state, waiting for her life to "begin"—the day when her "true love" would finally arrive and give her life a purpose—*loving him, of course.*

I still remember the first movie I ever saw in the theater. My mom took me to see *Snow White and the Seven Dwarves.* Entranced by the vivid colors on the magnificent screen, I watched as each of the seven dwarves was named and welcomed Snow White with song. (*All except Grumpy, of course. He was a dick, but I admired his authenticity.*) If Snow could find *seven* men to shack up with and still find time to cook, clean, and remember each of their names and needs, then surely *I* would be able to find *one* that was who I was meant to care for, right? Disney: fucking with women's minds since 1937.

But even those seven little men (*Well, six eligible bachelors—we all know Happy, with that twinkle in his eye, was the first gay Disney character.*) weren't enough for Snow. Nope. She was destined to find *another* man to care for—a prince. Lucky for Snow, she didn't even have to go looking. She just had to trust a random stranger's candied apple and fall into a coma. See, girls? Stay away from sweets—sugar goes right to your waistline and roofies will knock you out cold. After one bite, all she had to do was sleep it off until Prince Charming found her in the nick of time, ready to give her life with his non-consensual kiss! *Ah, romance.*

All of the schmaltz (*and future #MeToo cases*) in each princess's life, thereafter, would continue to make me swoon and reel me in. Belle from *Beauty and the Beast* was another one I couldn't get enough of. Every one of us curly-haired brunettes in a sea of straight-haired blondes finally felt seen, because until Belle showed up, even in the 90s, we were expected to use every heat tool on the market to straighten away our untamed ringlets. Belle gave us hope that we could wear our hair in its natural state *and* find a hairy, ugly man of our own who would magically become sexy as long as we remembered that it's what's *inside* that counts. Belle was our spirit animal.

So when Belle showed up on the block, exuding inner joy and giving the middle finger to sexy, narcissistic men who were easy on the eyes, young girls everywhere were inspired to think outside the patriarchal box. *But wait, there's more!* This new-age, Renaissance woman also loved to *read.* She adored the local bookstore so much that she read every book in the shop—some even twice! We were ready to cozy up with a good book just like our heroine until the damn townspeople began singing their judgmental songs. Apparently, Belle's nose was so deeply stuck in her books that she was completely ignorant to every asshole in town who was gossiping about and around her:

"Look there she goes—that girl is strange no question... dazed and distracted, can't you tell?"

"With a dreamy far-off look, and her nose stuck in a book, what a puzzle to the rest of us is Belle."

"She really is a funny girl, that Belle..."

WTF?! In this two-part number, Belle is singing about her appreciation for the town while dreaming of something bigger that's out there for her, all while the townspeople are throwing shade and Gaston is adamant that he's going to bone her. My young girl self instantly shifted from confident to confused. Wait, wait, wait. So we *aren't* supposed to follow her example? Apparently, being a literate female with an imagination was (*and is*) a threat to society.

Shit. If Belle couldn't break the stigma with her flawless face and pitch-perfect musical numbers, how was *I* going to do it? After that Disney rant, I guess I can blame society and the patriarchy a bit... yes, still feels good. But beyond the mouse, old white men, hormones, and my horoscope, I know that I also need to challenge myself to reflect on what I actually *did* have within my control. What caused me to obsess over boys to the point that, like Belle, I sacrificed my dreams to prioritize theirs?

When I use all of the strategies I've accumulated in years of therapy, it really boils down to one word—*belonging*. I wanted to *belong* to someone. I saw how my parents belonged to each other. I saw couples everywhere in movies and on tv *searching* for their "soul mates." Mom and I were obsessed with that TLC reality show *A Wedding Story* (...as I subconsciously begin humming the show's theme song: *"...and when the spark of youth someday surrenders, I will have your hand to see me through..."*). The *real* couples in that reality show seemed to *belong* to each other. They were so smitten that their lives were now complete that this miracle had to be celebrated with tens of thousands of dollars spent on dresses that would have less than twenty-four hours of life and centerpieces that no one would remember.

Snow White and what's-his-name, Belle and the Beast, Britney and Justin... *belonged* to each other. (*Damn you, Disney. See! It is their fault!*). On the news, we saw how Princess Di and Charles *belonged* to each other. I was blinded by the "love" that was captured through a shit-ton of editing, and I believed that I could attain that level of happiness and belonging if only I, too, sacrificed my happiness to be with the man of my dreams.

Now, after all these years, and guilt-free binging of Netflix's *The Crown*, I've learned that Charles was already in Camilla's DMs even before that blue sapphire was on Diana's finger. 51%+ of marriages (*including those on TLC*) ended in divorce, and those princesses' stories and many of the lyrics Britney sings to on Auto-Tune were written *by men*. Thank God my daughter (*and sons*) are exposed to empowered characters like Moana and Merida who refused to complacently follow the orders of men who told them to patiently wait to be saved. They didn't sit by like good little girls to assume their expected place within the predictable roles of society. Female characters like these are finally our modern equivalent to Odysseus—leaving their families behind to truly discover who they are and what they want out of life. That's where the comparison ends, though—they definitely didn't need to sleep with other people's wives and magical mermaids on their roads to self-discovery. Come to think of it, that *could* make a phenomenal coming-of-age tale of two lesbians looking for love. Picture Wonder Woman dreamily kicking stones along the beach on the island of Lesbos when, suddenly, a fiery-maned Little Mermaid leapt up to shore... their eyes meet... Now *that* would make for a fantastic Pride movie I could rally around!

Alas, this was the 90s. The burning bras of the 60s were now ashes swept under the rug of MTV and a generation of wanna-be-hos. I witnessed R&B singer Sisqo encourage a generation of women to wear their thongs out and proud—*which we did*—and Brandy and Monica fighting each other over a boy who was barely to be found in the music video—*which we also did but without a music video set*. At least Christina, arguably the most feminist of them all, demanded that he rub *her* the right way. By the time my savior queen P!nk came around, I was too brainwashed to hear her wisdom. My teenage mind was inundated with messages about being the right size, the right volume (*silent*), and the right "fit" for a man.

Please Excuse My Boundaries

If what I was watching and listening to wasn't telling enough, then the one-hundred—and I do mean an exact *100*—jagged-edged, Teen Beat magazine tear-outs of Jonathan Taylor Thomas (*That was his Christian name; he will always be JTT to me.*) that wallpapered one-quarter of my bedroom walls should have said it all. It was only one out of the hundred, though, that when examined closely, was caked in the Wet 'N Wild pink shimmer lip gloss that I applied to my lips each night before planting a goodnight kiss right on JTT's perfect lips.

I was more in the dark about my boy-crazy ways than JTT was about his *own* love for boys. Millions of girls' hearts would break years later when that "truth" came out. Clarifying point: I obviously don't know the man personally, but *God* do I wish I did. *I promise that if I did, I would tame it down—no restraining order necessary!* Several magazine covers and vague interviews at that time led us to *believe* that he's gay, but I can't confirm. Fingers crossed he's still interested in women (*Sorry, Hubby.*) I never did get a response to that letter I wrote on loose-leaf paper and snail-mailed to an address in my "teen heartthrobs" book of addresses. I'm sure I'm the *only* preteen who signed my name and kissed the salutation with sparkly pink lip gloss...

Kristy Jean

Souvenirs of Womanhood

    In my eighth-grade year, while Britney was singing "... Baby One More Time," I felt like she was preaching to the choir. I thought my middle school years had already hit me with surprise after disappointing surprise, but I was in for the shock of every young girl's lifetime at the most inopportune of moments in the most inopportune place.
    Watching the annual Macy's Thanksgiving Day Parade has been a long-standing tradition in our family, thanks to my mom. I don't think even she knows the reason for her obsession with both the department store and the annual event, but it has always drawn her in. And one year, far into her thirties, it drew her in so much that it inspired even *her* to finally set boundaries with her own mother.
    My mom loves to shop, so there's an obvious draw to Macy's right there. She's a fan of knee-high boots, strappy sandals, and any shoe that speaks louder than anyone in the room with its rhinestones, glitter, or feathers *("You never see feathers like this!" she has excitedly exclaimed in more than one shoe*

department.) As my mom says, "Shoes and purses *always* fit." So, with their seasonal boots and purses for every occasion, Macy's was a win-win.

As to her fondness of the parade, maybe it's because it takes place in her favorite place—New York City—in her favorite season of fall. Maybe it's because she loves creating any tradition, especially one that requires everyone to snuggle up with her on the couch. Or maybe that parade was a reliable source of hope every year in a childhood that was missing it so desperately. Regardless of the reason, my mom is the biggest fan of Macy's, Macy's Thanksgiving Parade, and *The Rockettes*. She is such a devoted fan that she defied every instinct in her body that kept her in line, doing exactly what her mom wanted her to do at the exact time her mom wanted her to do it.

Grandma expected everyone, and I mean *everyone*, at her house on Thanksgiving Day at 1 p.m. This meant, of course, that you had better arrive by *12:00 p.m.* to show that you are grateful, help set up, and begin sneakily picking at the crisping turkey skin so that she could slap your hand away. You know to bring *nothing* (*don't dare to ask*), eat and remark on how great the food is (*which it was*), forcefully tell her to stop cooking and sit down to her own plate (*which she never did*), and leave fully stuffed, knowing that you would return the next day for leftovers, because they were still *definitely* not leaving with you.

These were the expectations. No excuses. Until my eighth-grade year, that is, when my mom decided that she had kept her dream at bay long enough. She was done trying to please my unpleasable grandma, and she was done giving herself excuses for not going to New York. She was done dismissing her dreams just because they seemed unnecessary to my grandma and unimaginable to my co-dependent papa who never wanted her more than a two-minute drive away from him. This was the year that she told her family, "We're missing family Thanksgiving this year, because *our* family is going to New York for the Macy's Thanksgiving Day Parade." Shit just got real.

The Grinch's heart may have grown two sizes bigger when he learned compassion for the Whos in Whoville, but my mom's *balls* grew at least two sizes that day when she mustered up the courage to make that statement to my grandparents. While we're on the topic, I'm over saying that someone has "balls" when they act bravely. We should say they grabbed the world by the *vagina*—now there's an organ that has to endure more than its fair share of hardship and struggle! So my mom's *vagina* grew two sizes that day, and trust me, it was already mighty.

Though I could prove this in any number of examples, one of the best that comes to mind is when a persistent gas station owner wrongfully accused her of not paying for her tank of gas. Mind you, this was in the mid-90s when full service was being phased out and before you were required to pre-pay, so you could fill up and pay *after* inside the gas station. Ah, the days when we could trust people...

In her case, she chose the unnecessary but integrity-proving choice to pre-pay that day—*$20 unleaded, to be exact*—and returned to fill the tank on her red Firebird that she so proudly cared for. I heard the click on the pump, and my mom invited me to pick out a treat because she was going back in for a pack of smokes (*Don't worry, I got her to quit when I earned my license and told her I wouldn't hang out at home with her if she was smoking. Apparently, I've had smoking boundaries all along!*)

I grabbed a pack of Zebra Cakes from the Little Debbie stand and met her at the counter where I heard the owner *accosting* her, adamant that she needed to pay for her gas. I had to look away as her once-in-a-blue-moon Italian evil eyes came out, throwing *daggers* from across the cashier counter as this man now *greatly* regretted his decision. I watched as her pointer finger joined the argument and she declared in a calm, calculated, and truly ominous tone,

"You question me? I paid your clerk before I pumped. I've lived in this town, down *that* road, my entire life, and you question *my* integrity? I have a big mouth, and I will tell everyone about this day. You will be closed in a month."

At this point, I can't help but imagine her capping off this fantastic moment of defiance with an authentic "Italian Goodbye": flicking four fingers under her chin in the direction of the person who just pissed her off. I envision her sauntering out, a devilish plan surely hatching in her mind, because true to her word, *less than 30 days later*, the "For Lease" sign on the building was proof that her Calabrese Curse had power. Vagina 1. Balls 0.

Up until this point, I'd never witnessed my mom bringing that badass confidence in front of her own *mother*, though, so I'm sure you can imagine my grandma's reaction to this direct contradiction to *her* holiday plans:

"I didn't raise you like that! Fine, then. Go. We'll eat on the *good* China this year."

The first time you tell an overbearing parent, a narcissist, or in some families, *both*, that you are denying *their* expectations for *your* life, it's not pretty. Yelling. Disappointment. Judgment. Anger. Self-pity. Tears (*only my mom's, never my grandma's*). All the feels and all the reactions came out, but somehow my mom mustered up the vagina to hold her ground. I'm guessing that's why she purchased the tickets so far in advance—there's no clause in the airfare refund for adults who buckle beneath their parents' unreasonable expectations. *Big Apple, here we come!*

I had never experienced New York before, let alone the Macy's Parade, so I was over the moon! Travel continues to be the answer to so many of life's challenges. Feeling indecisive? Go somewhere new to clear your head. Feeling fearful? Go somewhere new to remind yourself how small and insignificant your problems are. Feeling doubtful? Return to a place that you connected with deep down in your soul. Travel continues to gift me with a sense of humility, adventure, and renewed motivation to live life to the fullest, and it all started with my mom's desire to show me the world.

What you don't see from the comfort of your cozy couch on Thanksgiving morning is that the Macy's parade requires a

TON of barriers, police presence, and cameras. This national treasure has very distinct boundaries. For instance, if you want to see the pre-parade Broadway performance "sampler" LIVE in front of Macy's, you have one of three options:

1. Be in the cast.
2. Be on the camera crew.
3. Be a higher-up at Macy's.
4. Be a celebrity.

Not checking off one of those life choice boxes this year? Then you won't even be allowed to watch that dramatic lip-syncing from a *distance*. You'll be sucking up subway air three blocks away while you stand on your tiptoes, claiming that you're sure you caught a glance of a Backstreet Boy—"*You know, the tall, gloomy one who has always looked like he could be another Backstreet Boy's father.*"

The marching bands are another quintessential Macy's Parade highlight, and my dad's favorite part. Students from all over the country dream of receiving an invitation to perform. If you venture out to the parade in hopes of hearing them play, though, you'd better stand many blocks away from the department store finish line, because marching bands aren't allowed to play within *earshot* of Macy's. Trumpet and tuba background sounds don't exactly complement the commentary and performance taking place LIVE for millions to view.

This experience helped me see that there are a lot of unwritten rules and unforeseen expectations when you travel somewhere new. But, as I learned, just like everything in New York, if you're patient, spontaneous, and willing to breathe in hot, sweaty subway air filtered through dirty grates, you'll *LOVE* it!

I grew to love the hum of the city and the complete anonymity that travel offers. The Macy's Thanksgiving Parade is like no other I had ever experienced, and not just because of the phenomenally talented people showcased throughout the event. It blew my young mind to realize what a massive undertaking it was for Macy's, the NYPD, the cast, crew, and so many others to put on a parade like this. With so many people involved, there was no time for "niceties" or apologies—after jumping in fear the first time I heard it, I came to love the crass way NYPD officers could make entire crowds move back with a look or a *"Get outta here!"*

To put on an event this extravagant with so many moving parts required clear boundaries that everyone was expected to follow, boundaries that ensured that *everyone* could enjoy themselves that day. I saw how boundaries were not just beneficial, they were *essential*. New York had a million boundaries, and I didn't have a single one... yet.

This was 1998, so after catching a glimpse of my all-time favorite boy band, 98 Degrees, lip-syncing (*parade staple*) their latest song, I couldn't believe we were actually here! (*Side note: My cousins pulled off an amazing surprise decades later when I finally had the opportunity to meet Drew—I mean, the whole band, but who am I kidding? He was always my favorite—face-to-face in Cincinnati!*) I made sure to wave to Santa at the very end, because let's be real, I was a 14-year-old Italian, Catholic school girl raised on guilt and superstition. My mom and aunt were notorious for spending the time between Thanksgiving and Christmas ominously reminding us kids, "You don't believe, you don't get."

We headed over to Hard Rock Café for our first Thanksgiving dinner in a restaurant, let alone away from home. The Macy's Parade *and* dinner at my favorite overpriced chain restaurant?! I was on top of the world!

I skipped into Hard Rock Café as an innocent, wistful child. The most challenging decision I had to make was how many cherries I wanted in my Shirley Temple and which shiny new Hard Rock collectors' lapel pin I would choose to add to my signature HRC jean jacket back home. And *after* dinner, I knew we were headed for the experience of a lifetime—ice skating at Rockefeller Center! I was beginning to forget the shifting reality of puberty—maybe NYC was bringing the change I needed to gain some perspective on how lucky I was. Life was truly looking up!

NYC was bringing change, alright. And it was all positive change until I felt a unique type of stomach ache, quickly excused myself to the HRC bathroom, and looked *down*. Aerosmith was making aggressive pouty faces at me from their wallpapered photo, KISS was blaring at alarming decibels in the bathroom, and all this as I sat in disbelief, wondering if I was dying.

Clarification for the men: No one tells you that your first period (*and the tail end of your future cycles*) gives an undeniable impression that you may be dying from the inside out. My confusion paralleled Tina Fey's story in *Bossypants*—she couldn't believe that this substance was her period, because every TV commercial had led us to believe that the magical Ice Blue Kool-Aid that was poured into pads was exactly what we should expect to drop out of our vaginas. I exited the bathroom with stomach pains and confusion, looking to my mom for an answer.

Me: "I have the worst stomachache, and things don't look right when I went to the bathroom..."

Mom: "It's your period!!!"

My inner thoughts: "What the *fuck* is that, and why are you so *Goddamn* happy? Did you say that it's going to keep coming *back*?! *How often*?! Would it have killed Catholic school to spend a minute of Family Life telling us that what appeared to look like your body was shutting down was actually your *period*?! I mean, if you're going to tell girls to keep their legs closed, then you should at least tell them how it all starts..."

Ah, the first signs that a girl is a woman: bleeding from her vagina and suddenly believing that her mother doesn't know *shit* about anything. My newfound appreciation for travel and life in general ended in that moment. Fuck ice skating. Fuck Hard Rock Café. Fuck becoming a woman. I wanted my own bed.

My dad looked so incredibly confused as we made a beeline

right past the merch counter at HRC and hailed a taxi to take us directly to the hotel. My mom and I already walk at a pace that would make anyone assume we're evading a fire, but this was different—he knew something was up.

As soon as the taxi arrived at our hotel, Mom told Dad that I really wanted to pick out a *souvenir* from the gift shop and that we would meet him upstairs—*Because nothing says "The Big Apple" like heavy-flow feminine pads.* We brought my souvenirs of womanhood upstairs, and shortly thereafter, I was in my pajamas, under the covers, given *unprecedented* permission to order the outrageously priced apple pie à la mode from room service because, well, puberty is a bitch, and my mom understood. The final lesson I learned in that rollercoaster of a day was that when your body physically tells you that your childhood is over, it's time to put on your "feeling bloated" sweatpants and dive into sugary salvation.

Kristy Jean

Taunting Richard

Remember life before cell phones and the internet? If not, I truly apologize that you missed such a beautiful time in history. That magical time when we had to look people in the eye and ask questions instead of secretly investigating their social media accounts to get to know them. We never had to worry about cell phones in every pocket, just waiting to capture us at our worst and instantly make our *inexperience* a *global* experience. Our greatest concern was seeing someone who knew our parents when we snuck a kiss with a bad boy or drank a sip of underage alcohol. None of us could even imagine giving a shit about being judged by someone on the other side of the world; it was bad enough knowing that your parents knew *everyone* in your community—and they all talked. We knew that we just had to be sly (*or naïve*) enough to dodge the adults, and we could take the story to our graves.

There was no way to know how that freedom, that opportunity to fuck up without the world peering in like the unassuming "cast" in *The Truman Show*, would disappear. We had the freedom to make mistakes, kiss the wrong people, and say the wrong things without those decisions literally following us *for the rest of our lives.*

I should really step down from my soapbox about technology catching us "doing bad," because I was *always* a card-carrying member of the goodie-two-shoes club. I was as squeaky clean as you were going to find in Catholic school. I got the right grades, joined the right clubs, and played all the right sports. I stood out just enough to be noticed but not so much that my choices would be judged (*Thank you, internet-free childhood!*).

So what's a parochial-school educated goodie-two-shoes to do when eighth grade ends? Well, attend parochial *high* school, of course. A high school that ended up costing more in tuition than my eventual bachelor's degree and part of my master's degree. I was excited about this next step in schooling, and St. Catherine's had a great reputation in the community, and my family, as a faith-based, college-preparatory high school. It would take years before I would notice the contradiction of a faith-based, extraordinarily expensive school located in the heart of our version of the inner city. I may not have had a silver spoon, but it was bronze, at minimum, and I was completely ignorant of the privilege I had.

My mom and her sisters also attended this same parochial high school, and my grandparents did whatever it took to afford tuition to keep their kids far from public school. So it comes as no surprise that my parents, aunts, and uncles, did whatever it took to afford the *inflated* tuition to keep the next generations out of public school as well.

We attended Catholic school in direct response to our family's legacy of *fear* and *guilt*. After spending nearly two decades working in public schools, I'm beginning to believe *all* families send their kids to faith-based or private schools less out of *hope* and *faith* and more out of *control* and *fear*. In hindsight, there were at least four reasons why our family sent generation after generation to Catholic school:

Reason #1: The media. Our local newspaper (*Younger generations, Google "What is a newspaper?"*) was riddled with stories of unruly students at nearby public schools—fights, weapons, and teachers physically assaulted by students on the daily. Some things never change.

Reason #2: My dad was a cop. He only responded to the *most* challenging schools with the *most* challenging students with staff who could only do so much before calling for police reinforcement. My dad is the OPPOSITE of a power-hungry, controlling person. He is much more receptive and supportive, so when he asserted two things—You will not attend public school, and if you *choose* to become a cop, we will not help you pay for college tuition—I listened.

Reason #4: The women in my family had the instilled-at-birth fear that when they saw St. Peter at the end of their lives, the first question he'd ask was which Catholic school they gave their offering and *offspring* to.

Though I was sent to St. Catherine's to embrace the Father, Son, and Holy Ghost, my focuses were more skewed toward my grades, sports, and *boys*. High school was the height of boy crazy, but I was always the good, God-fearing (*and pregnancy-fearing*) Catholic daughter who was one step away from carrying purse-sized Lysol to spray on public toilet seats, ensuring stray sperm were kept at bay—family myth or not, I wasn't taking any chances. I'm sure my irrational fear of restrooms has assured you by this point that sex was NOT even an idea in my mind at that age. I'd like to revise my previous list of reasons for attending Catholic school to add:

Reason #5: When you're taught that Jesus is omniscient, believed to be *everywhere*, the probability of chastity increases *infinitely*. Before the technology evolved, *Jesus* was our first nanny cam, Ring camera, and AI.

Though I have *zero* scientific data to prove this theory, (*And I knew a handful of guys and girls who completely debunked it altogether according to stories I heard in high school...*) for me and most of my girlfriends, the Catholic card was enough explanation for the boys to know—*You're not getting any.* So I guess I was what many would formally refer to as a "dick tease"—I wanted guys to notice me, but I didn't think beyond that initial attraction. (*Refer to my undiagnosed ADHD on this one and many other areas of my life.*) I wanted to be in a relationship to show that I belonged, and I wanted to give someone all of my love and attention—pure, *fully-clothed*, playing board games and going to high school football games to *actually watch the football game*, love and attention, that is.

Freshman year was an awkward mess of high academic expectations that I wasn't sure I could tackle, undefined hopes for my friendships, and barrel-curler bangs *with* short, naturally curly hair. I was a walking billboard of indecision, so finding someone to be in a relationship with me didn't exactly seem like it was in the cards. I definitely didn't know what I wanted, but I *did* know that I *did not* want to be completely noticeable—yet. So on a beautiful fall day when I *was* noticed at school, I was dumbfounded about what to do.

That fall day is still one of my most memorable moments in high school—the day my broken leg (*more on that later*) blessed me with the attention of a *trifecta* of gorgeous senior guys.

I was alone at my third-floor locker after crutching my way there down the long hallways from the scary elevator that brought me from the first floor. It was what you'd expect to find in a Catholic high school built in *1864*. I remember it as one of those rickety contraptions that you see in horror movies or old-timey New York City apartment buildings— the ones where the character has to strenuously slide the latticed gate aside before unlocking the actual door to the elevator. Then we see the character use all of her strength to shove the solid metal door away, quickly shuffling onto the elevator car before that very same door attempts to trap her in its wake.

I was alone at my locker that day, which means that I either braved the deathtrap elevator (*last inspected during the Great Depression*) on my own, or I had told whichever friend was my helper that day to go on ahead to class, explaining that I would just stop and kill time by my locker near my next class. I like this version best, because it captures the magic of that day as though it was fated to happen—the stars aligned and I swear the freaking angels (*our mascot, of course*) were singing.

So after crutching along to my locker down the long and silent hallway, I arrived at my locker with a sigh—no matter how much my dad helped to pad the armpit rests of those crutches, the rubbing irritated my skin, and the whole process tired me out. As I looked down to the bottom of my locker, thinking about how to maneuver my giant textbooks without falling on my ass (*before the time of laptops, my post-millennial friends*), I heard a voice come out of nowhere:

"Hey, Kristy. How's your leg healing?"

I looked up to find a *senior*. And not just any senior—our school's star basketball player with a million-dollar smile... and he was talking to *me!* I'd also like to mention here that he was the nicest guy around who would eventually go on to become a Division One college athlete and a Hall of Fame inductee at the very same high school where he was talking to me, a lowly freshman.

We'll call him "Senior A." Senior A knew me as "Tammie's daughter" because my mom worked in the school office prior to my enrollment, and I would visit here and there. Without needing to say it, I think she knew that it would be best for both of us if I didn't have my *mommy* in the main office, and all these years later, I can see that it probably wasn't easy for her to give me the space to grow. She continued to coach the pom-pon squad there at her alma mater, though, because we both knew there was no chance I would ever consider joining *poms*.

Before I knew it, a couple more students were in the hallway, and Senior A called over to "Senior B"—another dreamy senior with *piercing* blue eyes—to ask him if he had signed my cast... What in the good Lord's name was happening?! I needed someone to pinch me... there's no way this was actually happening. And then, as Senior B was mesmerizing me with his baby blues and I thought life just couldn't get any better, "Senior C," the towering six-foot-plus center for the varsity basketball team walked up to finish out this trio of gorgeousness surrounding me. *Me*! The short, regrettably feather-banged freshman with a bum leg who was *still* short of breath after crutching her way there.

They took turns signing my cast, and hand to God, I don't remember another soul in that hallway besides the four of us. But if there was another girl who caught sight of this magical moment, I imagine it would have played out like that scene in the movie *When Harry Met Sally*. I wasn't making orgasmic noises (*I didn't even know what an orgasm was*), but from the look on my face, I'm sure any girl in that hallway would have commented, "I'll have what she's having."

For someone who isn't very observant, I remember *every* detail of that day, probably because I recounted the event in *every* class period for the remainder of the day, week, and... *the next two decades*. That moment would go down as one of the most memorable of my high school career for two reasons:

1. Duh—the hottest seniors in school knew my name and spoke with me—*finally a silver lining for this broken leg!*

2. Their kindness and sudden presence actually helped me forget, for a few moments, the one truth that was truly devastating at that time in my life—my leg was broken, and I had no idea if or when I would once again play the sport that gave me so much of my identity.

Kristy Jean

This is a Man's World

Sports were the only thing I spent more time thinking about than boys and getting good grades. Being an athlete was a part of my identity before I knew that I should have one, and to this day, it's a core part of me that I don't even have to think about—it's in my nature, and I don't think I fully appreciated that when I was younger.

Regretfully, I viewed my athletic involvement much the same as I did the initial years in my educational profession; I was always seeking what was *next* to the point that I struggled to stay focused in the moment. Being present was a value that I wouldn't prioritize until much later in life, so it comes as no surprise that I left middle school a "should-have-been" MVP who was itching for a redemption chapter in high school.

Basketball tryouts were one of my first opportunities to start making a name for myself in this new chapter. The high school coaches were the same ones who I aimed to please every summer at the local basketball camp. The summer camp where I gave my all, never complained, won trophies for my efforts, and ensured that all of the coaches knew my name before I ever enrolled as a freshman—Catholic inner circle in full effect. So when I attended every tryout preparation session, I knew that I was coming in with at least a partial reputation to live up to.

Devastatingly, though, basketball was destined to break my heart once again when I *broke my leg* at one of the open gym sessions one week before tryouts. I remember hobbling off the court, very aware that it was my fibula that was broken—*damn you, anatomy class*. The doctor confirmed my suspicions as well as my greatest fear—basketball would be on hold for a *minimum* of half the season. My fate was in the hands of the head basketball coach; he would determine if the past I had proven was enough to assure me a future in the sport I loved.

Knowing that there were freshman, JV, and Varsity teams, I wholeheartedly believed that a true tryout would have landed me on the JV team. I was especially hopeful because I knew that JV had a badass female coach who was tough as nails and challenged her players to give more than they thought they had within them. But without the ability to fulfill the time-sensitive structure of tryouts, I could only imagine what he would decide.

My present-day self would have asked for a meeting with the head coach. She would have affirmed her belief that she had proven, pre-broken leg, that her ability levels earned her a spot on the JV team and that she would do everything in her power (*short of washing the team's gym socks*) to prove her place until she was physically capable of proving it on the court. But this was Kristy pre-boundaries, still seeking the approval of others.

I wouldn't dare speak up to the coaches, no matter how well they knew me by this point. Just like those fourth and eighth grade experiences, I was raised to trust teachers (*and coaches*) and earn my place by keeping quiet and working harder. I absorbed the fate that was handed to me and accepted the head coach's decision that he would *graciously* place me on the freshman roster without an official tryout. He insinuated that *with* a tryout, I would have made the JV team but that *without* one, this was the best they could offer me.

In an instant, my dreams of learning from the badass female coach were swept away. My life as an athlete was once again swirling unsteadily and that nauseous feeling in the pit of my stomach returned just as it had that day I was passed over for MVP. I received words of sympathy from my former middle school competitors, now teammates since we were all housed within the same Catholic high school. They, too, knew what I was capable of, and they respected that it was a shitty situation to land in.

The worst part of landing on the freshman team, though? The reality that my coach would be the brand new, fresh-out-of-college twenty-something who also happened to be my homeroom teacher—a man I already struggled to connect with while the senior girls drooled over him.

This, then, was meant to be the start of my basketball career in high school. I believe now that God has a plan and He doesn't give you more than you can bear, but my faith was rocky back then, as it is for most young people finding their way. So I just did what was in my nature—pleased the people who are in charge and waited patiently for my turn. I attended every practice, bum leg and all, showing my commitment and support, very aware that I would have to start all over again, proving my worth. I attended every game, knowing very well that my uniform would never be seen beneath my warm-up gear. I sat on the bench, cheered on my teammates, and befriended our team manager—one of my first high school friendships with a girl I didn't already know since I was *five years old.*

As my leg began to heal, I increased my support at practices and before games—rolling basketballs out, gathering supplies, and encouraging teammates. So by mid-season when my cast was removed, my leg was healed, and my doctor gave me the green light to get back into playing, I guess I had some expectation that I would be given an opportunity to prove my abilities *on* the court as I already had *off* the court. I was wrong.

That coach, also the bane of my frustration in homeroom every day, chose to make me *miserable* for the remainder of my freshman year, turning basketball (*the core of my existence... besides hot senior boys*) into a horrible curse I was required to endure. Game after game, I would give my all as I hustled and warmed up with the team—until I watched as he passed me by to choose his five starters to begin the game. I sat on the bench, cheering on my teammates and waiting for my moment to prove myself.

That moment never came. I would watch every quarter of every game tick away, wondering when I would get my opportunity. Even in the fourth quarter with ten minutes remaining in games where we had a major lead, he wouldn't glance my way. Not a single consideration for playing this talented, dedicated athlete who he was *told* to place on his roster because it would likely hurt his 20-something-thinks-his-shit-doesn't-stink, fragile *ego*, and my game time was the one thing he could control.

I vividly remember the day my final ember for this sport, the sport that had established the first piece of understanding my identity, officially burned out. It was my sophomore year, and my second year with this coach who followed our team to the next level—*lucky me.* We were scheduled to play at Waterford High School—an approximate 30-minute drive west by yellow school bus from our school near Lake Michigan. Blind optimism kept me motivated, as it would for the majority of my life.

Since I saw no game time in my freshman year, at practices in my second year, I doubled my efforts in an attempt to please this coach. At games, I cheered louder than anyone else. I gave my parents the thumbs-up as they sat in the stands, watching me sit on the bench game after game, reassuring them that I had a plan, and I was going to do everything *right* to *earn* my place on my high school team. Those familiar feelings crept up from that fourth-grade experience and my years of giving my all to middle school basketball only to be let down for not one but *two* MVP slots.

But Catholic high school was *nothing* like Catholic grade

school—especially in regards to the caliber of players I was competing against to gain game time. When you think about it, high school tryouts are the equivalent of blending a new family from nearly a dozen smaller families (*schools*) in your area. That's twelve captains vying for *one* captain slot. That's twenty-four starting point guards vying for *two* starting point guard positions. Needless to say, you have to have a lot of drive and more than a drop of ego to think you have a chance. And as I was learning, you also had to be willing to stroke the coach's ego. (Get your mind out of the gutter! This was long before Cosby, that Team USA gymnastics *very* physical therapist, and years of settlements paid out by the Catholic Church. I mean I *was* one of the first female altar servers back in my elementary days, but as history has shown, priests weren't interested in *us*.)

I checked every "box" that a coach would want to see in a player. I wholeheartedly believed that this game against Waterford was finally going to be my opportunity. Our opponent's record that year wasn't strong, so this was going to be more like an exhibition game for us than anything. Like an actress who finally landed her breakout role, I just knew that this was going to be the game where *everything* changed.

I watched the clock in school all day, waiting for the time to wind down when I could run to the locker room to change and gather my gym bag. The bell rang, and I ran up the stairs, filled with anxiety and anticipation. I changed, checked that my Nikes were securely *(and cleanly)* inside my bag, and flew down the stairs to board the awaiting bus. The ride out to Waterford felt twice as long, but we finally arrived. I gathered all of that anxious energy and put it into giving 200% during warm-ups. My doomsday warm-up uniform finally felt hopeful, knowing that at some point in this game, I would likely be able to remove it and once again reveal the number on my jersey that had stuck with me since second grade—#22.

I knew who the starters would be, so that was no surprise. The first quarter started, and we were all into it, cheering for our team. The coach already began to sub players late into the first quarter—a great sign that my predictions about this game were correct. He'd look down the bench, look back to the court, down the bench, back to the court. "Becky" (*Yes, the very same essay-writing, Madison field trip Becky*) or "Jessie" he'd shout, and they'd tear off their warm-ups and run up to coach, waiting to hear who he wanted them to sub in for. With a smile on their faces, they'd kneel down in front of the announcer and scorekeeper, waiting for the loud, brief buzzer that announced when a sub was coming in for a player on the court. I eagerly anticipated hearing even that God-awful buzzer, because I knew it symbolized my turn to step in.

But quarter one quickly dissolved into quarter two, and I was still in my white, iridescent, polyester warm-up. Andy Angel, our mascot, was still hiding beneath my warm-up shirt and, thankfully, he was the only one who could hear my heart beating as hard as it was. "What's going on?" I began to wonder. "Maybe the second half will be my time to shine, and he'll finally put me in..."

Quarter 3 heard more sub buzzers, but none for me. Is there no pleasing this man?! I was early to every practice, on time for every game, and I smiled a shit-eating grin every day while I sat there and took my penance. I was a good, Catholic girl who was turning the other cheek and doing everything Jesus told me to do. So what the *fuck* did it take?! (*The good Catholic girl never swore, by the way. She later learned to knock that shit off—life's too short to hold back.*)

Then came the fourth and final quarter. Our lead in points was so great that even early 2000's Green Bay Packer Brett Favre would have walked back to the locker room to start changing. Any quality coach who's trying to build culture on his/her team would minimally utilize a fourth quarter like this as an opportunity to try out various team dynamics and give other players the chance to prove themselves. A quality coach would have tried out a fresh batch of five players to see how they would collaborate to work the plays, scouting for a "B team" in case of injury or illness. A quality coach would have empowered his players and actually *coached* them to uncover signs of greatness to encourage. *I didn't have a quality coach.*

Instead, with two minutes and forty-five "I-don't-give-a-damn-about-you-but-I-know-private-school-parents-complain" seconds left in the game, that asshole actually called my name. He glanced down the bench and yelled—"Radspinner! You're in at guard!" (*I had a super German last name... before my married Italian last name... before my second and final marriage now with a Polish last name... Yes, I represent ALL of the United Nations.*)

I wanted to say, "Fuck you." I wanted to scream at him. I wanted to stand up, laugh (*to avoid tears*), and walk off that court. I daydreamed my own version of the great movie montages of the late 90s where the character who's pissed off visualizes all of the ways she could exact revenge... Until the character snaps out of it, puts on a smile, and does what she's expected to do. And that's what I did. *I pleased my coach at the cost of my pride.* I mustered up all of my "Do unto others as you want done unto you" energy, even though I knew that I could never be a narcissistic coach like this prick. I quickly removed my warm-ups and ran past my empathetic teammates on the bench who pity-slapped my back as I hustled past each of them. I watched my coach's guppy mouth tell me to sub in (*as though I didn't know—I'd only been playing ball since I was seven, but he never made the time to learn that about me*), and I humbly knelt below the announcers table, holding back tears.

Two minutes and forty-five seconds. To make this clearer for those who don't have the same love for the game of basketball, putting me in with less than three minutes remaining was a slap in the face. It's like that jerk boss who hands you an extra assignment right before the end of the workday on a Friday because he knows you're looking to advance in the company, and this way he can say he gave you an "opportunity." But God as my witness, I ran out onto that court, and I jumped into the action, and it felt *amazing*. I still loved the game itself. I loved the intensity, the demands on my physical and mental abilities, and the camaraderie of working together on a team when there is no time to overthink—you have to trust your instincts and *do*. The basketball court was my first healthy obsession. It provided me with equal parts physical health, mental challenge, friendship, and a humble boost to my confidence that only comes from working toward goals that you accomplish with others. The court was the first place I learned to trust my instincts and play the way that made sense to me—albeit an *overly aggressive* sense, but I had an *identity* on that court. I had moved beyond that shitty MVP situation in middle school. I was trying to move beyond this shitty broken leg situation. But it was like God had given me a gift that He never meant for me to fully open. I always felt like I was one ribbon pull away from truly embracing this present before someone yanked it from my hands.

So I played my heart out in those two minutes and forty-five seconds. On defense, I shuffled my feet and anchored my body lower than I ever thought possible. On offense, I was so textbook that I could have been in a Pistol Pete video like the VHS collection I sat through year after year at summer camp. Pouring sweat *on* the court before sitting in rooms without air conditioning to pour sweat *in a classroom* while learning from Pistol Pete. The summer camp that was hosted by the very high school I was now wearing a jersey for. The summer camp where I proved myself day in and day out. Where I proved that I was a starter and that I earned that spot on the team, but where I was now fighting to get even four fucking minutes of game time. Nothing made sense anymore.

I played hard. Our team won. After I made it through the line to high-five the other team to tell them "Good game," I headed back to the locker room, packed up my stuff, and ran to my parents' car without saying a word to anyone. Once we were in the car, it all poured out:

"I hate him! Less than three minutes left in the game, and he thinks he's throwing me a bone by *letting* me play?! I've worked SO hard! I've worked harder than I ever have! Why is he doing this to *me*?!"

In the past, my parents would have let me vent but then challenged me to own *my* role and take ownership over how *I* could have done better. This time, they were silent. They listened and gave me space to ball my eyes out from the back seat.

We pulled into the Burger King—just about the only fast food location in the small town hosting our "away" game and the final stop before merging onto the highway that would take us home. My dad drove through the drive-thru to get me dinner around 9 p.m., because being a student athlete means attending school all day, followed by packing, followed by a bus ride to your away game, followed by physical exhaustion (*typically*), followed by the need to refuel. But I couldn't eat. All I could do was cry.

I remember my dad pulling into the parking lot and my parents turning toward me. I asked, knowing they didn't have any more answers than I did,

"Why?! Why is my sport being stolen from me? What am I doing wrong?"

Their compassionately shared reply was, "We don't know."

My mind was racing. Excuse *me* for devoting my life to this sport. Excuse *me* for being a team player. Excuse *me* for playing so aggressively that I always walked away bruised and, more often than not, with at least one sprained finger. Excuse *me* for the unforeseen accident that broke my leg—*at your open gym*—and, apparently, my career in this sport. Excuse *me* for never giving your *ego* the chance to determine if I was good enough for *your* team. And excuse *me* for refusing to kiss your ass like so many others who knew just how to feed that ego of yours.

I was raised to let the coach "coach" and to put my head down and work hard. To let my efforts speak for me. To let my *game* tell my coach everything s/he needed to know about me. I give my mom and dad all the credit in the world for not being *those* parents that we see more and more today. The parents who not only think their baby is special but whom overstep their bounds, telling the coach how to do his/her job. The parents who steal the essential opportunities for their children to face adversity, grow a sense of humility and character and come to realize that the world does not revolve around *them*, and life isn't always *fair*. I give my parents all the credit in the world, because I needed to feel this heartbreak for myself—no matter how much I wanted to avoid the struggle. I wanted to believe that being "good" and working hard always equaled success and opportunity, but as we all know, that isn't always the truth. True character is solidified when you *don't* live for the "cause and effect" in life, and you think, say, and do in a way that is *your* most authentic self—not because you expect a *reward*.

My final ember for the sport that had become a crucial part of my identity officially burned out in those two minutes and forty-five seconds. I gained two hard lessons about life from that experience:

You can try your best and give your all, but sometimes *nothing* you do will make one damn bit of difference, because someone or something will be in your way, unwilling to waiver.

When you face unmovable challenges that are out of your control, the only thing you *can* control is how you *respond*.

I realized that I could either *give* my power away to others by faking a smile and exhausting my energy in pursuit of their approval, or I could say, "Fuck this. I *am* better, and I *deserve* better" and walk away. In this case, I chose the latter.

For the first time since I laced up my basketball shoes in second grade, I was giving up on the sport that had taught me so much about life and built up my character. But I wasn't giving up on *basketball*; I was giving up on *his* boundaries. Finally, I was beginning to realize that *I* had permission to set boundaries of my *own*.

So I held on until the end of the season—*because I was raised to see things through*—and then, I chose not to return the following fall. I came to realize that I was ignorant to the truth that I was mixed up in a chess match the entire time. I thought shifting my pawns around the board was making a difference—showing up early to practice, asking what I should work on at home, shagging basketballs to keep the team on point. But this "coach" apparently *knew* how he would put me in checkmate all along. For the first time in my life, I reached a *limit*. I never knew I was allowed to have limits, let alone that I had the permission to set them for myself. I learned that I was strong enough to walk away from a situation that no longer served me. Though it hurt like hell, there was something empowering about acknowledging what only *I* knew to be true for *myself*.

Had I finally found my voice? Had I finally drawn my first line in the sand as a young woman who knew what she wanted and what she was willing to walk away from? Not quite, but it was definitely a step in the right direction. I *am* still amazed that I decided to stop playing. Basketball was like my first true love. It was all I thought about day and night. When I had even a moment of free time, I was out shooting hoops and practicing my dribbling skills. Even my sense of style was directly influenced by what my idols, like Sheryl Swoopes and Lisa Leslie, were wearing in 1997, the early years of the WNBA. (*And, as always, any new gear North Carolina was putting out.*)

So what gave me the confidence to say enough was enough? Sure, I had volleyball in the fall, varsity softball in the spring, and I had recently sold my soul to the Racine Belles' traveling fast-pitch softball team (*kidding, but the commitment of traveling sports is no joke*), but at my core, I felt like I only *played* those sports; basketball (*I thought*) represented who I *was*.

So why don't I remember a "break-up" period after basketball? Maybe because it turned into one of those relationships that lasts far beyond its expiration date—in hindsight, you realize that you cried so much *in* the relationship that you're simply *numb* when it has actually reached its end.

Years later, I would come across this quote that inspires me to this day:

"I found that every time I asked for permission, the answer tended to be *no*, so I had to make my own *yeses*." (Issa Rae)

No matter how hard I tried, the answer kept coming back to me as a "No." It was time to create my own "Yeses"—in a very unexpected next step in my journey. Breaking up with basketball and facing all of this change as an athlete was challenging, but I had another athletic "relationship" waiting in the wings—which could also, coincidentally, describe the reality of my *romantic* relationships for the majority of my life...

Working Girl

While this basketball debacle occurred, other life experiences were taking place that likely helped me to develop the confidence I was now wielding. First and foremost, I secured my first j-o-b. Honestly, though, I can't even call it a job when I compare it to the grueling first jobs that many of my friends took on. My mom worked her way up through SC Johnson (*A Family Company*)—first as a tour guide, then to an office, and finally as a rep with big accounts to manage. This was back in the time when companies realized that a college degree does not always ensure a competent, loyal employee. My mom ran that shit with a high school degree, childhood trauma that she wouldn't face for a few decades, and a husband who left for work in Kevlar every day—Now *that's* a résumé worth reading!

Thanks to her role in the company, as her *offspring*, I was provided the opportunity to apply for jobs within SC Johnson that others my age didn't have access to. My first job found me as a dining room server-meeting preparer-hotel pantry re-stocker at The Council House, a hotel, conference center, and dining venue exclusively for SC Johnson big wigs.

At my interview, I recall sweaty palms and a professional outfit that I wouldn't be caught dead wearing to high school. But I was presenting myself to a supervisor who ran a space that housed a helipad, million-dollar paintings, a *chunk* of the Berlin Wall, and was frequently visited by none other than fourth-generation heir-to-the-throne Sam Johnson himself— This was not the place to wear the quintessential 2000s outfit of white pants, tank top, and *thong*.

The interview was my first experience speaking confidently about my abilities, looking someone in the eye, and assuring them that I was the right person for the position. I was hired a few days later, and on my first day, I'll never forget what the supervisor said to me:

"You did a really great job in your interview, especially with no prior experience. The one thing you said that stayed with me, that no other candidate said, is that you always arrive at least five minutes early to every responsibility. That's an important quality in any role."

I felt seen, heard, and reassured that I was on the right path. This was a new kind of attention that I had only experienced in honors' classes—my responsibility and intellect were proving that I had the potential to go far.

Working at The Council House was, in hindsight, an integral experience of understanding what it meant to be "professional." First, I was required to wear a polyester, navy vest and not-exactly-pencil-but-not-exactly-Amish-but-equally-polyester skirt along with a starched white blouse and, yes, *pantyhose*. You know that shit was invented by a man, right?

Besides learning that hard work often equals horrendous uniforms, this job helped me learn how to swallow my pride and do whatever it takes to make the customer happy. I served everyone from the picky lady who placed her specific order every morning for breakfast—hard-boiled egg (*Hold the yolk*), ½ piece of unbuttered whole-grain toast (*Is that 8 grains or 12?*)—to the future (*and current*) fifth-generation heir to the company, Fisk Johnson, whose guests ate filet mignon while he enjoyed his predictably humble cheeseburger and fries. I learned that being a professional meant accommodating them all, and work was my wheelhouse. I was already a people-pleaser, so showing up to a place every day that *paid* me to please others? That was a cakewalk! To this day, I can lose myself in my work to the point that I don't even break for lunch. There's something about checking off boxes and making people's lives easier that naturally drives me—which is also why I've had to wean myself off of my addiction and learn to set boundaries before I burn out.

I looked on as professional chefs pulled herbs from the garden while I polished actual *silver*ware—while wearing the mandated white gloves, of course. I watched our interior gardener care for the multitude of plant life all around the property as I restocked Toblerone bars in the hotel pantry. I learned to present fine foods from the left and refreshments from the right. Oh, and the best part? We indulged in the leftovers! My palate explored dishes like roast duck, filet mignon, jumbo shrimp flown in for special events, and crème brûlée to name a few. I was the youngest employee by far, and I was gaining life experience that was worth far more than my eight dollars an hour.

This first job opened doors and experiences like no prior opportunities could, and it inspired me to begin imagining what my own future profession would look like. I soaked in the pro's and con's from my coworkers who had far more experience in the service industry, realizing that I had my whole life ahead of me. *I* had the power to choose the path I would take, and little did I know that even though you have the *power*, that doesn't mean you have complete control over the *plan*.

Catholic Kids for Sale!

Maybe it was the confidence I was gaining in working my first job. Maybe it was pure stupidity. But this is the point in my high school career when I share with you that I voluntarily entered myself in an event that was so incredibly demeaning and inappropriate it could only have taken place in the sheltered structures of a Catholic school.

My school was always seeking money from the alumni, community, and anyone in general—apparently sky-high tuition and nearly minimum wage teacher salaries do not an adequate cash flow make. Sure, they had their festivals and galas, but I can't defend this one event because there's no way it exists in the present day. This one event was an auction—not for tangible prizes, but for *dates* with *students*.

Long before Tinder, Grindr, or Bumble, my high school was offering a night on the town with its most willing juniors and seniors—for the right price, that is. In the same auditorium where we ended mass singing "Lean on Me" while the stoners slept in the comfy chairs, our school held an auction... of students... to go on a non-consensual date... with other students... who bought them. Because nothing says blind ignorance like a Catholic school placing kids up for auction in front of their peers. We were required to wear a black top, khaki bottoms, and when our names were called, step to the front of the stage in front of a student body of approximately 800 students as the deacon grabbed the microphone to begin his auction chant, seeking any takers.

I heard my name, and stepped to the middle of the stage, the epitome of fashion in my black shirt and khaki Gap skirt, fingers crossed that someone would start the bidding. What the hell was I thinking?! This is still, often, my experience, though. I throw myself blindly into an idea that sounds great, I want to throw up when it actually arrives, and then I realize it wasn't *so* bad. Then, before I know it... *let's do this again*!

The deacon started up, "Do I hear ten dollars, anyone? Ten dollars!" Several moments of crickets felt like hours before a friend of mine shouted an offer. (*Phew! Let's wrap this up—I will happily pay $15 out of my own pocket to walk off this stage.*) My still-closeted-at-the-time best friend Matt gradually stood up and countered with all the confidence of a future queen who would run his own corner of the fashion world: "Twenty. Dollars." Then my boyfriend at the time chimed in (*more on him later*). I felt so grateful that these two young men were coming to my rescue. I knew it would be over soon. Or would it?

Suddenly, a bidding war ensued. Matt was definitely proving that best friend trumps boyfriend, because he had no intentions of giving up. My boyfriend likely felt that he couldn't give up, because what would *that* look like to the crowd of onlookers? Back and forth these two went. The intensity grew to the point that students were applauding when the bidding went higher. Counteroffers ensued until my boyfriend reached a bid of *$100*, and then there was a slight pause.

Finally, I could see in Matt's eyes that he was bored by this *boy* who Matt knew would only be a temporary placeholder in my life, compared to *him*, my best friend. Matt was over this fiasco. With one hand on his hip, he proudly raised a rectangular paper in the air, waving it like a pride flag in June when he calmly and resolutely announced to the whole student body,

"I've got a blank check. I can go all day."

Hoooooly shit. Who else could pull off a stunt like this but a gay man rushing in to save his best girlfriend? Ultimately, the boyfriend lost *(now and later)* of course—to the tune of a $200 check that Matt's mom so generously allowed him to write. Technically, "winning" me meant that Matt received a gift certificate to take me out for dinner at the Olive Garden along with tickets for the play to be performed by our high school theater group in this very "auction house." But the best part? Matt was a *lead in the freaking play!* Meaning that he spent a crap ton of *(his parents')* money just to beat my boyfriend for a date he *couldn't even take me on*! Power move. Queen 1, Boyfriend 0. And in true upper-hand bad-assery, Matt let the entire school day pass before giving my boyfriend *permission* to use the voucher and tickets to take me out... to see *him* perform on stage.

Matt taught me a couple of things that day. 1. Never. Ever. Mess with a Queen *(especially one who was growing up in a society that was nowhere near as open-minded as it is today)*, and 2. Friends will always be the last ones standing next to you in the end. I had a long road ahead before I would truly understand the power of friendships, but I'll be damned if that day doesn't go down in my lifetime as the most incredible way that a friend supported me without blinking an eye at what anyone else was thinking.

Oh, Mickey, You're So Fine

My mom continued to coach the pom-pon squad at SCHS, and during those first two years of high school, I stopped down after school every now and then to swing by practice and reminisce about all of those childhood years when I tagged along with my mom to the various high schools where she coached. Pom practices were always a comfort for me from a very young age. Whether we were out in Union Grove or nearby at Park High School, the dance world fascinated me unlike cheerleading or other female-centric sports ever did. In poms, you had to be athletic to dance for nearly three minutes straight with pointed toes and high kicks, and you had to be prepared to drop into the splits right out of a kick line. I saw the sweat on their brows and the determination of the squad to practice their contagions until they were just right so that they were a uniformed *whole* rather than *individual* spotlights.

One of my first memories of attending these practices centers around watching the captains choreograph their next routine in the back of their geometry notebooks. I watched as they sketched out formations of X's and O's like football plays, ensuring that every girl was accounted for and that the choreography aligned perfectly with the music. It was empowering to watch these young women so intently focused on something they were passionate about, working tirelessly to achieve their absolute best. Sure, they were focused on the crowd (*and the boys*) who would be watching them, but they gave so much at practices that I had to believe it was about more than just making an audience smile at halftime.

Even at elementary age, I remember standing in the back of their practices while the captains taught a new routine, realizing that I was able to memorize the eight-counts quickly. I would "mark" the routine as the squad practiced, slyly pointing my toes in sync with the kick line or mimicking the arm movements close to my chest so that no one knew I was trying something so seemingly distant from my usual athletic arenas.

Eventually, I found the confidence to publicly dabble in this artistic form of athleticism and creativity. During one of their practices, I found my place at the back of the gym, knowing that the formation would begin facing the home crowd in the opposite direction. Initially, they thought it was cute that this elementary kid wanted to be like them, like I was their little mascot, but at that practice, one of the captains noticed me marking the routine and was amazed that I actually *knew* the routine she wrote. Word spread quickly, and eventually, they asked me to sub in at practice when one of the girls was sick. I guess poms (*through my mom*) was my first real taste of female empowerment. No men were around telling them if they made the team or not. No men were deciding who would perform each night or if the music was a good choice. Sure, they performed primarily for the *boys'* games, but they were often gaining more attention (*and more trophies*) than the boys ever did, and the crowds cheered just as loudly for the halftime experience as they did for the game itself.

These women had complete control over the choreography, the uniforms, and ultimately, their bodies. They chose how sexy they wanted to appear and, *trust me*, there were many a chair routine that I'm sure incited instant boners from all the young (*and old*) men in the crowd. Only, the young men would inevitably have to sit *next to* these pre-Beyoncé bad-ass women in their World History class the next day, the poor bastards! These women seemed so powerful, and I never forgot that feeling.

I guess that's why, several years later, when the absence of basketball left a hole in my heart, I officially said "Bye, Bye, Bye" (*JC Chasez was always my favorite in case you were wondering*) to basketball in the fall and winter. And to *everyone's* surprise—*including my mom's*—said "Here We Go" *(NSYNC came a close second to JTT)* to officially trying out for my high school pom-pon squad. *Plot twist!*

Making the shift to poms from basketball was unheard of because it simply didn't make *social* sense. There was a basketball crowd separate from the pom crowd—how could you make that kind of transition in the latter half of high school? *Who did I think I was?*

Like all life-changing transitions, it was very hard to face, but it proved to be one of the best decisions of my high school career. I learned how to pivot in a big way—to go against the grain and listen to myself for a change. I faced confusion, questions, and doubters, but my supportive inner circle reassured me that I'd always done anything I put my mind to before, why would this time be any different?

I proved to myself, more than anyone, that I was exactly where I needed to be at exactly the right moment in my life. And nothing was more rewarding than the summer before my senior year when I was selected for the Badgerette All-Star squad at pom camp. That gritty, aggressive little basketball player applied that same tenacity to a *new* sport just as she was becoming a woman. And her inner child never smiled brighter than when this all-star squad, this team she never would have dreamed of being a part of, performed in the most magical place—*Disneyworld*. And she lived happily ever after... no prince needed.

Dear Asshole

By the end of sophomore year, I thought I had it all figured out: dates to formal dances, a quality friend group, a new sport added to those I was already involved in, and my driver's license before many of my friends. Cruising in my teal 1993 Pontiac Sunbird, blaring Nelly's "Country Grammar" out of my aftermarket Best Buy CD player while singing all of the lyrics (*with internet access to Lyrics.com, we were now invincible*), I was a rising phoenix, ready for whatever came next. By definition, though, sophomores are "wise fools," and even I wouldn't escape that fateful truth as I headed into my junior year.

If I thought *sports* gave me *purpose*, then I definitely fell into the trap of believing that getting attention from *boys* gave me my *identity*. Somewhere in my middle and high school years, I gradually stopped acting according to my own instincts and, instead, paid close attention to learn what I could do to gain boys' attention. I was still a dick tease through and through, though, so apparently I was on a mission that had no end game in mind—I just knew that it felt good to *belong* to someone, and that felt like a security I had never known. It's amazing how something that feels like *security* can so easily turn to *necessity* just before it develops into *co-dependence*.

I don't remember the details of how I came to date high school boyfriend #1, but I remember it having something to do with an upcoming dance and friends setting us up. He was a really funny and kind guy who was far taller than my barely 5' 4," and he made me feel special. He also came with the added red flag that would draw me like a moth to the flame in future relationships—he came from broken circumstances, and I learned very quickly that I *love* trying to "fix" what I don't have control over. Because loving someone means sacrificing all of *your* happiness in an effort to protect *theirs*, right?

So we went along holding hands at football games and "parties" (*I didn't touch a drop of alcohol until senior year—if sperm could jump, I only imagined what Smirnoff could do.*), and we got to know each other's families. I was on cloud nine... until I wasn't. I recall a conversation on the landline phone when he eluded to the idea of taking a "break." I cried. I *begged*. Even the most pathetic person in the world would have felt bad for me. We stayed together—*because high school boys don't know what they're in for when they encounter that first girlfriend losing her fucking mind*—and I continued my codependent pattern from middle school, afraid that losing him would mean losing my identity.

After a brief period, though, a new emotion rose up: apathy. One day, I just stopped giving a shit about trying so damn hard to make it work. I'm sure it developed a bit more dramatically than that, but I hit a point where the flame had fizzled. So I did what any self-respecting young woman would do in this situation: I kept one foot in the relationship and one foot dangling out there to test the waters and see who else might be interested, because I craved that initial, obsessive attention that came with a new relationship. Attention was my drug, monogamy my high. I sought my identity *externally*, and as my life's pattern would prove, I found it in the most unexpected places.

After breaking up in someone's basement party, my second foot quickly slid out of that relationship so that I could cannonball into the next. Enter high school boyfriend #2—the auction *loser*. He was a year younger than me, but he was more mature than most of the guys his age. This is best proven by the fact that he communicated his interest in me by inviting me out to his mom's minivan to listen to the song "I Can't Fight This Feeling Anymore." Romantic, right? He aspired to be a pastry chef—*I gained ten pounds in that brief relationship before losing all 100+ of his.* He was another kind, thoughtful guy who was doomed the minute he caught my eye. He gave me *too much* attention, and in the famous words of Ferris Bueller, "You can't respect somebody who kisses your ass. It just doesn't work." Apathy kicked in again, and not long after it began, I was off.

If I had been as reflective as I am now, maybe I would have paused to ask myself WTF before jumping into a new relationship. But, alas, this is *not* a sensible story, people; this is *me* and me in *high school,* nonetheless. In hindsight, from my much older and *wiser* pedestal, I have wondered where the relationship began to fizzle in these and several future relationships came from. If I could go back in time or—*Ooh! Even better*—apparate like Ghostwriter in my favorite 1992 PBS kids' mystery show of the same name, flip open to a page in my high school diary filled with bitchy and entitled remarks, and paranormally communicate the following to my younger self:

Dear *Asshole,*

I see you've started collecting boyfriends like Pound Puppies, so it's time to have a reality check. In a few decades when mental health and seeing a therapist is the norm (*and they've swept electro-shock therapy under the rug*), this is what we call "a pattern."

High School Boyfriend #1 and HB #2 were solid choices—so far you haven't picked an asshole, a narcissist, *or* a wet blanket—oh, don't you worry, though, *he* comes later! So you're two for two, *but* that means you broke two nice guys' hearts, and this is why YOU need to actually hold

YOURSELF accountable to reflect, know better, and then do better so that you're not a dick to another poor, innocent soul—*oh, don't you worry, though, you will!* Since this is such a dramatically foreign concept for an only child such as yourself, let me impart these reflective questions (*even though you're not emotionally mature enough to fully appreciate them... yet*):

1. How are you so *confident* in your decision to end these relationships? Were you at a breaking point of being too bored or jaded? Did your "attention" tolerance get too strong, and someone else was nearby to give you a bigger dose? Or did you have too many toys to choose from growing up, so now you play with *boys* instead of *Barbies*?

2. How much is *fear* driving your decision to get in and out of these relationships? Are you afraid of being alone? (*Rush into a relationship*) or afraid of being broken up with first (*Rush out of a relationship*)?

3. Remember those friends you used to make time for? Why do you place them on the backburner when you have a boyfriend? Is it your black-and-white brain that struggles to balance time with both your friend group *and* a boyfriend? (In all honesty, that was likely the truth—to this day, my scales are always tipping in an effort to gain both of my current needs: time with people I care about and time *alone.*)

4. What will you do when, *not if,* you end future relationships? Crawl back to the friends you ditched when you thought you didn't need them? What will it take for you to see that you can value *all* of these people in your life without losing yourself, and them, in pursuit of a boyfriend? You want someone to belong to so badly—why don't you see that belonging to your *friends* can be just as rewarding?

5. Ever heard of "ADHD?" Search it on Yahoo! (*About 10mg of Adderall should do... just a guess...*)

6. Oh, and "people pleaser"—give that one a search on Yahoo! as well. Maybe drop the phrase into a non-sexually titled chat room (*Rare, I know*) and see if a 50-year-old man pretending to be a fellow 16-year-old can give you some advice. (Don't ever *meet* this person in real life, though. In a few years, this will make sense: Google "*Catfishing.*") By the way, your chat name "sweetness_w_attitude" isn't helping your cause.

7. Got that definition for "People Pleaser"? Okay. STOP BEING ONE. What if your eventual apathy in relationships is a direct result of your initial efforts to make a guy like you by (naïvely) *pretending* to be what *he* wants you to be? Inevitably, time passes, and you can't keep the façade up any longer, and so you start remembering—Oh! I have my *own* hopes and dreams, and... wait... who are *you*? Why am I with *you*? Maybe that's why the people closest to you keep telling you to give yourself some "space" before another relationship? (*I know, your generation is told to "follow your heart." Knock that shit off.*)

8. Why are you about to jump into *another* new relationship? Just because a guy shows you attention, that doesn't mean that you need to pursue an exclusive relationship with him. You know, it *is* okay to smile, flirt, and... stay single. (*I know, I know—he's in a band... I'm talking to a brick wall of teenage rebellion at this point, aren't I?*)

Okay, okay. I've reached your mental and emotional capacity, I'm sure. Go ahead and scarf down some Bagel Bites to ease your ego, and then, for the love of God, please give a little thought to these questions.

Love,

Your Future Self (B.F.F.A.E.)

P.S. Quit being a bitch to Mom. Dad's right—you go too far; she actually does love the shit out of you, and there will never come a day when she doesn't expect you to be thirty minutes early to everything... even after you have kids... get over it. You'll both kick ass in therapy down the road anyway, so just buckle up in the meantime. ("Click it or Ticket," girl)

Bigger and Better Things

Apparently, senior year was prime time to flip my world upside down, as the opportunities I dove into were far beyond the norm of what anyone in my life expected—even beyond my pom-pons plot twist. I guess when you've tried so hard to fit in for three years, you might as well give up and just assume the persona of a complete *stranger*.

In no particular order, these are the choices I made that didn't even align with the *non-existent* identity that I *never* created for myself:

- Supporting acting and singing role in the musical *Annie Get Your Gun* (W.T.F. Thank God social media didn't exist back then.)

- Named "Miss Sunshine" at that Badgerette Pom-Pon camp and invited to their All-Star Squad to perform at Disney World. This one might not surprise you now, but for my family who knew me as a bit of a whiny brat, it seemed *laughable*. Proof: On the final day of camp, my mom was recording the closing event on her VHS mini-tape camcorder. When the coach prefaced one of the All-Star squad selections, she shared, "This camper was definitely the most positive and inviting person at camp..." It turned out that camper was *me*. The best part? Just as she was about to call my name, my mom turned the camera *off*! The recording abruptly begins again, shaking up and down as my mom was in an overjoyed state of absolute *shock*.

- Contestant in the Miss Racine *Pageant*. Oh, you read that right, *pageant*. College scholarship money was promised to every contestant just for trying, and since I had out-of-state, Big 10 dreams, I thought it would be worth it. I aspired to be a lawyer, so the speaking part was in the bag. My talent was a modern, pom-pon dance, because puppies would die if I tried to play the trumpet like the girl who got the crown, and my only other talent was shooting three-pointers, so there's that. While my choreography and performance *were* spot on, when was the last time you saw Miss America get crowned for her amazing *pom-pon routine?* Yeah, never. Also, my black polyester Kmart bikini with Bing cherries and boy shorts *definitely* wasn't doing me any favors, even with my sky-high *clear* plastic shoes. You'll be surprised to hear that I *didn't* place in the top three (*or five out of seven*), but I gained appreciation for the demands of pageant life and the brilliance of women who actually do excel in them. Don't worry, though, I left it to the professionals from then on.

- HB #3 entered the picture with a friend group I hadn't hung out with at any point in my high school years (*Did I mention there were less than two-hundred students in my graduating class?*). He was in a band; I played fast-pitch softball. He was Hot Topic; I was The Limited sale rack. His skin was as white as the suit he wore to our prom; my skin was a radiant, George Hamilton-esque tanning-bed orange to complement my coral-colored dress. We couldn't have been more opposite, but true to my chameleon qualities as a girlfriend, I sure did swap my Gap style for safety pins and pink Chuck Taylors.

Needless to say, my senior year was one for the books. I must have felt quite comfortable in my senior status, but it's still fascinating to me that I took on so many new and diverse interests and opportunities. The irony of all of this was that for the first time in my young life, I was doing all of these things based on my *own* interests and curiosities. Each hobby I took on required a lot of my time and energy, and I don't remember hesitating at any of the challenges nor the changes that they brought. Maybe I was leveling up my attention addiction? Maybe this was the first real evidence of productive ADHD? Maybe this was my unique way of feeding my other addiction—*goal-setting*—so that I could meet a goal in order to... move on to the next goal... so I can move on to the next goal...

I was having a small-town girl's *Eat, Pray, Love*—well, mine was more like *Eat, Pray, Live It Up!* Either way, I was stretching far beyond my norm, and though I didn't realize it, I was solidifying my *identity* in the smallest of ways. My athletic identity was already established, but the next to come was my own sense of style. I traded The Limited and Express for thrift shopping and sewing my own clothes and accessories. Thrift shopping in the early 2000s did *not* carry the positive connotations of "green" or "vintage" as it does today—at least not in my small town nor my small, melting pot of socioeconomic statuses in high school.

Shopping at Goodwill, in my letterman's jacket no less, was still referred to as "used," "second hand," or my favorite response when girls would question my look: "You shop there?" (*with a look of disgust climbing from their nose to their furrowed foreheads*). Somehow, their opinions didn't matter to me. I was beginning to shift toward worthy priorities—like getting the best deal (*still love a 50% off ticket color of the day*). Back then, I picked one-of-a-kind items that spoke to *me*, not the style of the season that someone at corporate styled in a window display for me to carbon copy.

Between my newfound ability to ignore popular thought and the way I was challenging my budding sewing, I can see now that I was claiming small boundaries through *fashion*. Without having to say a word, my clothes conveyed their own message: "This is who I am: take it or leave it." This seemingly small step ended up becoming a core part of who I am today, and I applaud that young woman, because we all know that *Mean Girls* was based on real-life bitches—especially the ones who *peaked* in high school.

Within the same world of style, I finally began embracing my natural curls. My mom used to joke that she emptied a bottle of Johnson's "No More Tears" conditioning spray on my hair after bath every night just to get through my snarled mess. So, of course, I valued those efforts by immediately *singeing* my beautiful ringlets as straight and as dry as angel hair spaghetti from '97-'02.

But in 2003, I was getting back in touch with my roots (*God, I love a good pun*), and I started learning how to care for and embrace my curls—mind you, this was still long before Pinterest, *TikTok*, or any other form of social media where you could actually gain quick tips and suggested products. Embracing my curls was like telling myself "You're wonderful just the way you were made"—it was another step in the right direction. Another step, though, that I wasn't mature or mindful enough to name as it was happening. I couldn't fully appreciate the way I was now setting boundaries by stepping away from pleasing others and instead asking *myself* what it was that pleased *me*.

Hindsight is such a blessing. That young woman wasn't aware that these choices were forming (*or solidifying*) her identity. Maybe if she had, she would have found her voice in more substantial parts of herself like integrity, self-esteem, and independence. Instead, these surface-level connections were only the tip of the iceberg that she wouldn't explore deeper for *decades* to come.

Senior year was definitely a whirlwind with signs of the hope of what the future held. As that year came to a close, I was officially heading off to Purdue University! I was going to get away and *reinvent* myself. What could possibly go wrong for a small-town girl with BIG dreams... *that weren't her own?*

Excuse

Kristy Jean

Shit Sitting

When I envisioned college, I aligned my expectations with the perception I gained from my experience: White girl. Born and raised in a hometown of 80,000. Private, Catholic schooling K-12. Enrolled in honors classes. Played Division 2 sports and traveling league softball. Had the time to take the lead in a variety of clubs and volunteer in my community. Held a few steady jobs that provided me with a little spending money and mostly built my savings account at the local credit union. I was *obviously* meant for so much more than this provincial life! I imagined that thriving so well in this (*privileged*) life *must* have meant that I was ready to spread my wings and get the hell out of here, *right?*

Wrong. So fucking wrong. Enrolling at Purdue University because I believed I just *had to* attend a Big 10 school, even though it didn't even have the major I would need as a future lawyer—***wrong***. Leaving after less than 24 hours because my case of the *holy-shit-what-the-Hell-did-I-do's* didn't kick in until I was unpacking in the dorm room with my parents—***wrong***. Moving back home with my tail between my legs, enrolling in the local state university, and remaining delusional that I just needed to go to a different, closer, but just as prestigiously expensive, school 45-minutes away—*wrong*. Enrolling at Marquette University only to determine that law *wasn't* for me and that teaching was my actual calling—*wrong*. Re-enrolling back at the University of Wisconsin-Parkside only months later with my tail *further* between my legs—*wrong*.

I punished myself (*and, let's be real, my emotionally and financially supportive parents*) over and over and over again, and for what? Because I simply couldn't accept who I was and what I needed. Because I couldn't help fighting the reality that I was a small-town girl who refused to admit that she felt most comfortable *in her small town*. My delusions led me to believe that I was supposed to hop on that *"midnight train going anywhere..."*, so when I didn't, shame washed over me, and I was too chicken-shit to go for it. And maybe it was never truly a part of the plan that was meant for me—no matter how hard I fought it. I had no one to blame for these sky-high, inauthentic expectations and unnecessarily large leaps except *myself*.

I graduated high school naïvely believing that the world revolved around me. I convinced myself that I was a big fish in a little pond who just needed to get out of this small pond so that I could swim in deeper, bluer waters and show the *world* what it was missing. I traded blissful ignorance for complete and utter *shame*, blind confidence for a shit-ton of fear-filled *excuses*. I was Eve in the Garden of Eden—my nakedness a startling realization. Sure, I'd been "naked" all along, but with the comfort of my home, my family, and a consistent sense of predictability, I simply didn't know what I didn't know until I tasted the forbidden fruit of someone *else's* dreams that I naïvely believed to be my own.

So I made grandiose assumptions that I knew better than *everyone*—including God. *I* was ready for adventure. *I* was ready to step fearlessly into the unknown. That forbidden fruit was ripe for the picking, and I was hell-bent in believing that once *I* took a bite, God would realize that *I* was far more capable than even *He* imagined—*His* plan was nothing compared to *my* plan. I hadn't even pierced the skin on that fruit, though, before I knew I fucked up.

There's nothing quite as sobering in life as those rare, fight-or-flight (*because the freeze eventually has to thaw, and then you're still left with only two choices*) instances when you have no forewarning that you're about to be thrust from 100% clarity and confidence to 100% scared shitless, ready or not. The effects of eating that fruit (*whether it was your choice or not*) tend to last far longer than you imagined. Realizing you're naked is only the *first* in many unforeseen discomforts God places in your path, waiting to see if you will crumble with *excuses* or rebuild and rise with *humility*. I was delusional about who I was and what I needed, and I would continue in my ignorant blindness for more than a decade. For me, crumbling seemed the best place to start.

So there I was, begrudgingly back at UW-Parkside after spending a year-and-a-half acting like I was *better than* this place and people who had welcomed me so warmly. I was in the depths of denial, projecting all of the inner pain I was feeling. I finally had to come to terms with who I, *disappointingly*, was and what I, *reluctantly*, needed. I entered the "real" world expecting one path to unfold before me, but the "real" world left me in its wake, embarrassed by the crushing reality that this wasn't the life I had hoped and worked for.

Life didn't make sense. I worked my ass off in high school to earn those BIG packets in the mail, communicating that exemplary institutions across the country wanted *me*. I attended a college-prep high school where I was *literally* prepared for these opportunities. I was given every accolade and acknowledgement that said I *should* want these opportunities and that I *would* be successful in them!

And yet, for the first time in my life, or maybe the first time since those confident childhood years, I *knew* something wasn't right for *me* because I walked the walk. I followed the illusion of moving far away and reinventing myself... until I tripped, stumbled, and fell flat on my face. I assumed I was coasting into a dream life that was uniquely my own, only to discover that it was never meant to be more than a dream—

someone else's dream.

The silver lining was that I no longer needed to look around to see what everyone else was doing and who they wanted me to be. I knew by the intense, *stomach-churning*, instinctual feeling deep inside of me that neither Purdue *nor* Marquette were right for me. In my first attempt to stretch beyond the safety of the hometown I was so resentful of, I let fear (*and a shit-ton of homesickness*) drive me right back to my comfort zone...

Unsurprisingly, though, I lied to myself about the rationale for my return, and I even began believing my own lies when I explained my failed attempt at a hero's journey to others. I made excuses for my return:

"It just wasn't the program I was looking for." (*True, but technically, I was aware of that truth way back before I even registered...*)

"Why pay $20,000 a year to become a teacher when I can attend our local state university and pay a quarter of that cost?!" (*True... but, again, I knew that before I enrolled...*)

Though these statements were true, the lie was embedded in the way I said they were my *reasons* for coming back home. They were not my *reasons*. They were my *excuses*. My excuses for avoiding the world. My excuses for avoiding the discomfort of being truly on my own. Excuses that would ultimately catapult me into confusion, shame, and depression as I wondered what the hell life was supposed to look like when the map I carefully crafted for years just went up in flames.

As my map burned to ash, I watched friends live out those same dreams I had only months before. They went away to school—and *stayed* away at school. They faced the discomfort, often with a healthy dose of alcohol—as we all did (*because only college students reference the days of the week with self-destructive names like "Tanked Tuesday" and "Wasted Wednesday" to give themselves permission to treat every day like a weekend*), but *they* made it... and *I* didn't.

Thank God MySpace was the only half-assed social media platform at the time. If Instagram, Facebook, or TikTok existed back then, and I had to choke down smiling face after smiling face of every person who was proudly living out their dreams for the world to see, I'm sure I would have sunk further into my high-functioning depression. I have profound empathy for young people today, as they face the barrage of guilt and shame-inducing messages on social media today. I don't know how I would have managed.

Like so many 18-, 19-, and 20-somethings, I felt like the predictable structures of society began to crumble at my high school commencement. After graduation, it was as if the world tilted its head in confusion, looked at me like a dog wanting to play fetch, wondering why the hell I wasn't throwing the ball—"*You've always known how to play this "game" called school before, so why do you seem so confused now? Throw the damn ball!*" But what society doesn't understand (*or teach you*) is that it has always *told* you what to do in the past:

Go to school.
Don't be a dick.
Get good grades.
Join some group activities.
Make friends.
Date boys to prove you will get married one day.
But... Keep. Your. Legs. Closed.
Be happy.
Be grateful.
Repeat.

But the worst part about the end of high school is that you speed-shift from a few rare opportunities to make your own choices into this new world where *every choice imaginable* is suddenly made available. Oh, and by the way, just because you make a choice, that doesn't mean that it will choose *you* in return. You are now Indiana Jones in the *Raiders of the Lost Ark*. You can muster up all of your experience and confidence to chart a course you think is best as you carefully step from the temple entrance to that golden idol statue, but all the experience in the world still can't remove the impending, and very likely possibility, that one wrong step equals death by ancient spikes impaling your skull.

Though most of choices at this point in your life aren't necessarily life or death, and you're far too young to have the credentials of a paleontologist-adventurer, you *are* at an age when it feels like your choices have black-and-white consequences. Those paths might accept you, but more than likely, they will chew you up and spit you out. Colleges will say no. Social groups will say no. Professors will say no. Bosses will say no. Cry your eyes out on your own time—life doesn't come with Kleenex. You can prepare your little heart out, but at the end of the day, life owes you *nothing*.

That is scary shit for an 18-year-old to face, because you're still a decade (*or two, or three, or four...*) away from the realization that there is a *beauty* in life not owing you anything. You owe it to *yourself* to build a life you're proud of without expecting one to fall into your lap. But just as a beautiful garden grows from a foundation of stench-emitting manure, so too will your mindfulness only grow when you've been planted in, waded in, and clawed your way out of heaping piles of shit. Sit in that shit and grow from it.

Kristy Jean

Buzzed Betty

So what's a small-town girl to do when she's feeling lost and unsure where her life is headed? Well, return not only to her *hometown* but also to her old *habits* of focusing all of her attention on a *man* she can support with *his* dreams, of course!

I was a serial monogamist. I didn't date jerks, thank God. No, that's one standard I actually continued to hold strong to. What I still lacked, though, was my own identity. And since I lacked my own, I was naturally overeager to help a *boyfriend* embrace *his*.

Which brings us *back* to HB #3 who will now be referred to as Bachelor #1 (*Because I've learned that being an adult means renaming things to make them sound more important and make you sound like you know what the hell you're talking about.*) Returning home meant recanting my previous "we should break up because we'll be so far away from each other, and I'm never coming back" excuse for breaking up. I definitely *was* coming back, so we rekindled our relationship through the transition to college. Somehow, we kept our relationship going through separate universities, separate cities, and very separate interests.

This was the early 2000's, so communication looked like burning minutes on my Motorola Razr (*Yes, there was a time before unlimited cell phone minutes, and it sucked.*) on long phone call conversations. Since I was back to living at home for my freshman year of college and Bachelor #1 was attending another state school an hour away, my dad—*God love him*—agreed to drive me to the McDonald's parking lot halfway between our home and my boyfriend's campus. There, we would meet Bachelor #1, and he and I would drive the remainder of the way to his dormitory for the weekend.

My dad would later reference this pre-Uber experience as "Feeding me to the wolves," but he knew I was stubborn, so it was either I drive my 1993 Pontiac Sunbird alone with limited cell reception out in the county, or he drove me halfway to be sure I was (*mostly*) safe. Needless to say, he's an amazing dad. He never fought me on decisions he knew were idiotic and not necessarily in my best interest. Instead, he gave me his two cents when I was willing to listen, let me fall on my face when I wouldn't, gave me space to learn my lessons, and swooped in to buy me ice cream and talk about it when I was ready to process my choices. I love my dad.

Eventually, though, my dad realized that this long-distance relationship was lasting longer than he expected. Gas prices were increasing, and he was ready to let me feel the full impact of keeping up this charade, so eventually it was left to me to drive my "Teal Mobile" out west on those same country roads every other weekend with Jason Mraz as my only companion.

My obsession with "belonging" to someone was so strong that I happily drove out to that campus more times than I can remember. Sure, he visited back in our hometown from time to time, but I saw those drives as my opportunity to live an altered version of the dream that recently crashed and burned. I didn't see that I was making excuses for not living my fullest life; I saw those drives as "Option D"—since Options A (*Purdue*), B (*Marquette*), and C (*Parkside—which I was still refusing to fully appreciate*) didn't pan out the way I *expected* they would.

This was my chance to live on a campus (*that I wasn't attending*), use a meal plan (*that I wasn't paying for*), and attend events just like a real-life college student (*who wasn't too chickenshit to leave home*).

I definitely grew as an individual, though, because of the time I spent jamming to Jason Mraz's latest albums on my hour-long commute and the experiences I had around campus with or without my boyfriend. I was away-*adjacent*. It was as though college was the weekend sleepover that I knew would end by Sunday, and then my week would resume to its predictable comfort zones once again. Permission to enjoy these weekends came without the pains of homesickness, because I was surrounded by people I knew. It also comforted me to know that I could *sample* moving away without having to make an actual commitment to moving away myself (*or, worse, help my family re-understand that it was something I might actually want for myself...*)

So, my Jason Mraz albums and I became regular travelers to a campus that neither of us belonged to in order to spend time with Bachelor #1. The majority of his bandmates relocated to the same school/area so that they could keep the dream alive. And where there's a band, there is an immense amount of band *practice*. When you're the girlfriend of a guy in a punk rock band in high school, your support looks like many hours sitting in a band member's childhood basement making "merch" and attending their shows in other people's basements and church halls. When you become the girlfriend of a guy in a band in *college*, it means many hours sitting in the *living room* of the band's off-campus rental house, making "merch", and attending their shows in the campus' generic coffee shop and surrounding church festivals.

I think it's important here to clarify the difference between a "groupie" and a "girlfriend," especially because I was the *latter*. Groupies show up where they think they can find the band, wear slutty clothes in hopes of sleeping with *any* member of the band, *buy* the merch to show their dedication, and move on to another band to obsess over. Girlfriends have sat through a million practice sessions to get ready for the event they've already heard about a million times, wear slutty-*adjacent* clothes to make the other guys in the band jealous, and *make* the merch that the groupie *bitches* buy with their *whore* money. What I meant to say was that girlfriends never get jealous or defensive... okay, minus the unprotected sex, groupies are winning this one.

    I spent endless hours on that hardwood-floored living room, surrounded by padded walls that were hung to minimize the sound that was surely echoing down the college town roads. I sat on the communal futon and crocheted, offering feedback when it was requested. I wrote in my journal. I smiled proudly as I genuinely enjoyed the music they created and the company of this group of good guys who were passionately chasing their dreams. I retreated to my boyfriend's bedroom to read, write, email with friends, and complete schoolwork for my own college classes an hour away.

    My classrooms were only an hour's drive from Bachelor #1's campus, but they felt a million miles away from this pseudo-away-at-college experience I was vicariously living through my boyfriend's *actual* experience. I didn't have the balls—sorry, old habits die hard—I didn't have the *vagina*, to move away... *yet*. But somehow, I excused that lack of lady parts by commuting two hours round trip and assimilating to Bachelor #1's campus for less than forty-eight total hours every weekend.

    Did I mention they were an alcohol-*free* band? Yup—dry as the Sahara. A house full of 20-something-year-old guys and not a drop of liquor in sight at an age in life when most people are experimenting with tolerance levels and late-night regrets. Well, besides Bass Player #3 (*Why does the bass player in a band seem to rotate the most? I blame Ethan Embry's T.B. Player in "That Thing You Do" for starting the trend—such a classic.*) Well, our bass player was a closeted alcoholic who participated in band practice *sober* but would suddenly disappear around sunset, only reappearing around the time when our routine delivery of late-night Topper's Sticks was less than a mile away.

Maybe the rest of them were old souls who were far more mature than Bass Player #3 and I ever were. I eventually found, though, that adulting is overrated. I'll choose those future alcohol-induced stories that still bring me to tears with laughter over *maturity* any day.

So there was the sober ska band, and there was *me*—the girl whose family parties had always required stocking the basement fridge with Bartles & James, Miller Lite, and on the special occasion of *every* holiday, my grandma's secret recipe Korbel's brandy slush—I can't imagine what the secret was, because you could definitely smell the brandy two rooms away. (*I love Wisconsin!*)

I distinctly remember one Halloween when my costume was nearly as amazing as the a-ha moment I had at the Halloween party hosted by my neighbor and friend a few apartments down. A few drinks in, I would realize how many excuses I had built up for falsely playing Sober Sally in his college town while being my more authentic Barely-Buzzed Betty in my own hometown. Yes, he was fully aware of this double lifestyle, and we both pretended like "out of sight" was also "out of mind," until reality finally kicked down my door.

My costume that year was a thoughtfully curated, right down to the length of the pearls, Holly Golightly. Everything from my thrifted little black dress to the oversized black sunglasses (*already worn daily as an essential accessory—I missed my most authentic fashion era by a few decades*) and the glistening tiara on my head screamed *Breakfast at Tiffany's*. I was one pastry and a cup of coffee away from standing on a desolate 5th Avenue in 1961. Costume fully accessorized, I joined my friends at the apartment party where alcohol was required more than costumes. The party was in full swing, and the costumes (*nor the wopatui flowing from the Gatorade dispensers that were health-code approved, I'm sure*) did not disappoint.

We were in college. We were told these were the best years of our lives, so why *not* live them up and collect a few regrets? Adversity is the greatest teacher, after all. I was in a safe place. I was with safe people. I was drinking something I was legally allowed to drink. So why did I feel like absolute shit inside? (*Especially since the gut rot of sugary, alcohol-infused fruit usually only comes much later in the hangover, never during the drinking itself!*)

In that moment, time slowed down as I assessed my surroundings. There I was, sitting on a couch, dressed adorably, with a Red Solo cup in one hand and a never-to-be-lit cigarette at the end of my period-appropriate cigarette holder, realizing that this was *my* definition of fun at *this* time in my life. So what was that feeling that kept drawing me off balance? Again, I was usually a Buzzed Betty, not a Trashed Tasha (*though she was a blast!*). If it didn't have to do with the impact of my second glass of this concoction, then it must have had something to do with this long-distance relationship's boundaries, or lack thereof.

And then it hit me—I was shaming myself for drinking just because it was a boundary that my *boyfriend* was against. I never hid my casual drinking, but I also never drank *with* him. I was shaming myself for an experience that didn't mean that much to me, in reality, but it was the precedence of the thing. We were on the same page that I wasn't going to stop drinking just because he was adamantly against it, but I guess there was something deeper that didn't click until I was sitting at that party *literally* in someone else's shoes.

Alcohol consumption may have seemed like a small difference of opinion in that young relationship, but it was only the tip of the iceberg in our very deep differences. He had a very clear boundary about refusing to consume alcohol. He had clear boundaries about being in a band and what that commitment meant. He had clear boundaries about attending his college on his terms. And in that moment, I realized that for every one of his boundaries that I could list, I had *none*. I lived in a very easily swayed mindset, ebbing and flowing with the breeze of opinions around me. I was the opinion-less girl who prided myself on being spontaneous and "going with the flow," but that, I was realizing, was an excuse to avoid doing the work to establish my own identity. As proven by my spot-on Audrey Hepburn-esque mannerisms for the entirety of the party, I was quite content to assume *other* people's identities.

My first thought was, "Is it *really* a relationship if one person has never existed as their truest self?" My next thought was, *"How long has my cup been empty?"*

I dove head-first into supporting his boundaries and his dreams so that I could avoid uncovering my own. This made me a "super supportive girlfriend"—until I was the bitch who broke up with him. I slid that classically beautiful "Promise" ring from Tiffany's, *irony of all ironies*, across the counter of my low-paying, hourly job and into his hand. Because of the gentleman that he was, though, he told me to keep it—likely in hopes that it would find its way back to my left ring finger... and a relationship with him.

To his dismay, though, the relationship was over, and it turned out to be a milestone in my seemingly boundary-less adventures in romance. For the first time in my life, I realized that I'm hardwired, as my dad would say, "When your mind is made up, your mind is made up." My mind was made up about this relationship, and when he realized that, he wrote a *dagger* of a song that only a songwriter with a broken heart can throw into the world. Not only was it well-deserved as the girl who wanted so badly to believe she could be someone else that she stuck around too long, but it had some kickass symbolism and a catchy beat!

In hindsight, Bachelor #1 never stood a chance. Come to think of it, none of them did to this point, but maybe that's the bittersweet truth behind the relationships you choose early in your life. They're not meant to stand the test of time; they're meant to challenge you to figure out where *you* begin and *they* end. And if you're lucky, you come to that realization before you ignorantly coerce your partner into buying an engagement ring, force him to move in with you as soon as possible, or "say yes to the dress" at Kleinfeld's in New York. I'd love to say that this is a list of "two truths and a lie" but, alas, in less than a decade, they would *all* become my truths.

At that time in my life, at the end of my relationship with Bachelor #1, I'm quite sure others were able to see what I simply couldn't: I was on a very *gradual* journey to uncover who I was. But that shit is HARD, real, and dirty work, so to soften the blow, I chose to rest in the cozy comfort of a relationship that kept me anchored to my *past* confidence, as I resisted peeling back the Band-Aid on my complete denial of reality. This would prove to be the pattern of my downfall in two more relationships and one marriage. Life's a bitch when you don't have one of your *own*.

In the course of my time with Bachelor #1, a few years in college had passed. Somehow, years of comfort-zone living in my hometown while tasting the freedom of someone *else's* college commitment gave me the space to build enough confidence to challenge myself to the next level of maturity. I was finally taking small steps to set boundaries around my needs. I was now ready to begin defining my *own* goals, and there simply wasn't a place for him in that reality. I wanted to blame him, but I just couldn't. I hung on too long out of fear, and, in hindsight, that wasn't fair to him. But that's the catch-22 of relationships, right? The paths we walk as a couple will challenge us to grow into who we're meant to be, but that doesn't always mean we grow *together*.

Kristy Jean

Badass Brains

Eventually, I settled into my identity at the very university that I spent three years resenting. Life on campus provided a strikingly different experience than my first year at *home* and my second two years in an off-campus apartment with my cousin and a friend. As would become the theme of my life, I embraced college completely *backwards* in comparison to the traditional experience. I lived at home my freshman year, transitioned into off-campus housing my sophomore and junior years, and moved *on campus* in my senior year.

I was still resisting the shit out of my current reality. I kept telling myself that I was just in a horrible dream and that life had to get back on track at some point... right? I blamed everything under the sun for the fact that I had now spent three years in a life that was never "supposed to be" mine, and I was quick with a million excuses for what was "keeping me" from the life I was *meant* to live.

Little did I know that life was trying to teach me that I wasn't doing it *wrong*; it was just time to put my big girl pants on and admit that this was the life I *actually* needed. The only thing that kept me from moving away was *me*, but I made excuses that my family was *too* co-dependent, my parents were *too* supportive, and those schools were *too* cliquey, but in all reality, God was blessing me with an amazing life that I had *zero* perspective to appreciate—until now.

    Trying to move away was my first *deeply* authentic experience in facing life on my own, and I ran right into my mommy's lap just as I did in that first basketball game. Rather than make that connection for myself, realizing that I just needed more time before I'd be ready, I threw a subconscious tantrum during some of the best years of my life. My decision to move back home was actually in alignment with who I was (*and am*), but denial was safer than admitting that truth for some reason. When did I absorb the lie that the only way to truly "make it" in this world is to move away from your hometown, and why did I allow it to steal so much joy away from me?

    Denial consumed so much of my life that I found myself slipping excuses into the most random conversations. I could be at a party, talking to friends about this professor or that professor, and suddenly my verbal denial diarrhea came out as, "...Yeah, that's why I'm thinking about moving away for grad school once I'm done with this place..." *What?*! Graduate school wasn't even on my radar yet, and that 1st-8th grade teaching license was going to need a few years of earning a predictably low-paying salary before I could even *consider* taking on grad school loans. In nearly every interaction, I wanted people to see my justification and excuse me for coloring outside the lines of the "right" way to live out early adulthood. What I didn't realize was that those lines—*society's lines, my high school's lines*—were never meant for *me*, and I wonder how many others feel that exact same way.

    So, *this is the true story of seven strangers, picked to live in a house and have their lives taped—to find out what happens when people stop being polite and start getting real...* Okay, so it wasn't MTV's Real World, but holy shit did this selfish little only child get a heavy dose of the real world when she chose to move on campus. This is *actually* the true story of seven college students who met through the university dance team and keggers at the track team's apartment, who chose to move into a tiny-ass apartment of their own, and watch Rom-Com movies on VHS while drinking Boones Farm to find out what happens when people *stop* being polite and *start* getting real! (*That last statement actually proved to be the exact same as our favorite 90s show...*)

If you haven't realized yet, I have a black-and-white, mostly linear mind. The majority of people wired this way are logical, predictable, and good with numbers. For me, on the other hand, being wired this way means that as soon as you *think* you have me figured out, I will do the exact *opposite* and wonder why you're giving me that confused dog look. Case in point, I ran scared from the opportunity to live with *one* girl in *one* dorm room *hundreds* of miles away from my hometown and traded that for *six* girls in *one* apartment *five miles* from my hometown. The fact that the latter option was my comfort zone is where you either nod unsurprised (*as my husband does*), or you cock your head to the other side, wondering why you ever tried to understand me at all.

We lived on a mostly commuter campus, so each of us was constantly coming and going. Six of us held down part-time jobs around our classes, and, honestly, I don't even *remember* who the seventh girl was because she was a late addition by the university to our apartment, and we never saw her. Maybe she was holding down a full-time job?

I dove into a variety of jobs that, in hindsight, were painting a path to my future in education. During the school year and summers, I worked in daycares, summer camps, and the tutoring center on campus. These jobs didn't offer duck à l'orange like my first gig, but they did teach me:

1. I'm fantastic at getting little kids to nap (*paid off in my future as a mom*), as proven by the $1 my grandma paid me every time I got my baby cousin to sleep and my "nap whisperer" status in the four-year-old room at the first daycare where I truly realized my knack for educating kids.

2. I can make friends with anyone. (*The tutoring center was a diverse mix of people who excelled in everything from academics to Dungeons and Dragons to Guitar Hero to henna tattoo art.*)

3. I am not built for summer camp or any other round-the-clock, day-after-day, unstructured childcare. Fuck *that*. Sure, I can play Chutes and Ladders and teach kids how to sew a cute little stuffy by hand, but that novelty wears off after a couple of hours when you look around and see that the game was never picked up, two game pieces are somehow missing, and scraps of material are littering the *entire* floor. I thrive on structure, so I realized that teaching and lesson planning would be my strong suits, but put me in a room of kids with a bunch of play shit, and I'll lose my mind before the hour is up. I love my kids beyond life itself, but as I tell anyone who will listen (*including my husband when summer days at home get loooong*), God never intended for me to be a stay-at-home mom. That requires *real* "vaginas," and I am in awe of them and theirs.

My diverse jobs and the experiences I encountered with my roommates at this time in my life placed me in situations where I was beginning to question *everything*. They forced me to challenge who I was, what I stood for, who I wanted to be, and who I *didn't* want to be. And though doing that kind of personal growth work suuuuuucks at any stage of life, it's definitely a little more bearable when you've finally allowed yourself to live in your comfort zone with people and places that make you feel safe. An environment where you can fall, crumble, and cry over a $7.99 bottle of Moscato d'Asti because your roommates assure you that you "deserve it," and they'll never let you drink alone. Can you believe that with all of this work in personal growth, I was somehow expected to attend *classes*?! The audacity of these colleges, I tell you.

My first two years of "gen ed" classes kind of sucked. Everyone aiming for an undergraduate degree has to get through them, though, and, if you're me, your Poli Sci 101 night class proves early on that studying law wasn't all that you imagined it to be and that you should finally, *finally* stop fighting your destiny to work in education. The second half of my experience, though, was filled with courses and professors who *inspired* me—especially my badass female professors and supportively challenging male poetry professors.

As a female growing up in the 1990s, I was exposed to a paradox of contrasting experiences. In Catholic school, I still experienced nuns as teachers, men as priests, and stereotypes about women doing all of the cooking, cleaning, and making everything perfect for their families. Simultaneously, I lived in a home that was progressively different. Sure, my mom stayed at home with me until I began elementary school—*a reality I'm grateful for but couldn't even imagine for my own family as we raise our kids in this current decade*—but it was a *choice* my parents made together, not an *expectation* because she had a vagina. When my mom did return to work, I keenly remember the way my parents shared all of the chores and responsibilities. When it came to laundry, for instance, my dad was the one whom I remember taking on that chore. Until the day when *thongs* and *bras* entered my wardrobe—Victoria may have had a secret, but there was no keeping mine from my dad. At that point, he simply couldn't bring himself to face this reality that his baby girl was becoming a woman. *"How do you even fold these things?!"* I once overheard as my dad was navigating a basket of clean laundry. It was that day that we both determined *(in a look without words)* that we would save ourselves any further confusion and awkwardness, and I would take on my own laundry. My parents also shared the responsibility of cooking, and they had an unspoken norm that whoever *didn't* cook was the one who stepped up to hand-wash the dishes.

Even my Catholic high school had progressed to the *19th century* in the message it was now sending its young female students. Sure, abstinence was still touted as the *only* option—keep those legs crossed until you have a ring on your finger, *from a man*, nonetheless. And they tried to enforce saving space for the holy ghost between couples as the homecoming dance trends continued to challenge the system set forth by the pastor in *Footloose*. But in contrast to the experiences my mother-in-law, mom, and aunts had in that very same school decades before, the school board was now touting its "college preparatory" claim to tuition-increasing fame even for *us*, future Suzie Homemakers.

So you can imagine the mind-blowing experience it was for me to *feel* the ground shifting under my feet when I had the honor of participating in public university courses led by brilliant women with doctorates. While I was blessed to have many, there were four who still stand out in my mind for the influence they had on challenging my excuses and view of the world:

- A passionate Latina who opened my eyes to diverse women writers and injustice around the globe

- A fierce women's rights activist who challenged us to step away from society's restrictions and give our own definition to femininity

- A brilliant Lit professor who challenged me to digest more British literature than I care to remember, but who gave me the confidence to read, analyze, and appreciate *anything* thrown at me

- A boldly confident, wise-beyond-her-years professor who could quote Chaucer over a pint of Guinness and was the first to *assure* me that I was a writer

That last professor led my senior thesis course on medieval romance; the capstone of my bachelor of arts in English. As an English major, I wrote a TON of papers, but my final assignment for this course nearly broke me. The objective: write a *minimum* 20-page paper around a self-determined thesis that ties in at least three of the medieval texts we read, analyzed, and/or translated from Middle English (*What a fantastic assignment! Okay, dork moment over.*) Any guesses as to the thesis I crafted and developed into an over *thirty*-page paper that my professor and I shared a "holy shit, we feel empowered" moment around?

"Women in medieval literature utilized their *sexuality* as a *weapon* to gain *power.*"

Come on! That is a *badass* thesis for a 21-year-old who was just about to graduate and head into the real world! And it was 100% inspired by that boldly confident professor and all the others who opened my mind and my world through the literature they so passionately shared with us.

I also had several male professors who valued my, initially, shallow interpretations of the poetry and literature they shared with me—*Dickinson, Plath, Whitman, Homer, and Thoreau to name a few.* And because they invited my initial, juvenile analyses, I felt comfortable exploring deeper meaning in literature. In hindsight, their encouragement set the foundation for my lifelong admiration of these classic authors and my motivation to continue seeking *more* works that gave me that same sense of connection and realization of how small I was in this great big world. Though some of my professors have since passed, their legacy continues to add to my own appreciation for literature and my desire to *revise, revise, revise,* until my written expression sounds just right.

Not-so-subliminal soapbox moment: If you're passionate about an English degree (*or any other dream*), fuck anyone who looks at you, *as they did me,* and ignorantly asks, "What would you even *do* with an *English* degree? Teach? Write *stuff?*" Okay, I will admit, you actually do *teach,* because when you're fresh out of college, you need a j-o-b (*Or, in my case, it could actually become an incredibly fulfilling career*), but ignore those assholes and go for that English degree! You have the rest of your life to *work.* And if you look around, you'll realize that the majority of people never even *use* their specified degrees the way they thought they would anyway. Spend your youth engaged in your *passion.* Sure, you *teach,* but then again, you also *write*—because that is who you *are,* not what you *do.*

These English courses in the second half of my college

career teamed with my education courses, as I pursued both my bachelor's degree in English and teaching certification. I was so blessed to have this balance between both pursuits that were proving to be my equal passions. And unlike many who gripe that they learned *nothing* about their careers in college, I can proudly say that I did. It was because of inspiring education professors who saw us less as "future teachers," and more as citizens of the world who needed authentic preparation so that we were resilient enough to face the *bad* shit while we were doing a ton of *good* shit.

Kristy Jean

I'm Not Your Mommy

My latter experiences in colleges were opening doors to new friendships, new thinking, and the challenge to start focusing on my *own* goals... until another bachelor came along, of course.

Just when I thought I was empowered enough to walk away from my "support men's goals so much that you naïvely take on their identity as your own" phase, that bitch roped me back in. Are you familiar with that *phase*? The one where you answer every question from your partner indecisively because you're waiting to see what *they* want first? Yeah, that unnatural instinct kicked back in and coerced me into my next relationship (*and a couple more after that...*). How long is a *phase* anyway? Is it plausible for a phase to last throughout middle adolescence, teen years, and even into your *20s*? Asking for a friend...

Bachelor #2 came out of a random encounter on a random night out with an old friend who randomly reached out, willing to take me under his wing post breakup to help me explore the *opposite* of what I had lived in "punk-band central." All I knew was that a group of people was gathering, and we had to meet at my friend's friend's house. We arrived, and I didn't know a single person. But those weekend travels to my pseudo-university had built up my courage enough to willingly engage with a complete group of strangers.

I could *instantly* tell that this group was far from the crowd I was accustomed to hanging out with in the first half of my college years. First, we were all of drinking age by this point, and second, we were all itching to *abuse* that Uncle-Sam-given right. The first sign of this truth was the limo parked in front of our gathering place, pre-arranged to drive us safely to and from downtown Milwaukee—a mere 45 minutes away. Apparently, no one was even contemplating playing designated driver tonight.

Between the limo ride and a slew of bars and clubs, I got to know Bachelor #2. He and his brother lived in the home where we initially met, and it seemed that the adventures of this night were just a regular occurrence for this crew. *Nothing* was serious, and *everything* was fun—at least that was how it seemed to me. And after a lot of *seriousness* over the past few years, *fun* was exactly what I needed at this time in my life. Watching future Bachelor #2 and his friends living this exciting and extravagant life definitely enticed me, so I ignorantly did what I always do—soaked in their lifestyle "as is" without a single pause to wonder if it truly fit *me*. Women's lit be damned, my past repeated itself, and after flirtatious interactions that night and weeks of commiserating in conversation about our *individual* heartbreak so much that it became *shared* heartbreak, we clumsily began a relationship that was damned from the beginning. My sense of belonging was once again fulfilled in a man, and I hitched a ride on *his* journey so that I didn't have to do the hard work to figure out what *my own* exciting life could look like.

The fact that we were both licking our wounds after the recent demolition of serious relationships, apparently, wasn't red flag enough for me, because before long, we shifted into an exclusive relationship, which always proved to be a great indicator of longevity in my past! Dad was right again—"When your mind is made up, your mind is made upm" often to my own detriment. Dammit.

I quickly forgave many lingering connections with his ex-girlfriend, even the fact that she was present on that random limo ride to Milwaukee—"We share common friends," he said. The fact that she *broke up* with him but was still *hanging out* with him and his friends should have been a glaring neon sign that told me to stay the fuck away, but I have a sick tendency to gravitate toward a challenge. I also have a sick tendency to give life-consuming problems that I *should* run away from cute names like "a challenge." So, of course, I also excused the fact that when this ex-girlfriend learned that *I* was in the picture, *she* suddenly had "needs" that only *he* could support.

I excused him for helping—*"I just have to drop this off"*—or when he wouldn't answer right away when I called because he was wrapping up an urgent call with her, "She just calls when she's having a *really* hard time." To this day, I genuinely believe (*maybe naïvely*) that it was all emotional co-dependency and not physical cheating, because I didn't have a reason not to trust him. And yet, I also have a sick tendency to let the smoke of assumed positive intent slowly grow to a five-alarm fire that somehow only leaves me burned.

I also excused a lot of his self-serving behaviors, because, well, he bought me expensive gifts (*a very new experience for me*), and I genuinely wanted to support him and the admirable dreams that he seemed to have such clarity in pursuing. Without a doubt, it was his clarity of purpose for his future, entrepreneurial endeavors that made me gravitate toward him. He had a vision for his future, even if he was stumbling over the steps to get there. I couldn't blame him, though, because I was still stumbling over my past, avoiding the gift of being fully aware of the opportunities in my present. I admired his drive and his focus, and I guess I was hoping to soak some of that energy up, dreaming of the day I would find my *own*.

I wonder now, though, if I truly *wanted* to support his dreams or if I wanted to be the *"awesome girlfriend"* who supported his dreams. There's an integral distinction between those two types of girlfriend: The *first* supports her significant other's dreams because she genuinely cares for him and wants what's best for him, as she confidently lives her own life in tandem. The *second* says and does all the "right" things to *look* good and keep the focus on him so that she never has to face her own shit. I'm sure there was a dose of the former in my decision-making, because that's just in my nature. But I had a hell of a lot more of the latter going on at the same time, as I obsessively sought my identity *through* the opinions of him and his friends. I concocted excuse after excuse for my own lack of self-discovery, redirecting the conversations back to him and his admirable goals.

He was earning his degree at the same university where I lived on campus, and he was genuinely talented in the business he was growing. So, with his dream set and the convenience of our geographical proximity, I found every opportunity to encourage and help him pursue his business goals. Travel to Milwaukee for a late-night business pick-up even though I have a paper due tomorrow, because you'd love my company? Of course! Sit in your basement while you inventory product? No problem! Spend weeks planning your amazing birthday surprise and then take you on said surprise—a day trip to Chicago to explore one of your favorite places as I embed all of your favorite things along the way? Well, duh! But when I needed you there for one, special event at my grandma's home, and you were not only "running late" according to your text, but then when I called you wouldn't be able to come at all because you and your brother, *both in your twenties*, "got in trouble" with your MOM?! Um... *what?*

From the beginning, there was always something that just wasn't right about the two of us being together. We weren't really friends to begin with, and I think that ultimately spells disaster in most relationships, because you have no idea if your values line up. The fact that he still kept ties with his ex-girlfriend, whom he had no *actual* ties to, should have also been a huge warning sign, but not for me... at first.

There was one ex-girlfriend encounter I clearly recall

because though I excused it quickly after communicating my discomfort, I vividly remember a *new* feeling about this relationship. For the first time, I was jolted enough by an experience to step, however temporarily, out of my hopeless romantic emotions. I might not have known who I was or what my future would hold, but I knew that *more* of this experience, and *more* of him, did *not* fit into any definition of my future.

This situation was also the first time I remember speaking up while still *in* the relationship, verbally communicating my *own* boundary. I was always accustomed to setting *zero* boundaries throughout the duration of my relationships only to set one, final boundary by *ending* it after there was nothing left to salvage. Maybe I was uniquely spineless or devastatingly fearful of being alone, but to communicate what I was thinking, feeling, and needing as the moment took place was a HUGE milestone for me. It was the first time I actually told my significant other that I was *not* okay with a situation, with genuine hope that it would help us grow. This was a far cry from my usual response to shitty situations in relationships—pretending like everything is okay, building resentment, and throwing him a curveball when I decided I was tired of his shit. Revolutionary, right?!

We were on the road home from another business trip to Milwaukee, and we had genuinely enjoyed our day together, stopping for a delicious lunch and exploring a few unique spots (*his favorite places, of course*). He was driving, and I was (*naïvely*) basking in the joy of knowing that we were feeling more and more like a "real," long-lasting couple each day. Until, that is, when his phone rang.

He looked at the phone, glanced at me in his periphery, and, after a brief pause, answered it. Other than his response of, "Hey," he said very little at the onset of the conversation. And yet, when he did add brief remarks, his voice was shallow and sweet. He was talking someone through something, and it seemed like he was filtering his words very carefully in my presence. Either he was a secret agent or he was talking with someone whose needs were so important to him that this person had apparently won out in the "should I, shouldn't I?" game of answering his phone in front of me. I connected the dots and realized that these "helpful" conversations were those that he was still having with his ex-girlfriend when I wasn't around, but this time, *I had front-row tickets.*

This was the ex who broke up with him for another guy and was now regretting her decision. The ex who moved on to something better but who needed his help to help talk through the struggles she was having—free therapy and free access to keeping him on the hook, just in case. She wanted to have her cake and eat it too, and he fed her right from his own fork. She wanted him to talk her through the struggle of seeing him *move on* with someone else, because she naïvely believed that she would be the only one *who would...*

Upon this realization, with my past history of keeping my mouth shut and pretending like everything is okay, one would assume that I would quietly stew in the passenger seat, waiting for his conversation to end *and then* let him have it. One would be correct, except that my Italian genetics suddenly kicked in, bringing a new response from my mouth and hands. You know how a fifteen-year-old Hispanic girl becomes a woman on her quinceañera? Well, it's my belief that Italian girls have their own coming-of-age transition into womanhood as well, but there's a lot less tulle holding up her dress, and there's no reason for a crown, because though she does embrace her Italian Princess identity, the crown would inevitably break mid-transition. See, an Italian girl becomes a woman the first time someone wrongs her so deeply, so personally, and so carelessly for her needs that she can't help but invoke the spiritual powers of her ancestors. Something about that moment assures her that *better* men have earned custom "cement shoes" as consequence for far lesser offenses than what this man just did to her, and so he, too, deserves the wrath that this Italian princess *held back* in her girlhood, waiting for this very moment.

So I did what any sane, Italian *woman* would do in that situation. I loudly barked, "Who is that?!" as my hands took on a possessed quality, gesturing toward the phone as though the direction of my question was uncertain. His eyes widened, and I knew two things happened in that moment: 1. The ex-girlfriend heard me, and 2. I was officially an Italian Princess. I didn't know that I possessed this power within me, but my curiosity was piqued, as visions of shattered glass ceilings and clear boundaries danced in my head.

What he did next still makes me shutter. Immediately after my rhetorical (*and passive-aggressive*) question caught him off guard, his ass responded to me with the worst sound a man could allow to slip from his mouth when a woman realizes he's done her wrong. In what I vividly remember in my mind as a slow-motion scene in a movie when you know that shit is about to go down, he removed his one remaining hand from the steering wheel, lifted his knee to stand in its place, and formed a pointer finger that he *raised to his lips*. Yes. Yes, he did. Not only did he make the universal symbol for "shut the fuck up," he also had the *balls* to look in my direction and utter, "Shhh!"

Hell. Fucking. No.

In that moment, I didn't need to think it over to determine *if* he was right. There was zero room for benefit of the doubt on this one. I let him have it, and I didn't give a damn what he (*or she for that matter*) felt about it. The words flowed in a stream of directives to *never do that again* along with a wealth of condemning adjectives to describe his behavior. In that moment, my prioritization of *his* goals and *his* dreams dropped off of my list, as that visceral feeling inside triggered a reaction to act out of self-preservation rather than staying small to appease a man. In that moment, without a second thought, I instinctively chose *me* and *my* needs, because I felt it in my bones that this was wrong, and it didn't matter how anyone felt about it or how much they wanted to explain away the experience from *their* perspective.

His response and this experience were wrong for *me*, and for the first time, I listened to and trusted that voice inside of me. She had stayed quiet for some time now, but in that moment, she kicked my ass in gear to be sure I noticed and felt something that would ensure I didn't allow his excuses to wash away this experience.

For the first time in any relationship, I didn't pause to filter through my "Be quiet, be supportive, and always fix problems" mindset. In that moment, the words leapt from my mouth so quickly and so furiously that I don't even remember what I said. I only remember recognizing anger, *true anger*, for the first time in my life, and it was empowering. In that moment, I felt disrespected, and I mustered up the *vagina* to say something about it, never giving a damn about how he would react.

My first boundary was set—no one has the right to take away my voice for their own self-serving purposes. No one has the right to quiet (*or silence*) *my* life in order to live *theirs* out loud. If I had to be alone, then at least I knew that the discomfort of that existence was better than diminishing the fact that I have a *right* to exist. *Alone* is a choice. *Lonely* is the byproduct of accepting someone else's shit. I was coming to realize that it was empowering to accept the former, and I was finally beginning to wonder why I was putting up with the latter.

And yet, new habits are hard-earned, so while that small voice raged in that experience, she inevitably quieted once again as soon as she felt that twinge of fear around being *alone*. She gave in to his excuses and explanations, but this time she made him sit in it to see how *she* would respond, and *that* was new. You have to win the battles to eventually win the war, right? Unfortunately, I was still at a stage in life where, even in my relationships, I always wanted to seek peace over conflict. I still hadn't learned that conflict is the beginning of any worthwhile boundary.

There were several other encounters that differed from this one in details but aligned in the way he was ignorantly careless of my needs and focused on his own self-preservation. During one incredibly snowy winter that created prime conditions for skiing and snowboarding, everyone was itching to get out and experience this rare, fresh powder.

I was newer to snowboarding, but I fell in love with the sport quickly. Back at my pseudo-college years prior, Bachelor #1's landlord was a ski and snowboard instructor, and he collectively passed on his used boards and bindings to the house. I had zero exposure to any snow sport beyond ice-skating and sledding, so I decided that snowboarding—where you literally strap your feet to a board while hurling down a very steep hill—was worth a try. (I'm the girl who can barely walk and chew gum without chewing, remember.) Needless to say, that first time, I fell on my face *and ass* more times than I can remember—and that was just getting off the ski lift! But that experience was a test of my resilience and inner strength, as I had to face the discomfort and persevere to see what was on the other side. This was definitely my kind of sport, and I eventually personalized it with all white board, boots, bindings, goggles, jacket, and snow pants. Because nothing says "I prioritize safety over style" like an entire ensemble that would all but *ensure* the safety crew could *not* find me when, not if, I took a digger in a ditch.

Bachelor #2 had skied since he could walk and was a natural at the sport—just another example of our "opposites attract," right? We were both eager to join his friends and head to the local "mountain" (*In southeastern Wisconsin, we call them mountains, because any hill taller than a barn counts.*) to embrace the winter wonderland that day. He and his buddies pitched the idea of skipping afternoon classes to get out there while the snow was still falling. I had an exam I couldn't miss, and if there was *one* boundary that was ingrained in me since I was a child, it was that your education comes *first*.

Because couples usually do things *together* and in *each other's* best interest, I made the incorrect assumption that he would wait for me, as I would have waited for him, and we would head out *together* a little later. He had a "better" idea—How about he goes with his friends, and *I* drive out later, *on my own*, after my test? Win, win! Yes, great idea. Let me drive my rear-wheel drive, POS, nearly vintage car forty-five minutes west on snow-drifted, county roads after dark *by myself*. You know, after he and his friends drove out there together in their four-wheel drive, sport-utility vehicles.

I was baffled by his selfishness. He was baffled by my confusion. We agreed to disagree, and I headed home to study while they took off without me. I took my exam and then returned to my *completely* empty on-campus apartment, because my roommates had all hit the road to head home for the long weekend before the storm really hit. I cracked open a bottle of Moscato d'Asti, tossed a frozen pizza in the oven, and was just about to press play on my VCR, hoping that *You've Got Mail* would quell my anger and remind me that love *does* exist—somewhere out there—when, suddenly, my phone rang:

Caller: "Good evening, is this Kristy?"

Me: "...Yes."

Caller: "I have arrived for your transport."

Me: "I'm sorry, you must have the wrong number."

Caller: "I don't believe so... I'm parked outside the campus apartments. I was reserved by [Bachelor #2] to drive you to Wilmot Mountain. Is that correct?"

Me: (WTF?! Did his guilt-ridden ass actually rent a town car to take care of something that he was too selfish to do himself?! That silver-spooned bastard! Always used to having his cake and eating it too, so what did he do? Threw money at the problem! I'm disgusted. I'm furious. I'm... *in a Hallmark movie?*)

Maybe it was because I was halfway through my bottle of wine, or maybe it was that damn romantic comedy duo of Ryan and Hanks, but either way, my twenty-something self was suddenly *swooning*. Also, I mean, the car *was* already paid for, and my stuff *was* already packed, and I *deserved* to go snowboarding on a beautiful night like that, God dammit.

Driver: "...Ma'am?"

Me: (*Fuck it. You only live once.*) "I'll be right down!"

I gathered my all-white ensemble and hustled out the door. The snowflakes were enormous, pouring out of the sky, creating a snowstorm that kept all *sane* people in the comfort of their homes. But I've never prided myself on being a super sane person, and what a story this was going to make—*if I got there safely*. The adrenaline rush of this surprising gesture propelled me out the door, down the snow-masked stairs, to the sleek black town car where the driver kindly opened the door for me and placed my belongings in the trunk.

Suddenly, I found myself inside the warmth of a Lincoln Town Car with champagne amenities, riding toward my thoughtful/asshole (*undecided in this moment*) boyfriend and company. I felt like *Pretty Woman*—clutching my Oakley goggles and giggling to myself. This was long before Uber, Lyft, Google Maps, and the like, so my cop's daughter mentality instantly flashed in my mind as I realized that I was in a *random* car with a *complete* stranger in the middle of a *snowstorm* that wasn't letting up. Would I even be able to tell if we were going in the right direction?? Visions of being turned into a lampshade gave me a mild moment of panic, but then I realized that my Motorola Razr had decent reception and a mostly full battery—ah, the false safety that technology provides!

Eventually, I *did* safely arrive, gave him a brief "who do you think you are?!" look, then, embarrassingly, gave one of those adorable fake punches to his chest when he walked up to tip the driver before I decided to enjoy the best powder I've experienced in Wisconsin. I knew it was a short-lived joy, but I deserved it—*I could rest on my morals later*—and luxuries are few and far between when you're a college student. Tonight, I was going to enjoy the sport I was learning to love—on *his* dime.

Obviously, Bachelor #2 and I were on very separate paths, each trying to figure out who we were and what we valued. Ironically, we were both learning how to stand on our own two feet apart from our overly involved families, and in that way, I think we served the purpose of stretching each other to grow up a little bit more. Our relationship was part adventure, part enabling, and it left me heartbroken to have to be the one to end it, leaving both of us confused about what we just endured together.

It was the first time I ended a relationship *without* staying longer than I could have. Usually the end of my relationships felt like a *relief*, because I held on too long past the expiration date. This end was different. This was a boundary I established before I "had" to. I chose being alone; I chose myself. This relationship was unique in the way I read the signs a little quicker this time. And so, from the seated discomfort of the futon beneath my lofted bed, I broke up with him. We both sat there in silence for a few minutes, and then, he was gone. It was a sobering milestone to realize that I just made a decision that I really didn't want to make but that I made it because I knew it was what was best for *me*.

That break-up *broke* me. I'd never chosen to be alone before without the potential of someone in the wings, so this struggle was REAL—like snot running down your face as you cry into your pillow, *real*. The truth is that I wasn't distraught over the ending of that specific relationship; I was distraught because for the first time since *middle school*, I was single, and I didn't know what that lifestyle looked like. I was experiencing personal growth, and I've learned that those experiences always make you feel very lost, like there isn't a light at the end of the tunnel. "Dark before the dawn" and all that beautiful language for when life sucks balls.

There's no doubt now that I was scared to figure out who I was apart from my family, friends, and a romantic relationship—that's still scary as an adult sometimes. There are moments when I want to blame my fear on my "only child" status—that experience can be very isolating even when your parents kick ass and your cousins are *like* your siblings. And there are other times when I want to blame it on my tight-knit, immediate and extended family, because they made it equally impossible to *have* room to breathe, and their love made it so that I didn't *want* room to breathe. It seemed that always needing someone with me was a dangerous security blanket. It led me into a complex reality and misguided relationships—I felt like I simultaneously *needed* someone and *wanted* to get away from everyone. This is still an awareness that I grapple with to this day.

In hindsight, I genuinely believe that I was on the verge of a breakthrough that would have led me to greater independence—if only I would have waited that pain out a few months longer. But this is *me* we're talking about, and I'm an impatient spirit who loves attention, so why *not* toss one more relationship in there before I find my "forever *for now*" and end up with a ring on my finger?! Bachelor #3 came into my life in an even more unlikely way than Bachelor #2, but I guess that's the reality of dating in your 20s—I mean, who meets people at work anymore? (*P.S. That's a gift of thinly veiled foreshadowing—more on him later.*)

Be Still, Dammit

Bachelor #3 was older but just as mixed up as I was when I met him on the dance floor at a country bar out in the county, west of the interstate. My cousins and friends were always great at trying to rally around me after my now infamous, crash-and-burn relationship endings, so they talked me into coming out for sand volleyball and live music. It was such a blessing to have those relationships to bank on, and I only wish I had prioritized them more. It took many, *many* years before I would be able to wrap my brain around having friends AND a romantic relationship. For whatever reason, my black-and-white brain always struggled with balancing the two, and since I was rarely single, I feel like my friends often got the shit end of the friendship stick.

This particular night out was an adventure that took place a few weeks after I broke it off with Bachelor #2, so I was *still* ugly crying, but maybe I just had to throw myself into a night out with friends to find some sense of normalcy! Nope. I was wrong. I cried between swigs of Miller Lite. I cried in the bathroom. I cried on the phone to my *mom*. I cried and cried until I switched to vodka and the band kicked up.

I talked myself into just letting go—to just being present with my cousins and friends and to stop lamenting over a relationship that never truly made any sense. *How pathetic was I?* So many excuses for not living a present life. So many excuses for not living *my own* life.

So there I was, confused as hell about how to live my "best" life without a man defining my existence, dancing freely with my friends and throwing caution to the wind when Bachelor #3 made eye contact with me. Fuuuuuuck. *Here I go again.*

He seemed a little more mature, had a winning smile, and a dance partner sounded like just the thing to keep my mind in the present, right? But as with everything in my life, I neither know how to *stay* in the shallows nor appreciate the *purpose* of staying in them for my own safety. So assuming that I could enjoy a single dance with this stranger and then just move on with the night is laughable even from my far-distant comfort of hindsight.

To this day, I don't jump; I *dive* headfirst into everything (*yoga, event planning, that one time I thought bangs were a good idea...*). And I give all of my immediate energy to whoever I am closely connected to at the time (*new friends who need more from me than I have to give, colleagues who are excited to learn, the 95-year-old alum who I interviewed for my school's centennial celebration and who is now my best friend...*). And so it was with my dance partner who would soon become Bachelor #3.

I craved attention, and he gave me 100% of his. Just as I sought distraction from my heartbreak/ fear-facing, I *later* learned that his fixation on me was a direct result of seeking his *own* form of self-healing in response to his struggles with anger and depression. I was naïve, so of course *I* obsessed over the way *he* obsessed over *me*, telling myself it was a beautifully healthy connection to have and that it was so *different* than the last that it *must* mean this one will be unique!

If we had gone on that show "Baggage," hosted by Jerry Springer, a shit-ton of red warning flags would have been apparent when he opened his luggage, and also when I shared my big secret (*to him*) that I was addicted to monogamy. If we had, maybe we would have dodged this bullet. But we didn't, and so our *unique* relationship began.

Our story started with me spending more time at his grown-up house over my on-campus apartment and my lovely seven roommates (*Well, six... seriously, where did that girl go every day?!*) who I never made sufficient time to get to know deeply—*go figure*. I mean, my roommates and I did have our drunken nights of fun, though. Like getting a ride *to* the bars without planning for a ride *home*, because we knew damn well that one of the college guys would give all of us a ride back to campus. Like hopping out of the car in Wisconsin winter because the train going by was not moving fast enough for our overflowing bladders and that snow looked like it could use a new shade. Like late-night top ramen and nursing each other back to health and trying to make sense of each other's stories in the morning. Like drinking wine and getting so deeply into craft stamping—*Yes, this was when rubber and ink stamping really gained a following in the mid-2000's*—and holiday greeting card making that we spent all of our $9/hour wages on ink, stamps, and embossing tools. We were a beautiful blend of seemingly mature but mostly insecure, and that always made for an unpredictable experience.

Ultimately, Bachelor #3 and I found commonality in our shared love for the outdoors, and he had far more experience in "roughing it" and exploration than I ever had. For all of my faults, I do have to say that I am quite proud of the way I became a little more worldly, and a little more open to new walks of life because of these relationships. Bachelor #1 opened the door to the world of being in a band and embracing a passion for music. Bachelor #2 opened the door to the world of fine dining and experiences, embracing a passion for entrepreneurial living. So what about Bachelor #3? He opened the door to the natural world, of putting yourself in nature in a way that had maximum potential if you brought minimum expectation. And eventually, he would be the bachelor I was with when I was finally at an age and level of inner confidence that encouraged me to stretch beyond my comfort zone and officially "move out"—five years after I intended to.

Kristy Jean

Delayed Departure

Most people feel that pit-in-their-stomach draw to stay close to their comfort zones—especially when home is all they've ever known. So that homesick feeling that encouraged me back to my roots didn't exactly make me unique, but I shamed myself into believing that it did. Rather than face my fears and see something through when my courage was tested, with barely two feet on the ground at Purdue University, I listened to the supportive *(and enabling)* voices around me, bailed on my move out of state, and ran back home. Life up until that point had been so easy for me that it was nearly *predictable*—go to Catholic school, make friends, get good grades, play sports, date a nice boy, *keep your legs closed*, go to college, pick a major, have fun, repeat. So when high school ended, and I was faced with a LOT of unpredictability all at once, it was like the world turned to quicksand and there wasn't a safety rope in sight.

I've learned that you can "relive" moments in life in your mind, but you can't relive the way you *felt* in those moments, no matter how hard you try. When I graduated and found that the routine of life was losing all ground, I remember the details around me, but I can't reimagine how it viscerally *felt* to be me at that time. "Homesick" or "alone" are easy labels to slap on that time period to describe the feelings I remember, but I know there were deeper roots and feelings that I've never uncovered. I simply can't go back to that version of myself, so the best I can do is unpack what I remember in order to learn what my *past* self and experiences have to teach me about this version of me *today*.

What first comes to mind is that my mom's dad, my papa, literally planted a narcissistic seed within her when he convinced his teenaged daughter,

"You can't leave me. What if I die while you're gone?!"

So there's *that* trauma. My mom had that fear ingrained in her until the day he died, too, so I'm sure there was a touch of that in both her parenting and the vibes I got from my family as a whole. Though my parents never gave *me* that same expectation or impression, (*On the contrary, they promoted that I forge my own definition of what it meant to "follow my heart".*) I wonder how much my mom had to grapple with that childhood trauma as she was raising her own child alongside my dad.

My grandma gave me those same fear statements that Papa (*her husband*) had given to my mom all those years ago. She gave them to me right near the end of college graduation, when I found myself on the precipice of deciding what the hell to do with my life now that school was over—*again*. Ironically, though my mom was unable to attend college, Grandma gave me this well-intentioned burden at the very same age that my mom was when Papa placed that burden on her:

"You can't move that far away from me. I'll never see you for lunch anymore..."

And so, the generational guilt trip continued. (This was also the inspiration for the version of guilt I lovingly named "Grandma Guilt" in my first book, *Decision Permission*.)

My crossroads were complete—my parents paved one path, telling me to "follow my heart," and my grandparents steamrolled a perpendicular path right through theirs, coercing me to be grateful and stay put. Even after four years of college, four years to move on from my own failed expectations of what I would do with my life when I was eighteen, my heart was still telling me that I had something to prove—more to *myself* than others. I needed to challenge myself to see if all the smoke that had been blown up my ass—"*You're smart; you're independent; you have your own ideas, and you're going to make a difference!*"—was anywhere close to the truth. Sure, I was able to pull off all of that shit in the comfort zone of Catholic school and a university in my own backyard, but how brave would I be when those comforts were *removed?*

Potential is safest when it hasn't been challenged, after all. I realized that I lived through college without ever having to live through *any* monumental fears or discomforts. Sure, I had lived out some of that potential in my accomplishments and friendships, but all of those milestones were checked off in a space where safety net after safety net was waiting for me if I fell.

So now that Bachelor #3 and I had played house for a couple of years, I wondered if my truth was that I just needed a *slice* of comfort zone along for the ride, aiding me to face those initial fears on the road to pursuing my dreams. Why had I concocted this tale of the *fiercely independent young woman branching out with nothing and no one from her past* as she carved a new life? I was blessed to have a great childhood with nothing to truly run away from, so what was I running *to?* And why did it feel like it was always just out of my reach? Maybe Bachelor #3 could be that slice of comfort zone, since I was my own catalyst, to finally move beyond my hometown and break that generational guilt trip.

Moving to Milwaukee wasn't the boldest move (*45 minutes away*), and sure, I had a safety net in moving there *with* someone and knowing I could always *go home*, but I had learned the hard way that if I'm the *queen* of setting unrealistic goals for myself, then I'm also the *princess* of viewing my blessings as setbacks. I set myself up for disaster when I concocted those extreme thoughts about moving hours away with nothing familiar but the clothes on my back. I wasn't chasing *my* dream; I was chasing the young adult dreams I had seen on the likes of *Dawson's Creek* and other teen dramas on TV. You know, the ones where the main character battles an internal conflict—out of their element and unsure how they're going to adapt to this new situation. When, suddenly, the depressing music cuts out and the joyful music cues up, because after only *two minutes* of crying, there's a knock at the door, and it just so happens to be a new best friend! Surprisingly, this new best friend has all of the same interests as our main character, and before long, the new best friend invites our main character out for ice cream where she makes introductions to *three more* new best friends, creating an instant comfort zone that our main character can settle into. The final scene cuts to our protagonist calling home to say she just *knows* it's going to be "all right." A small smirk curls in the corner of our main character's mouth, and we believe everything she just said will come to fruition. Fade to black, before the streaming platform quickly moves us on to episode two, and we're left believing that discomfort should (*and will*) only last a *maximum* of two minutes before *our* beautiful new lives will begin!

    So moving to Milwaukee wasn't the boldest move, but it *was* bold in that I was finally admitting to myself that my expectations needed to be taken *down* a few notches and that my supports needed to be dialed *up* a few notches. Moving to Milwaukee created the circumstances that would allow me to face those fears that were still haunting me years later—finally allowing me to put my excuses to rest. Maybe taking a slice of your comfort zone with you is actually how *most* people make big changes. One large question loomed over me, and I needed an answer: Did I *love* the predictability of my hometown, or was I just *led to believe* that a predictable life *is* the best (*safest*) life? I had to find out for myself.

    Bachelor #3's job was also located in downtown Milwaukee, so why *not* move there together? Oh, I don't know. Maybe because *my* 50-minute commute (*60-80 minutes during a Wisconsin winter, which could very well consume half of the year*) to work—*back in my hometown, mind you*—was a bit extreme. I mean, was there really any danger in driving my used but improved "Blue Mobile" (*Chevy Cavalier—RIP, Teal Mobile*) on that round trip every day? I mean, can you really put a safety measure on proving yourself... *to yourself?*

The more I reflect, though, I distinctly remember that, for the first time, I was gradually redefining what it meant for me to "follow your heart." I started to realize that following *my* heart often meant doing the exact *opposite* of what it seemed the majority of society and the people in my life wanted (*or expected*) me to do—Ain't that some shit. It's challenging enough to wrestle *yourself* into submitting to your *own* unspoken needs, but then try to explain all of this to your outspoken Italian family! I was like Fredo, except I wasn't actually a traitor, and I get wicked motion sickness, so no one would have been able to get me on that boat in the first place.

I now realize that I benefited greatly from the strong women I embraced in my life. Women I knew, women in movies, in music, and leadership roles—they kept showing up in their *truest* forms, reminding me that I had an obligation to myself (*and future women*) to figure my own shit out so that I could lead by example. I was finally beginning to understand my own value *apart* from everyone else. Maybe moving to the city wasn't actually about being with my boyfriend, and maybe it wasn't to *prove* anything. Maybe it was just the right option at the right time for *me* as I was finally listening to *myself* and working on telling the world to *shut the fuck up*. Because—wow—did I begin to thrive like I never had before.

Get Your Ass Moving

Our 550-square-foot apartment on the northeast end of downtown Milwaukee was a shoebox for sure, but it was my (*I mean "our"*) shoebox. I painted it a bold blend of tan with deep navy accent walls that were so dark they were nearly black. Before you judge, let me remind you that this was long before Chip, Joanna, and their Magnolia influence. I had to do the best with the only source of interior decoration inspiration we had at that time—TLC's *Trading Spaces*. The only difference between my experience and the weekly experiences of the chosen few clients on that show was that I *didn't* know any of my neighbors, and I had *zero* budget. On top of that, let the history books remind us that Pinterest was also a far cry from existence. So, yeah, I did the best with what I had and painted my (*"our"*) rental—*Who the hell paints a rental?*—because apparently I was ensuring that I couldn't take back this choice *nor* my (*"our"*) security deposit.

We were sailing along in our nautical shoebox of an apartment that had—*bonus*—a tiny sliver of Lake Michigan visible to the east! To view said sliver, one would have to simply press one's head against the top corner of the window, crane one's neck to the right, and peer through the branches of the trees and across the park before oohing and aahing at the sight! This also had to be done carefully in order to avoid awkward eye contact with the residents in the neighboring apartments whose own windows were approximately fifty feet from mine (*"ours"*), because they *too* were imitating Garfield, suction-cupping their faces to the window to catch a glimpse of the water we were all too lazy to walk outside to view. No matter the view, I was ready to live my city dream, and I refused to excuse myself from experiencing it any longer.

Besides my new commute and the hours spent on that "old" college futon (*repurposed as my "young adult" living room couch*), lesson planning as a new teacher, I had too much time on my hands to concoct excuses *not* to live the life I promised myself I came here to live. So I challenged myself to find a summer job that was interesting and unique to living in the city. After a few grueling rounds of interviews, I landed a unique gig at the popular science museum Discovery World, just a few miles away from my apartment. As a newly arrived city girl, there was no way I was going to *drive* to work. So I got a tune-up on my good old, generic Walmart bicycle I'd had since high school, bought an *enormous* "U" lock (*as though this bike was something worth fighting for*), and planned a route from my apartment to my new summer job in the heart of the harbor. My options in this apartment, I learned, were to keep my bike *inside* my 550-square-foot apartment, transporting it up and down the elevator every day, or to store it in the basement where I would have to MacGyver it into my 4'x3'x6' caged-in storage space. The very same storage space that already accumulated non-seasonal clothing and bins of God-knows-what that we assumed one would need in a tiny shoebox apartment. I chose the latter—*my rusty bike clashed with my bold décor.*

So now that I had a plan, I was ready for my new adventure. To say that my "commute" to Discovery World was breathtaking is an understatement. My ride consisted of traveling through Veteran's Park past cute pups, residents flying sky-high kites, adorable old couples in pedal boats on the small pond, and that big, blue Great Lake—*Lake Michigan*—passing me by as though it was an animated painting, following me for the entirety of my travels. Riding your bike to work in a city must sound like a very practical and mundane thing, but for a girl who grew up driving *past* the lake all my life, it was a whole new experience to cycle *alongside* the lake. I'm still in awe of this incredible body of water, and it brings a sense of calm every time I'm near it. My carefully devised route (*prior to the Siri and Google Maps phenomena*) made all the difference in those first months living in the city, because that experience provided me with my first sense of pride since moving to the city that was gradually becoming my new home. I didn't ask anyone's permission, and I didn't make excuses not to put wheels in motion (*literally*) and make this relaxing commute a reality for myself. When I think back over those rides to and from that apartment, I can't help but smile, just as I did back then, because that little gesture was a big first step in proving to myself, *and no one else*, that I had everything within me to make my dreams a reality.

Riding my bike in my new surroundings was proving to be a great way for me to explore opportunities in the city. Since riding my bike had become a new comfort zone, I decided to extend my bike travel to navigate nearby Brady Street—an eclectic and popular block just around the corner, known for its indie shops, one-of-a-kind restaurants, and studios used for a variety of purposes. Riding along the lake through a designated park is one thing, but venturing into the busy streets of the bustling city was another. I remember my nerves as I attempted to ride my bike on the sidewalks, maneuvering around many a pedestrian or parked delivery truck. There was NO way I was going to careen down the road; as a driver myself, I already knew that those super narrow bike lanes were an afterthought for the plethora of visitors who were fighting for a metered spot before brazenly opening their car doors without a care in the world. Riding the bike lanes would spell disaster for this rookie cyclist, so I determined that maneuvering along the sidewalk was daring enough. Though I was white knuckling it even on the sidewalks, I would challenge my inner voice by saying, "What's the worst that can happen?" and "No one knows me anyway!" I never knew how influential it could be to talk *back* to your fears—how essential it is to remind ourselves that fear is only *one* of the voices in our head, and since we are its creator, we can kick it out just as easily as we let it in. Repetitive phrases, or mantras, like these motivated me to get off my ass and go try something new—excuses be damned. Little did I know that this ritual was only the beginning of the peace that mantras would offer me throughout my life, long after my years in the city.

To get to the end of Brady Street, I had to confront the reality that my apartment was at the *top* of the hill, and getting to all of the fun places on the street required (*what felt like*) a rapid descent *down* the hill. "What's the worst that could happen?" eventually grew to asking myself "What destination is *worth* facing this fear?" I found a beautiful purpose at the furthest west end of Brady Street—a dance studio by the name of DanceWorks. It was a modern studio right on the banks of the river, and the dancers walking in all looked so posh and confident. Their style and presence embodied Brady Street, and I craved that energy—hoping one day to embrace it myself. With pom-pons being my only dance background, and zero dance classes in my past, I began to excuse this opportunity away as something too far out of my reach. Well, that, and I was making *pennies* as a new teacher while living in a rent-inflated city, so class fees sounded impossible. But then I asked myself, "Are you really just going to sit on your ass over these next few months, doing the same shit you could have done back in your hometown? Then why in God's name did you move here?" Damn. I hate it when she's right. I couldn't argue with that logic; I had the will, but I needed to find a *way*.

I began by riding down to DanceWorks to try out a single hip-hop class that seemed most interesting, nearest to my skill level, and was only scheduled every *other* week, which would help to save on cost. The teacher was freaking fantastic, and she had a portfolio of experiences that assured every student that you were lucky just to *view* her choreography. My only hip-hop experience had been as a white girl on a Catholic school pom squad where we were able to choreograph a hip-hop number at our dance camps in the summer. All these little white girls with bandanas around their heads and eye-black on our eyes. It was as if they cloned Julia Stiles in *Save the Last Dance* but they left out anyone with the *actual* ethnic background to tell us we looked like idiots. If Left-Eye saw us, she would have encouraged us to keep chasing waterfalls and never look back... And yet, no matter how green I was to this form of expression, I found freedom in those classes in the way the teacher and the students all embraced purpose over poise and energy over execution. We were there to share our drive and our humanity with one another—and we got one hell of a workout in the process.

    I was beginning to blossom in those classes, but my bank account wasn't sufficient to keep this up long-term. Typically, this would have been a place in life where I would have turned to my parents for help that they, undoubtedly, would have offered. But I was finding new pride in defining and living this life *I* was creating, and I decided that I would find a different way. I was paving alternatives to the "easy button" in other areas of my life, and I would do the same to honor this passion.

    Lo and behold, I locked up my bike and headed inside the cozy lobby, waiting for class to begin, when I saw a sign posted: "Earn Free Classes!" You've got my attention. The basic premise was this: Clean the studios; dance for free. While I held a variety of jobs up until this point, cleaning dance studios wasn't remotely close to one of them. But my military/police officer father had enough experience to ensure that he kept a tight regimen on the cleanliness of our house—even if he didn't push his only daughter *too* hard in her own chores. I wanted to dance, and this was my way in. I filled out an application.

Cleaning the studios gave me a new lens of appreciation for the teachers, dancers, and the studio itself. I got to see "behind the scenes," and I felt even more at home in this building that was once so foreign and seemingly out of reach. Though I only spent about a year engaging in this experience, it became a core memory of what it feels like to face my fears without an immediate support system around me if I fail. It was a time in my life where I was proving to myself, *and only myself,* that I had the ability to uncover who I am and what I need if only I continue to push myself to explore new experiences.

So I was ready when "Haley 909" entered my life—appropriately named in my OG Apple iPhone because we met on the elevator in our apartment building where I learned that she lived in apartment 909, two floors above me. I learned where she lived because Matt (*blank-check best friend from high school*) and I hopped on the elevator en route to Pride Fest at the Summerfest grounds, and apparently my *white* top and the *torrential* downpour of rain struck this beautifully blunt stranger as a *disaster* waiting to happen. Though she was a few years my junior, this veteran city girl shared her concern for me and my potential wardrobe malfunction, immediately offering the solution of an umbrella in her apartment that we were more than welcome to follow her to retrieve. I wasn't crying, she didn't knock on my door, that busted-ass elevator had no music, and we never did go out for ice cream, but I'll be damned if that *Dawson's Creek* scenario didn't play out for me that day. What those shows forget to tell young women (*and men*) is that no one is going to knock and make it all better—*you* have to get off your ass and put yourself into the world (*or an elevator while appearing helpless*), open to what the world will share with you.

And then, as they say, the rest is history. She became my new, lovely, vegetarian best friend who introduced me to ahi tuna and networking with fellow twenty-somethings in the city. It felt so natural to spend time with her, and another first rose to the surface—I made intentional time to hang out with her, regardless of what my boyfriend was up to. I just know that we were fated to meet and embrace one another at that place in our lives, and I'm so very grateful that she supported me as my Maid of Honor (in my *first* wedding), and I supported her as a Matron of Honor (in her *only* wedding). The universe has an amazing way of placing the right people in your life when you need them, but the trick is that you have to be open to them—*fully open*—giving energy of hope and wonder about where God, the universe, and life will take you.

    Summer gave way to fall, and I begrudgingly returned to my lengthy drive back toward my hometown for a new school year, teaching middle school students. This time, though, I returned walking a little bit taller as a "city girl" who had far less fears now than she did three months ago.

Kristy Jean

You Have a Pattern

The teaching career I dreamed of reaching had finally begun, and I was living in the city, expanding my understanding of who I was and what I was truly capable of accomplishing. It was a time in my life when I *should* have been single—focusing on friends, career, and new experiences—but being in a relationship *was* my comfort zone. I can see now that having a constant guy in my life served a purpose beyond the obvious of searching for a *spouse*. There was a pattern in the trajectory of my relationships, and it definitely embodied the lack of self-awareness I experienced for a large portion of my life:

1. Kristy is feeling lonely or disappointed in a relationship.

2. A man catches her eye and/or gives her attention.

3. She proceeds to date said man.

4. Unbeknownst to the man, Kristy starts the relationship in a warped state of 100% focus on *him* and *his* needs, never communicating her own.

5. Kristy loves feeling needed, and the guy loves the attention.

6. Kristy begins to feel overwhelmed in being needed all the time. The guy is clueless, because Kristy says nothing and never rocks the boat, and he doesn't know how to ask her about her needs.

7. Kristy starts to communicate her frustrations (*not very clearly, I'm sure*), but the man feels confused because everything has seemed so *great* up until this point.

8. In response to his confusion, Kristy either retracts her statements out of fear that the relationship will end and she will be alone, or (*if he is fumbling over his words*) she doubles down on re-clarifying her frustrations, creating a dramatically draining environment for both parties.

9. Kristy begins making intentional effort on herself, reflecting on her own happiness and how she can be a better "her" and "girlfriend" moving forward.

10. Kristy gradually loses interest because he gets too comfortable and increasingly ungrateful. At the same time, the communication from both directions absolutely sucks, and a lack of communication is always proof that one or both people have not figured their *own* shit out in order to bring *their* best selves to the relationship.

11. The guy keeps trying to "get back" what he thought *was* their happy time, and Kristy: A. Cannot understand why he hasn't grown at the same pace as her, B. Cannot understand why he has the misconception she *wants* to go back in time, and C. Wonders how he hasn't yet realized that when her mind is made up, *her mind is made up.*

12. The relationship ends.

13. Somewhere between 1-2 years, Kristy and the ex bump into each other and have one of those interactions like Vince Vaughn and Jennifer Aniston in *The Break-Up*—both looking healthier and happier, amicable and subconsciously aware that their relationship was all a part of getting them to where they are today. This has been true for 90% of my relationships, and I actually think that's a pretty badass sign of maturity on both (*all*) of our parts.

At this point in time, while I was living with Bachelor #3, we were sitting somewhere around a 9.5 on the KJRT—"*Kristy Jean Relationship Trajectory.*" And since my linear brain mirrors my linear life choices, you know where this one was headed...

The downward spiral really began because we were in very different places in our lives. I was young, motivated, and reaching for my first professional successes. He was several years into the rat race, jaded, and self-sabotaging until his self-fulfilling prophecies became his reality. I'm sure I blamed him as I clumsily ended the relationship, found someone to sublet our apartment (*who didn't mind the boldly painted walls, thank God*), and told him not to call me anymore, because breaking up is hard enough without me having to hear *your* feelings—that's icky.

I'm sure there's no *good* way to end a relationship, but I do know that I *sucked* at ending each of these past relationships. Sure, I actually told them face-to-face, which, in this day and age, is probably less likely when texts, DMs, and, *I'm certain*, future AI break-up robo-calls will become all the rage. But immediately after those face-to-face endings, I felt a sense of relief and personal closure, whereas my exes all seemed to believe that our relationship could be saved... I was so confused. *Why couldn't they see that there was nothing left to salvage?*

Hindsight is a luxury that offers me the opportunity to

"do the work" to examine my past and realize the "KJRT," but in the moment, it was so incredibly difficult to know when to work *harder* and when I'd worked hard *enough*. I guess that's true in most areas of life—the path from Denial to Acceptance (*and revenge dancing in between*) never seems to follow the same route twice and, more often than not, two people in a relationship on the verge of crashing and burning often find themselves at different stages of grief when it does.

Relationships have a lot to teach us about the excuses we're making and what we assume we should be excused for. Without these (*and one more significant relationship*), I never would have learned that:

A. It's my responsibility to communicate and advocate for myself and my needs from the very beginning of a relationship.

B. I need to be with someone who will challenge me to say what I'm thinking even when I'm saying nothing at all. (*I later learned this from my Auntie Gidget—he comes at the very end.*)

If insanity is doing the same thing over and over again, expecting different results, how many times do I have to try (*at anything*) before I *realize* I'm insane? I mean, it would really help to have a sliding scale from "*Success is right around the corner—keep trying!*" to "*Bitch, you're crazy—stop the madness!*" Is that too much to ask? And then, with those two ends of the spectrum established, could I also get a *midpoint* in that scale that defines *who* should change? I mean, if all of the trying is actually working, and we're *not* insane, will those results show in the way *I* change, or should I expect that the *other person* or the *situation* changes? Or should *everyone* and *everything* change because all of the trying demands growth in *all* directions?

Okay, I'm getting a little deep here. How about just giving me one step right *before* "Bitch, you're crazy" so that I stop hanging on to people and situations longer than I should? I could really benefit from an earlier warning point that checks in on me—*"Hey, girl. This probably isn't worth it."* That step seems less aggressive, gives me glorious visions of Ryan Gosling memes, and still offers the opportunity for me to redeem myself *before* padded walls are required.

Reality and self-truths are hard pills to swallow. So often, it takes several years, several pounds, and several poor decisions before I acknowledge that it's time for me to put this person or situation in my past. Boundaries often seem impossible because relationships *(and that scale itself)* are *subjective*—there is no "right" and "wrong"; there is only what's right and wrong for *you* at that place in *your* life. Boundaries don't begin because we're so fucking happy that we're skipping through fields of daisies playing Duck, Duck, Goose with our "Yeses" and "Noes"—*Duck, Duck, Boundary!* Boundaries begin because we allowed someone or something to get away with pissing us off for so long that we just couldn't take it anymore. Boundaries begin when we finally understand what we do *not* want, what we will *not* stand for, and who we will *not* tolerate anymore.

I was still a far cry from that place in my life—knowing who I was and what I needed. If I had, I would have known how critical that awareness is *before* you leap into a big decision, because then, and only then, are you able to show up as your truest self *from the beginning*—from the beginning of a friendship, relationship, new career, etc. Ignorantly pretending to be someone you're not, especially in the beginning, is a dangerous way to start any new relationship or experience, because you're building a lie that will only snowball until it becomes an avalanche. And you know what they say when someone keeps exploring hazardously snowy mountains: *"Bitch, you're crazy—stop the madness!"*

Ultimately, if we make the time to process these situations, we *earn* lessons that teach us about our patterns. Then we do whatever it takes to knock that shit off the *next time* so that we don't repeat the same mistakes. Unless you've earned your lessons *but* remain naïve to the red flags early on—then you're me, *one last time.*

God's Vision Statement

When the Milwaukee relationship ended, so did 50% of the rent. Living in an expensive city while burning gas commuting to a low-paying teaching job in a smaller town with a far lesser cost of living left me to conclude that it was time to move back to my hometown to save money. I would move back to the same place, but I wasn't the same *person*—that was the beauty of the "unnecessary" experience that I chose for myself.

It was around this time that I was already "talking" with one of my co-workers at school. We'd worked together for a few years at that point, and he'd been there as I went through the beginning and eventual end of my relationship with Bachelor #3. Our transition from friends to dating was a rocky start to say the least. I was jumping into another relationship shortly after ending the last, and he was an eternal bachelor who often questioned if the timing was right. I was "carpe diem" to his "carpe comfort zone," so after several months of dating and realizing our differences, we inevitably... *got engaged.*

While Husband #1 and I were newly engaged, our top wedding planning priority wasn't what you would expect to find on most couples' top ten lists. Where other couples focus on the venue, DJ, music, and food, we gave all effort and attention to finding the right *church*. And by church, I don't just mean a location for the wedding; I mean a Bible-based second home that we could compromise on, assured that the church we chose was able to reflect both of our faiths. A church where we could not only begin our marriage but where we could raise our future children.

I was raised Catholic. He was raised Northern Baptist. And for anyone who has been raised in any form of organized religion, you know that they *should* all get along, since it's in God's vision statement for all of us, but every denomination thinks it has living life "right" figured out better than the others. So Christian *non*-denominational it would be. Now to find one (*out of the hundreds within a five-mile radius*) that met our spiritual needs.

Church shopping was interesting to say the least. I actually wrote in my blog about it at the time, because as a good little Catholic girl who only ever experienced the four walls (*plus stained glass, altar, and gigantic crucifix*) of the church she was baptized and confirmed in, I was amazed to see so many interpretations of worship. I even had to make up nicknames for the pastors to try to keep the variety organized in my mind. And we definitely only met *pastors*, not priests, because "Catholic" was no longer on my radar—with gay friends, a mouth like a trucker, and an unwillingness to sign a contract about how I would raise my unborn children, I came to realize that path *wasn't* for me.

There was "Touchdown Pastor"—the man who made more references in his sermon to the Green Bay Packers than he did to the Son of God. There was "Burn in Hell Pastor" who preached that Muslims and other "non-believers" would burn in Hell while *we* rose to the Kingdom of God. And then we visited a Pentecostal church. For those who know, I see you smirking, and yes, it was as crazy as you're imagining. For those who don't, I'll have you know that this was the *one and only* Pentecostal church that I would ever enter—*and quickly exit after only twenty-five minutes.*

The pastor kicked things off innocently enough, sharing about a children's fundraiser they were leading to help their youth ministry. But before you can say "crazy town," the pastor started *invoking* God. Suddenly, the lady in front of me began to sway back and forth, back and forth; the tiny faux flowers on her purple hat bouncing as if a slight breeze caught them as they grew in a meadow. But before long, those flowers were in danger of breaking off at their fake little stems, because her body was *thrown* into a fit of full-on *convulsions*. I quickly found my phone and nearly dialed "911," except that one quick look around the congregation proved that while her *physical* health was actually just fine, she and a large majority of the congregation's *mental* health needed saving. A good twenty percent of the congregation was suddenly running in the aisles, waving their arms to the sky, and speaking in *tongues*.

For those new to the world of religion, "speaking in tongues" is believed by some to be an alternate language that God hurls into your body like Zeus with a lightning bolt, and then suddenly you're speaking this language that NO ONE AROUND YOU understands. It's like your brain instantly downloaded Rosetta Stone: Pentecostal language, but even those who speak your same denomination of faith don't know what the fuck you're saying.

That homeless person on the corner muttering to himself? He must be crazy, they say. But that middle-aged man in the third pew, dressed in a three-piece suit, sputtering words that sound like he's either lost his ever-loving mind or is preparing his Tolkien language for a Lord of the Rings session at Comic-Con? *He's* different. *He* has clearly been overtaken by the *Holy Spirit*, bless his heart.

Purple-hat lady was approximately three inches from smacking me in the face with her erratic, swinging arms when I finally snapped out of my *growth* mindset about this denomination and instantly *fixed* my mindset in the understanding that this place was a fucking train wreck that I couldn't peel my eyes off of. It was time to jump, tuck, and roll the hell off of this train before they tried to recruit me as one of their passengers. We snuck out the back just as the Elvish-speaking "elder" cued up an unintelligible monologue...

But the one that really takes the cake *(That's right—there was a group that even trumped Frodo and the gang)* was the quiet, unassuming Lutheran pastor in the quaint, white church with the beautiful steeple. The congregation sang classic hymns—traditional in Catholic *and* Northern Baptist. *Check!* The pastor was kind while offering a challenging message because we *all* needed saving and we are *all* sinners. *Check!* The people were welcoming and not in a pushy, *"We've never seen you here before! Edna, look at this couple—They've never been here before, right? You should join our parish. We need more young people. Do you bake? We have a bake sale coming up, and we need cookies. Marge was our cookie baker, but she passed away last year, God rest her soul..."* kind of way. *Check!* So when the order of service flyer showed that we were nearing the benediction, *the final portion of the service,* I was already adding this church to my Google calendar for next Sunday.

And then, the pastor decided it was *story* time. It wasn't meant to be a horror story, but as soon as it was over, I ran scared, deleting this church from my calendar *and* my Google Maps history—I needed to stay as far away as possible.

Pastor: "As we wrap up for today, y'all. I want to share a story that might connect with you today. Back in my younger days—*I hear you snickering, Mark! You're no spring chicken either, my friend!* (*points at Mark who seems to have been Pastor's best friend forever*) So back in my younger days, I served as pastor at a youth Bible camp, and from time to time, I would encounter young people who just weren't right. Young people who I just knew had *demons* in them that they needed released."

My inner monologue: *I'm sorry, did you say "demons??" Well... hey, I get it. I work with middle school students. He can call them "demons"; I'll chalk it up to old-school ways. Okay, Pastor—I'm still listening...*

Pastor: "There was one particular student—we'll call him Steven—who had *demons* like I had never seen before. This boy went on a tirade during our camp prayer one day, yelling the most obscene words while his body was convulsing as though it was possessed!"

My inner monologue: *Shit, maybe this kid was just Pentecostal. Surely, they would have put this kid on a pedestal for the way God was communicating through him. You say "possessed," they say "prophesizing", Pastor—potato, potato! Kidding aside... where the hell is this guy going with this story?*

Pastor: "And suddenly, the boy was off on a mad dash down the path toward the water—the small, communal lake at our camp. And I knew then... I just knew... that Steven was being controlled by the *Devil* and his *demons*. Steven was going to drown himself in that lake if I didn't stop those demons from taking him under! So I chased after Steven, and in those days, I was quite quick on my feet—*Mark, don't start again! I know this waistline doesn't show it now, but I'll show you my track and field trophy from 1971 at our next Bible study!* I ran as quickly as I could, and I caught up with Steven just as the Devil himself was about to plunge that poor boy into the depths of that lake. And you know what I did, good people? As God as my witness, I *tackled* that boy. He was no little boy either, no sir. I summoned all of God's strength to tackle that big boy and bring him to dry ground where I invoked the Holy Spirit and shouted a series of prayers before yelling into his possessed face, 'Demons, be gone! Demons, be gone!' And do you know what happened that day, good people? That boy was SAVED! The Lord Jesus worked through me, and we saved that boy from the Devil that day. And all God's people said..."

Congregation: "AMEN!!!"

My inner monologue: *What. The. Fuck?!*

We skirted out the back door just as the pastor and his team of elders shifted to the front of the church, standing at attention like God's Army recruiters, inviting anyone in this church who felt *they* had demons in *their* lives that needed to be stricken from *their* bodies to "come on down!" This once seemingly stable, Bible-based church suddenly became the *Price is Right* of exorcism. One by one, individuals rose from their pews, receiving pats on the back as they (*and their demons*) sauntered to the front of the church for all to see. Once there, the elders physically supported the person while the pastor "struck" the demons from their bodies with a palm to their forehead and the phrase, "Demons, be gone!" All of that demon exorcising was so exhausting that the person would instantly drop to their knees, caught by the elders supporting them on either side.

All of this *LIVE*, physical interaction was too far from my Catholic upbringing of sit, speak, kneel, repeat. This pastor was triggering my trauma from that Pentecostal church, so I was definitely out and never looking back—I'll take my demons with me, thank you very much. I couldn't help but wonder how Steven turned out, but I wasn't sticking around to ask.

Needless to say, it was a long, arduous process trying to dial in on a church and congregation with an interpretation of faith that met our own, let alone one that didn't make me *lose* my faith in humanity altogether. And then we found a non-denominational sanctuary with "Bible Church" in its name. Good sign—Bible-based *should* mean that their focus is on God's word and not a literal or singular *interpretation* of God's word. The pastor was enthusiastic, imparted many interesting historical facts as he read from the Bible during his message, and gave a very tangible challenge each week before we headed out to "Do good" in the world all week long. Awesome.

A few Sundays later, we wanted to learn more about becoming members and getting married there. I should state, for the record, that I am an eternal optimist *to a fault*. This trait has burned me many times in my life, especially back then, because I made excuses for everyone and everything with a naïvely hopeful heart.

I had just survived church speed dating *hell*, and yet, somehow, I still optimistically thought that the church version of "Mr. Right" was just around the corner. I excused those past church experiences as anomalies, even though those crazy examples made up *80%* of the churches we visited. I was still making excuses to justify every damn thing that didn't align with my sunshine and rainbows view of the world—including allowing others to make me feel like shit as they presumed to know the "right" way to have faith.

My "Suzy Sunshine" personality was in full force when we approached the pastor that Sunday to tell him of the impact his sermon was having on us, that we were engaged to be married, and seeking a church for our wedding and future family. Suzy was caught off guard, though, when the pastor's face showed signs of confusion and potential frustration as he made a stern clarification—"You don't have to be members to get married here, but we *do* want to ensure you are *true* followers of Christ before we would welcome you to be married here."

Internal excuses for another man I should have immediately walked away from in 3... 2... 1...

Inner monologue: *Okay. Yeah. That makes sense. It's like a test—we have to prove that we love God and believe in Jesus, because this pastor doesn't want to marry just any couple who has been to his congregation for a couple months. Yeah. I completely get it.*

God help me, I swear I'm smarter than this. So when the pastor arranged for us to meet with a different pastor (*there were several of them—all deliberately men, all blindly narrow-minded*) to start the conversation, I was up for the challenge! Hindsight clarification: No one should ever have to *prove* their relationship with God to any other human being. That's fucked up, but it's a core expectation in *many* denominations of *any* religion that you say and do very specific things before people believe that *you* are the same version of saved as *they* are. Set that boundary early and often, friends—explain your shit to *God*, not other *humans*.

But I was still in my naïve, people-pleasing little world, so when this other pastor called to plan a meet-up somewhere casual—*Starbucks*—and only had specific availability because he was also the official pastor of the MLB's Milwaukee Brewers, I thought, "Cool! We'll be able to relate to this modern pastor and help him understand who we are!" Wrong. So fucking wrong.

We were greeted at Starbucks with a smile and an offer to buy our lattes. We swapped friendly banter until our orders were ready, and the three of us sat down to settle into conversation. "Tell me about yourself, Kristy!" I started in just as any normal person would—about my family, my school experiences, and my recent engagement. I shared until I was stopped short by the pastor,

"Wait. You *didn't* start by describing your relationship with Jesus... Let me be sure I understand—you went to *Catholic* school, so you were raised in the *Catholic* faith, then, correct?"

"Yes..." I responded.

The pastor replied, shaking his head in disappointment,

"I thought so. Wow. Okay. Then you will still need to be *saved*. See, I was *saved* on a *street curb*. I was strung out on heroine and alcohol, getting my face kicked in by a guy I got into a fight with in the bar a few steps away, and I *saw* God. I *felt* his warmth and I *knew* I was saved—my life has never been the same since that moment. The next day, I entered rehab and committed my life to Jesus. So I *know* when people have been *saved*, and since you don't have a "saved" story, I will keep praying for you until you do."

Jesus Christ! Who the fuck did this guy think he was—the second coming?! I would have to *prove* myself to this man? This recovered junkie, who has now dubbed himself St. Peter, determines who's in and who's out? Who did this guy think he was—the *God* whisperer?

Tears welled in my eyes. I couldn't name how I was feeling, but I knew deep in my soul that nothing felt right about this situation. Confusion swept over me—but I <u>am</u> saved. "Saved" means that you believe Jesus is the Son of God and that He died to save us from our sins. "Saved" means you make efforts to grow your personal relationship with God and, like any other relationship, there will be ups and downs. He'll never leave you, but sometimes you will distance yourself from Him for one reason or another. But He is patient, and He will wait for you to find your way back to Him.

I thought of John 3:16, Romans, and all of the other books of the Bible with verses that, quite frankly, I never *actually* remembered from Catholic mass or school. Sure, we referenced them, but there was always a big focus for kids to be *good* and *confess* to the priest behind the curtain. In my youth, I never realized the priest was unpacking Bible verses in his homily, because the *actual* verse read from the Bible was always so brief. Needless to say, I understood where this prejudiced pastor was getting his stereotypes.

But stereotypes never save space for the individual. They are broad generalizations meant to simplify what, in its nature, is incredibly complex—in this case, a person's *faith*. His stereotype didn't account for the way my Catholic upbringing established a routine, a rhythm, a "hum," if you will, that would continue to sound as I grew older. *That* was the gift of being raised in faith—in *most* faiths. The gift that is instilled when you are very young that you have a purpose that is bigger than *you* and *your own* happiness. The gift that life isn't here to serve *your* needs; *you* are here to serve *His* needs. Did the rules of the Catholic approach fit me? hell no. And I obviously have no problem raking some of its practice through the coals, but to condemn its believers as somehow "less than" just because of the *crucifix* around their necks?

That rings a little too closely to the persecution of millions of people just because the *Star of David* hung around theirs...

His stereotype didn't account for *my* story—*my* faith. It didn't account for the personal relationship I had grown with God in spite of *and because of* my Catholic upbringing. There I was, in my early twenties, reading my Bible regularly—*and not because someone demanded it of me*—but because I had recently developed a curiosity, a need for a sense of purpose, and I was finding something *new* in a way I hadn't before. Reading my Bible was like meeting up with an old friend after much time had passed, realizing we could pick up right where we left off. Only now, we were both a little older, a little wiser, and with newfound awareness of the sources of our challenges in the past.

But this man was telling me that I was *wrong*. Not just wrong in the sense that I said or did something wrong— "wrong" as in 100% shaming the shit out of me like only Brené Brown can understand. Shaming me, myself, and I for being, *in his opinion*, rotten to the core *because* a priest baptized me as a baby, and I was raised in a Catholic church. In his eyes, I was nowhere near a salvation-ready human being, because I still needed *saving*. He directly stated that my upbringing in Catholicism meant that I was not saved *yet*, but that *he* would be willing to step in to help *me* get there.

That *destroyed* me. The little girl and the adult girl in me crumbled in response to this person, this *leader of the church*, so resolutely giving me an identity that couldn't have been further from the truth. As he rambled on, unaware of the shit storm that he was creating, I wept quietly—giant droplets raining down from my eyes, crashing onto the tiled Starbucks' floor next to crumb traces of my iced lemon pound cake that I started but simply couldn't finish.

The fact that *I* couldn't finish one of the few cakes that I actually *do* enjoy was further proof that this pastor *wasn't* speaking to what I truly needed. Because if I knew anything about myself at that point, it was that I was notorious for spilling (*hence the crumbs*), I always finished my food, and I *was* saved because of the inner relationship I had with God—

not because this asshole thought he was the second coming of Christ. (*Side note: All three of these statements are still true today...*) But in that moment, I went into "freeze" mode, because I walked into that Starbucks believing that I was entering into an *opportunity*, not an *ambush*.

I just wanted to get the hell out of there to process what in God's name I (*we*) had just experienced. After "Saved Shaming" me for forty-five minutes, while sipping his *humble* black coffee that he could surely turn into wine if the need arose, he prayed *over* me. Not *for* me—*over* me. I felt like I was in a nightmare or, minimally, an episode of *The Twilight Zone*. I took in my surroundings, waiting for someone to shout, "You've been Punk'd!" or, the OG version, "You're on Candid Camera!" At nearby tables, though, I saw college students procrastinating over their schoolwork, one insecure couple *redefining* PDA, and an elderly pair slowly sipping their espressos, appreciating the moment. Somehow, all of this was going on around my table for three, while I felt like the world was burning all around me. As Jesus (*Part Deux*) prayed, summoning our Lord and Savior (*who must have been looking down, shaking His own head at this point*) to purify my soul, I glanced at that elderly couple, wishing I could run into their arms and ask, in the most respectful way possible,

"You're older, wiser, and closer to those pearly gates than any of us—is it *true?* Is what he says *true?*! Am I *damned* because I've always loved God in a way that made sense for *me* instead of the way this pastor, this 'man of God' says that I *should?*"

But I didn't, because I was still frozen in place. So frozen that I don't think I moved a muscle as this idiot's attention shifted from me to my fiancé. My fiancé did *not* endure this same shaming. He was raised Protestant, so he did have one thing in common with this crackpot—he had all of the common words, experiences, and even his very *own* "saved" story—all of which, apparently, checked the boxes on the pastor's secret "saved" list. "Brewer's Jesus" was pleased with my fiancé's response to his inquisition, so he was off the hook.

But me? The Italian Catholic puttana sitting before him? Though he was busy blessing locker rooms and forcing his story onto anyone who would listen, he was willing to make time to take on *my* unfortunate case, helping me unlearn a shit-ton of Hail Mary's and the names of all of the saints—apparently, I wouldn't need any of them anymore.

For my faith-finding or atheist readers, Mary was Jesus' *virgin* mother who God *chose* to bestow with the one and only Immaculate Conception before she gave birth in a *freaking* manger because everyone in Bethlehem refused them room, and she was a badass *(I think they just didn't want to hear a woman screaming through an unmedicated labor)*. And this woman—*THIS WOMAN*—is not to be raised on a pedestal in all Christian, non-Catholic, traditions! Are we really surprised that a patriarchal religion started by men, pastored by men, and guided by strict guidelines to elect only *male* elders would shit on the *mother of God?* Remember, it's only the "Father, Son, and Holy Spirit"—still no room for that teen mom in this trio.

As to the saints, they were real people who actually walked the Earth and devoted their lives to doing above-and-beyond, selfless acts. Canonizing them requires a shit-ton of paperwork following very clear criteria, and they have to be dead for a certain amount of time to make it count. Once canonized, Catholics turn these people into stained glass windows and print them on medallions that you can pick up for $49.99 in your local Catholic gift shop—*$59.99 if you want the ones blessed in Vatican City by the Pope*. From there, you learn to pray to each saint for very specific reasons. Keep losing important crap *(like me)*? St. Anthony's your guy. Even my adorably indoctrinated son walks around the house mumbling, "St. Anthony, please help me find my Pokémon cards..." thanks to his saint-loving Nana and my hybrid version of Christianity. Found yourself knocked up? Call on St. Anne—she'll help you through, but she will likely expect that you *keep* the baby, so avoid the "should I/shouldn't I" prayers. Still ignorantly praying to saints because you're still not saved via a *Protestant* upbringing? Apparently, you're fucked. I guess singing "Ave Maria" or calling out to Saint Padre Pio—*patron saint of healing and suffering*—wouldn't be appreciated either...

When that "Pitchers' Preacher" finally finished praying *over* me, I jumped up from my seat, ready to run to the car. But at that moment, he put his hand out as a signal for me to stop moving away from the table. Ooh, if I could go back in time with the confidence, wherewithal, and female empowerment I've gained, my *hand* and my *mouth* would have been *MOVING*—you know what I mean—but instead, I paused like the good little, *not-good-enough-Catholic-girl*, and listened as he posed a *challenge* to us. WTF?! Your very *existence* has posed a challenge in my life!

He proudly advised,

"You both need to be in God's Word; I mean, *really* deep into God's Word on a daily basis. *I* read and study my Bible up to two hours a day, minimum! So I challenge both of you—if you can read your Bible every day for the next two weeks... I'll have this $25 Starbucks gift card for you!"

Fuck you. Fuck you for your attitude. Fuck you for shaming me. But fuck you even more for ruining *Starbucks* for me! Was this guy working on commission? He should have come with a disclaimer—"*Sponsored by your hometown Milwaukee Brewers and Starbucks franchises throughout southeastern Wisconsin.*"

So many things I *wish* I would have said. So many truths I *wish* I would have trusted my inner self to believe. But I was at a place in my faith journey where I was impressionable and undecided. I waivered between listening to that inner voice and feeling the need to excuse my interpretation of faith. I mean, this man *was* a representative of the church, a man of God; *he* must know more than *me*, right?

It took several days for me to process this experience, and when I did, I came to the mature conclusion that *this time*, adversity wasn't going to be a catalyst to change *me*. Instead, *this* adversity did the exact *opposite*. It helped me affirm that I *didn't* need to make excuses for my upbringing, my faith, nor my sense of self. This experience helped me see that I was actually quite *proud* of who I had become, and I didn't need some radical pumping nonsense into my ear, because for all the Biblical knowledge and personal experience that he had, I knew he lacked knowledge in the most important topic—he didn't know *me*.

While I still struggled to view adversity as the lesson-provider that it can be, challenging moments like these affirmed for me that I could grow *in spite of* difficulties that I faced in life. I didn't have to shrink in response to the overpowering voices, judgments, and opinions of the world—maybe the only way I would grow was by asserting *my* place in this world and finding a way to be *unwavering* in my beliefs. Over the next decade and a half, I would learn that adversity was actually my greatest teacher—if only I stayed *open* to its lessons.

Maybe that struggle in church shopping was an omen from God. He was like,

"Listen, you suck at hearing your *own* inner voice, and your brain is often too cluttered to even listen to *me*. So I'm making this one hell of a challenge so that you minimally learn to never listen to idiot pastors who use my name in vain, and *maybe* reconsider this whole 'getting married' thing..."

My God says "maybe," because He always gives us space to *earn* our lessons. Well, I came out 1 for 2 on that challenge!

Thankfully, God sent me renewed faith through that same *Catholic* church from my childhood, in the form of Father Ron. Father Ron didn't meet us in a Starbucks; he met us at the rectory. Father Ron didn't condemn my fiancé for his Protestant upbringing; he stayed curious and asked questions to understand, not judge. And Father Ron's final statement to us (after agreeing to marry us in the *Catholic* church through a *service* instead of a *mass* so that everyone felt welcome, which is still unheard of in many churches) was,

"I'm sorry you've had such unfortunate experiences with church leaders. How wonderful it is to see two people of faith who want to continue in their spiritual journeys. I would be happy to marry you."

Now *that* is God speaking through His people.

So we were married in the traditional Italian way—Catholic church, same Italian hall where we celebrated my First Communion, and of course, tons of Italian food for dinner and parting gifts of Jordan almonds and home-blended olive oil to go.

The irony of all of this church shopping is that it actually made me *stronger* in my faith. I can see how many people would look at these ridiculous experiences and think, "Wow, *there's* further proof why we should *all* run away from religion!" But instead, it showed me that *no one* has it perfectly right, because *perfect* doesn't exist. At the core, though, every religion, church, and person did believe some things in common. They believed that God is everywhere, and Jesus died to save us. So I decided that whenever we finally found a church that fit our family, it would ultimately have to have *those* values. We couldn't obsess over all of the nuances; instead, we needed to stay anchored in those truths as we continued to search for our own family church; a place where we could get quiet, connect with God and others, and walk away feeling challenged and motivated to do the best we could in this jacked-up world.

Kristy Jean

Labor Pains

The lessons of marriage were meant to be earned right after the *honeymoon*, in our case. Within our first year of marriage, we both learned that marriage was *work*. In hindsight, it was so much work because neither of us had done enough of our own, *individual* work to know how to bring our most authentic selves to the marriage.

Of course, there were joys along the way, but we made too many excuses for our incompatible relationship long before we were even married. If I had it to do all over again, though, I would walk that aisle and face the struggles that lay ahead, because I know without a doubt that life's greatest challenges are truly what make or break us, and I will always *refuse* to break. Also, this next chapter of my life, while difficult within my relationship, was the most beautiful, because I had the amazing opportunity to bring two sons into this world.

In 2013, I gave birth to my first son, Jonah. When you read this one day, Jonah, I regretfully share that I hoped you would be a *girl*. I was actually worried when they told me that it wasn't a *glitch* or *blur* on the screen in your ultrasound picture—you were a boy, and the doctor had *no* doubt about that. Once again, though, God knew better. Because as soon as I let go of society's stories around "having a girl" and "raising girls" and the "cute outfits" you can buy for them, I realized I was a *boy-mom* through and through. Further proof that I didn't know *shit* about myself at that stage of my life—*and they were going to let me bring a BABY home?* WTF—first-time parents everywhere, you felt that too, right? Like, they saw us struggle to figure out the damn car seat, and yet somehow they still let us take a *living being* home to just "figure it out"?! Parenting is a fantastically fucked up life experience where you're never ready, never prepared, but you always, *always* have these moments where you could just cry (*and sometimes you do*) with such gratitude that you, of all people, get to raise this phenomenal little person.

Jonah fought to avoid coming into this world. Labor was a complicated process. Eventually, I found my voice and stopped listening to the nurses and my delayed doctor who was calling in to check on me from another building. I finally listened to my body and my unborn child as I stammered back that he was *stuck*, and they needed to get that damn vacuum thing that they taught me about in those scary-as-hell weekly birthing classes, because that was the only way his big head was going to straighten out and make its way into this world.

During this time, my only-child mother was anxiously pacing in the waiting room with our other parents, but since she doesn't like to wait, and she would place me safely in a bubble if she could, I found that the nurse kept leaving my bedside during my labor... *to respond to my mom's questions and fears.* Yup. I was in the middle of one of the many lovely birthing strategies—this one involved the nurse holding the ends of a rolled up-towel, and I held the midway point, like tug-of-war while your vagina is dilating—only to hear a *knock* at the door, and we had to *stop*.

Turns out the nurses out front were getting an earful from my mom, and they needed *something* to tell her so she'd stay calm. This, I think, is the irony of a matriarchy. My mom *never* would have wanted *her* mom in the delivery room (*except maybe to share a cigarette, since they both smoked right through their pregnancies—I know, explains a lot about me, right?!*) But I know she really wanted to be in the room for mine. I barely let my husband in the room with me! I know I come off like a super outgoing person, but ask anyone who knows me, I could go a week or more not talking to a *single person* if my family wasn't around. I like people, to a point, but it's taken me forty years to fully like *myself*, so I guess I'm just making up for lost time.

My mom didn't want her mom in the delivery room, because she thought her mom was a bitch who would have told her to "suck it up" or say something stupid like, "Epidural? Really? In my day..." My experience was the exact *opposite*. I love my mom. I genuinely appreciate her thoughtful care for me and my family, but I am naturally built with quite a bit of that "suck it up" mentality, so when she brings the layers of mushy gushy and wants to hold my hand, I genuinely don't know how to process that type of love because that's not what *I need*.

I often find that my mom tries to love *me* the way *she* needed her mom to love *her*, but what she doesn't realize is that she loved me *so well* as a child that I don't have childhood trauma to heal from as an adult like she did. My dad and I "get" each other in this way. While he has his own shit from his childhood, he and I have always had this common understanding that we love each other unconditionally, and we both *show* that love through acts of service and quality time. My dad has always shown me love by cleaning the snow off my car, running back home for the millionth time to grab softball gear I didn't realize I forgot until we arrived at the field, and showing up for every single event I've ever taken pride in. So though my dad was likely just as anxious in that waiting room, *he* knew that *I* knew that all I had to do was ask, and he would have run out to get me an entire *pint* of ice cream if I wanted it—even before seeing his newborn grandson. Because I don't think I realized it until just now, but my dad has always loved me the way I *wanted* to be loved—challenged me when I need to be challenged, supported me when I need to be supported, and given me space to figure out my own shit so that I could come back and tell him what I learned.

Soapbox moment: We need to stop this trend of telling women to marry someone "like their dad." First, ew. Second, it's not about the *dad*; it's about how he sees (*or doesn't see*) his daughter. And when I say "see," I mean like yoga *Namaste* "see"—sees her for who she is, what she wants in life, and how she wants to be loved. THAT'S what we need to tell our daughters, sisters, and friends—Don't find a man (*or woman*) "like" your dad; find someone who listens to you and loves you as you *are*. And don't stop searching until you're done making excuses for assholes—have some patience while you search for your person, because s/he is out there. And in the meantime, keep working on discovering who you are, what you need, and how you want to be loved.

So my mom was showing love in her own way (*those poor nurses*), and my dad was showing love in his way, and then, on the evening of April 24th, they Hoover-ed Jonah into existence. His little cone head and beautiful, hazel eyes (*like his mom's*) made every minute of labor so worth it. "Hi, monkey..." were the first words I spoke to him when they placed him in my arms, and the nickname has stuck until this day.

We brought Jonah home, and I was completely unaware of the impact that the traumas of labor were having on my mental health. Physical signs were as obvious as the mile-long ice pack *pad* they gave me to heal up "down there"—you can use your imagination on that one. Being a naïvely independent person, I made a lot of excuses to avoid facing my own health needs—

"I'm fine!"

"I *want* to get up and feed him."

"I'll just nap on the couch next to him to catch up on my own sleep."

I sunk into what they call the "Baby Blues." (*A man MUST have come up with this fucking watered-down name for what is actually PTSD*.) I wasn't sleeping, and I couldn't stop crying. Our family rallied around us to babysit *me* while babysitting *Jonah*. I simply could not function, and I shamed the shit out of myself.

"Maybe I wasn't meant to be a mom."

"I wish I could take him for a walk in our new stroller, but I'll never be able to do that."

Scary shit. I was never suicidal, and I never got into a harming state of mind; I just had this resolute belief that I was now a hermit who was unable to leave her house. I deeply believed that every other new mother in the world was able to function just fine (*as social media leads you to believe*) and that there was something wrong with *me*.

When it got to the point that I was eating less and less except for the spoonful of peanut butter that my mom told me I *minimally* had to give to my body each day, we all realized it was time to get in touch with my OB-GYN again. Though I loved my doctor before (*not during*) and after delivery, her absence during my labor struggles left me unsure how she could help, but I trusted the people who loved me, and we set up an appointment.

She greeted me with her same, beautiful smile, because usually our visits were so positive. When she saw my pale face and red eyes from days of crying, she comforted me immediately. I told her my shame story. And because *I* was too deep into my depression to talk back to it, *she* talked back to that story for me. She told me of her home village in Nigeria. She told me that new moms aren't even allowed to care for their babies for the first few months, as the women in the village care for the baby *and* the new mom so that both have a healthy start in this new chapter of life together. WTF?! Here I was in America, weeks into being a new mom, already getting emails from my employer asking when I would return—placing my own health needs at the bottom of my list.

Her words helped a little, but her prescription of *Ambien* helped a LOT. I slept like I hadn't slept in over a month. Little by little, my mind came back "online," and I was able to recall the depressing thoughts I once had, but it was as though I was remembering what someone told me, in disbelief that I actually *felt* those things not so long ago. It didn't seem possible that I actually *believed* those untruths because my mental health was so incredibly unstable. To this day, when I find my thoughts tending toward negativity, I remind myself that our brains are so much more powerful than we give them credit for. Our brains follow patterns and different levels of adaptation, but *we* are the ones who can talk back to those thoughts—telling our brains how *we* want them to function and focus. And no matter what it takes to get us to that place—*medication, exercise, nutritional changes, spa treatments*—we need to embrace that truth so that we feel empowered to speak back, fully aware that *we* are not our *thoughts*. *You* are not your *thoughts*.

Baby Mama

Shortly after my doctor's intervention, I was able to fully enjoy being a first-time mom. I loved my quality time with Jonah, and I could clearly feel the truth that I was meant to be a mom all along. Once I finally settled into motherhood, though, it seemed that my comfort zone was not going to last long. I grew up in an already established matriarchy, after all, so forming my *own* family apart from "the" family that had claimed me since birth was quite the challenge. *And* I was the first grandchild to have a child of my own, so inevitably, I was fucked.

Anyone who comes from a big extended family knows that traditions are more than fun, annual experiences—they're *expectations*. For instance, while our days-long celebration of the Fourth of July was fun when I was a child, with a newborn, it seemed absolutely ludicrous. I should clarify that the Fourth of July and Christmas were neck and neck when it came to going all out in celebration—*and Christmas was losing*. The Fourth was always a multi-day event that included spending July 2nd preparing for the massive annual party, July 3rd spent in the Farm & Fleet parking lot *(tailgating for the local fireworks, of course*), joining the local parade route at 4 a.m. the next morning in order to get "the best spot," and then *the final event*—the 12+ hour party that we prepared for over the course of several days. It was a marathon, and a fun one at that, but how do you tell your amazing family that while you are grateful for *your* childhood, that does not necessarily mean that you want the same for your *own* child?

Simply put: You don't. You *imagine* what your boundaries would look like and then you *imagine* how you would even start the conversation, and then you give up and give in. You have many lengthy conversations with your future ex-husband, trying to rationalize all of the family traditions and attempting to honor the fact that you now have your *own* family *plus* your husband's family to consider *on top of* the matriarchy with all of its energy and expectations. You don't tell them, because you love them, and you know that though it's not technically about *them*, you worry you'll hurt their feelings if you do. So with a newborn in tow and a less than strong marriage to lean on, I dissolved any dreams of boundaries and tried to keep up with the matriarchy.

Family dynamics are so interesting. My situation wasn't unique—each new generation must feel the strain of figuring out how to break away and hold on at the same time. It's easy to excuse the behaviors and expectations of the family you grew up in because that's all you've known. But then how do you assert your *own* boundaries in the face of all that tradition?

When I was a new mom, my own mom, newly "Nana," tended to reference all of the things that her *own* mom got away with when *I* was born:

"I attended dinner every week with *you*, so now *you* can make it work with *your* family."

"*My* mom spoiled *you*, so *I* get to spoil *Jonah*."

"*My* mom made *me* attend every holiday event, so *you* can make it work with *your* family too."

There were so many aspects of her mom that she absolutely couldn't stand, and yet, now that she found herself in the same stage of life that her mother once was, *she* wanted the "perks" that my grandma felt entitled to.

It's so confusing, and yet, it makes so much sense. Each of us can only speak from our own experiences, and I'm sure that though she *hated* the pressure that her own mother gave her as a new parent, she also saw the benefit *I* gained from all of those quality times with family. However, I quickly realized that I would have to have my own equivalent of the "Macy's Parade" talks with my *own* mother...

So there I was in my boundary-less attempt to blend all of the adults, make everyone happy, and, oh, care for my newborn. And I felt stuck right in the middle, as most women find themselves, trying to balance all of the people and all of their expectations. It suddenly felt like each group assumed that I could give them 100%, but everyone (*including me*) seemed to forget that A. Jonah was the only one who *needed* 100% of our attention, and B. I deserved to have *my* needs met as well. Part A was definitely taken care of, and I grew to affirm that more and more—*nap times, appropriate foods, and where I was willing to take him and for how long*. Part B, though, I'm still asserting with myself and my family, but I've worked on clarifying my boundaries and becoming a better communicator over the years, so they understand my needs a little better now. Part A became a non-negotiable, black-and-white. Part B still remains negotiable and a gray area, trying to navigate the truth that I don't need boundaries *from* any of the lovely people in my life; I need boundaries to retain my *own* sense of balance that ultimately has *nothing to do with them.*

For someone who loves her alone time, giving birth to the very first grandchild on *both* sides of the family was shit planning on my part. Everyone wanted to see the baby and spend time with the baby, and though I'm very aware of how blessed we were to have so many loving people in our lives, it was just plain overwhelming. I adored time alone with

Jonah, and yet, I felt the obligation to make everyone else happy. Between holidays, birthdays, and family gatherings, I was learning what it meant to be anxious (*a feeling I never felt before*), and I realized that even though every event always *ended* well with everyone happy, getting to the finish line as a mom who was barely keeping her "nuclear" family afloat was exhausting.

I grew to realize two things at this time in my life:

1. My child is my priority, and I am capable of facing the fear of disappointing others and their opinions in order to ensure what I, *instinctually*, know is best for him.

2. I am not a victim, and I don't have offenders in my life. It is up to *me* to communicate *my* needs; I can't expect anyone to read my mind nor know my situation. Unconditional love means respecting boundaries, and they will respect mine—even if it's uncomfortable for everyone at first.

Those two realizations suddenly made me curious about my own mom. I felt some of her resentment as I set these boundaries, and I wondered if she was connecting the dots back to her own childhood. This is when my mom and I started what we now lovingly call our "Come to Jesus" talks. My mom will be the first to share that these usually come about when she's over-spoiling the grandkids or offering parenting advice that wasn't requested. I will be the first to share that these also come about when I'm being a bit of an insensitive bitch *(Oh, yes; she's in there!)* or when I'm too task-focused to remember that the people who love me just want time *with* me.

These "Come to Jesus" check-ins are always born in one of three ways:

1. My mom has talked a situation over enough with my dad so much that she's finally encouraged to ask *me* to "get coffee."

2. I have talked a situation over enough with my (*current*) husband so much that I'm finally encouraged to call *her*.

3. My mom is having such big feelings that she is struggling to communicate that *either* my dad calls, "Hey, Kiddo... How's it going?," or my mom *and* dad ask me to a *meal*. Those are rare, deep, and always, *always* end with us feeling a sense of healing and common understanding moving forward.

One way my mom and I are identical is in the way that no matter what fresh hell is going on around us, we will always seek to find a way *back* to each other. That's why we ended up spending the next 10+ years getting very real with each other. Through separate and shared therapy, we uncovered the roots of our feelings. Her feelings were a paradox of adoration and resentment of *me* because I was her only child, and she never felt empowered as a young mother to set boundaries with her *own* mother. My feelings were rooted more in my ticking time bomb of a marriage, my obsession with people-pleasing *(everyone except my mom, apparently)*, and the way I would push her away because I didn't yet have the words to communicate how I needed her to love me *differently* now that I was a mother myself.

I love time with my mom, and I love her sage advice, but I didn't need the coddling, curious check-ins, nor her worries placed on my shoulders. And what I learned that she needed was for me to explain my thoughts and feelings (*without being passive-aggressive or screening her calls...*) so that she could respond accordingly. Sometimes the result is both of us smiling, and other times the result is a bit of an "agree to disagree," but we *always* find our way back to each other through these talks, and we *always* leave with a clear understanding of where each other stands. Because the beauty is that while the *feelings* change, the unconditional love never will.

Many mothers from the Baby Boomer generation seem to feel a sense of shame when they finally begin taking care of themselves after the kids are grown. After retirement or the kids are out of the house, women in that generation seem to feel like they're selfish for practicing self-care because society always told them to put themselves dead *last* on the priority list—even though they were raising kids while still feeling like kids themselves.

In contrast, my generation has rewritten that narrative. Society *and* our families seem to be on the same page (*for the most part*), encouraging us to find our passions, assert our independence, and take pride in our efforts. Growing up in the 80s and 90s, though, the scales tipped a bit *too* far in the opposite parenting direction, as we were told we were "special" and became a bit entitled with the ease of microwave meals and the distraction of multiple televisions throughout the home. My generation is the "look at me!" generation—we're addicted to proving ourselves, but at least we're hard workers. Because after us came the "participation trophy" generation—those kids were fucked from the start!

Regardless of the era, mothers and their daughters have the most uniquely painful and evolving relationships; it's no wonder so many of us struggle to find a middle ground. I've witnessed moms who think that love is *making* their daughters happy. I've witnessed daughters who think love is *making* their moms happy. I've witnessed moms who think tough-love means distance and authoritative interactions. And I've witnessed daughters who think their moms did (*or didn't*) do their jobs for eighteen years and should permanently get the hell out of their lives, thank you very much.

I give my mom a shit-ton of credit for doing her own "work" to grow *with* me as best she could, considering the mother she had—one who expected her daughter to stay in the box that she made *for* her. As years have passed, we've swapped therapy notes with each other—often over vanilla lattes, exchanging "thank God you finally figured *that one* out for yourself so that *I* didn't have to say something" smirks.

We continue to face and work through our shit. Third

only to my relationship with God and my relationship with my husband, ours is one of the most honest and vulnerable relationships in my life, and it's only come from both of us swallowing our pride, reflecting *within*, and then trusting that the words coming out of each other's mouths come from a place of genuine love and hope.

A Million Reasons

Once you have kids, life hands you a magnifying glass that you never asked for. It's like some sort of twisted door prize for choosing to raise children, as it uses sleepless nights, unexpected tantrums, and *for-the-love-of-God-is-he-potty-trained-yet?!* adventures to magnify the weakest points in your marriage—and your ability to care for *yourself*. Because before kids, you have all the freaking time in the world to argue, cry, get defensive, repair, and move forward. But after kids? Diaper changes and late-night feedings suddenly soak up all of the time *and energy* you once devoted to "fixing" your marriage and adjoining relationships. I became keenly aware that the only human I should be *taking care of* was my *child*, so why did I feel like I was caring for *adults* too?

When we moved to Kenosha, my new city of employment that was also closer to our families, I was happy to be closer to work, but it meant that the three of us would now be in three separate *counties* between two schools and daycare. Still, the transition had moments of joy, genuine moments of happiness, but often I found myself struggling more than ever to enjoy caring for and playing with my son while our marriage was showing signs of struggle that needed individual work—fixing that I couldn't do alone, no matter how much I tried.

As an eternal optimist, there must have been enough moments of joy to give me hope, though, because shortly after our move, we learned that Andrew would round out our family as our second baby boy! Andrew, when you read this one day, I need you to know that being an only child really makes you either want to have a *bunch* of kids or, also, only have *one* child (*if any*). It's hard to imagine siblings when you never had one yourself. But, Drewski, I just *knew* someone was missing from our family. I even remember sitting at the dining room table one evening while eating dinner, and I could *feel* that a presence was missing. That presence was you, buddy!

Andrew was born 25 months after Jonah—two spring babies. When both partners in the marriage are educators, you hope for spring babies so the maternity leave leads right into your summer. I prayed for happy and healthy, but I *crossed my fingers* for spring birthdays too—*it seemed a little too crass to waste God's time on a shallow prayer*. My prayers *(and superstition)* worked, because now there were four, and our family was complete... *except we weren't.* I felt whole as a mom to these two amazing boys, but I struggled to give them more than 60% of who I *could be*, because of the challenges we were facing in our marriage.

As in most cases that end in divorce, there were years of *trying*. I began writing a blog as an outlet. I told myself that I just needed a path for self-reflection, growth and a way to connect with others. I went to yoga classes. I told myself that I just needed to get my ass moving and increase endorphins. I threw myself into work, gaining approval and recognition for my teaching and coaching abilities. I told myself that I just needed to find my purpose. *I.... I.... I...*

Finally, *we* went to therapy. I told myself that we just needed a neutral party to help us figure out this puzzle, because hell would have to freeze over before I'd tell my never-before-divorced extended family nor happily-married-for-thirty-plus-years in-laws that we were struggling. I started my master of science's program to become a school administrator. I told myself that I just needed a professional challenge—one that would stretch me in my current career that was beginning to feel too predictable.

And when marriage therapy was seeming futile, *I* finally went to therapy—*alone*. I went just for *me*. I found a female therapist in downtown Milwaukee. Yes, I was now living nearly an hour south, and yet Milwaukee still called to me. That city will always represent a time in my life when I carved out my own little space in this big world. So I didn't give a shit what gas prices were nor the truth that I was giving myself an unnecessary commute; Milwaukee just *had* to be the place where I could heal from pain, reconnect with that once confident woman, and bring my best-self to my marriage.

I still remember my nerves when I drove to my new therapist's office for the first time. It felt very symbolic to drive away from our home and away from my two, young sons, but you learn as a mom that if you continue to drain yourself to serve everyone else, you truly have nothing left to give. My car speakers blasted Lady Gaga's "Million Reasons" before it faded into "Wild Horses" by Natasha Bedingfield, and tears flowed down my face for the duration of my drive north. I prayed over and over again, asking God to give me strength and direction. Jeremiah 29:11 is still where I find courage in moments when I have none:

"'For I know the plans I have for you,' declares the Lord, 'plans to prosper you and not to harm you, plans to give you hope and a future.'"

Raised Catholic, you never learn to memorize Bible verses like Protestants do, so I'll admit that the oppressive pastor *was* right on that one detail. I never understood why Catholics haven't honed in on Bible verse memorization, especially when you consider that Catholics are *killing it* in the memorization department—you could put a Catholic in that soundproof crying room, blindfolded during Mass, and we'd still sit, kneel, stand, and recite the Apostle's Creed at the exact right moments. In my hybrid faith, I was now finding comfort in memorizing verses like Jeremiah's. Proverbs 31: 25-26 continues to ground me as well:

"She is clothed in strength and dignity, and she laughs without fear of the future. When she speaks, her words are wise, and she gives instructions with kindness."

I cried, sang, and prayed all the way to Milwaukee. Hitting those busy interchanges gave me a boost of confidence—I've always been a proud "beat cop's daughter," navigating roads bravely *(sometimes at the speed limit...)*. I got off at McKinley, right near Fiserv Forum where the Milwaukee Bucks play, and it was like I was back home in a way. But not a physical home, and not that living in this city with that ex-boyfriend ever fully felt like home, but Milwaukee will always give me the *feeling* of home—of a time when I made intentional time and effort to uncover what it meant to be *me*.

Parking is always a pain in the ass, but after I figured that bit out, I asked Siri to give me walking directions to the building, because I was out of practice winging it as a city girl. I had to laugh, because my new therapist's office was inside the very building where Haley and I met for after-work drinks and apps years prior. It was the reassurance I needed to walk myself toward the elevator and press the button that would take me to the fourth floor.

The waiting room was incredibly beige and incredibly quiet except for the white noise machine that ensured privacy for the patients pouring out their souls behind the four, distinct office doors. It felt as though I was on a game show, waiting to see if I would enter Door #1, Door #2, or *Let's see what's behind curtain #3!* No matter which door my Google-searched and reviewed therapist was behind, I hoped she had answers... or would at least *help me* find answers. (*I've learned a lot about therapy since then.*)

She opened her office door and welcomed me in—*Door #1!* I immediately soaked in her stylish space and the gorgeous view of the eastern skyline from the oversized picture window opposite the door. It was a sight to take in—it gave new meaning to "picture window" in my mind, because this view gave the same feeling as an inspiring piece of art. I found the seat that, unbeknownst to me, would be *my* seat each time I returned for my follow up sessions. I don't know if they use a certain blend of essential oils in those offices or if Kleenex has a subliminal form of advertisement, but all she had to ask was, "How *are* you today?," and I completely lost my shit. Balling my eyes out and using up her tissue as if they were coupons that would alleviate the cost of this session in her swanky office.

Eventually, I calmed myself enough (*about my emotions and the pay-before-you-leave bill*) to share my story and express myself clearly—in metaphor, of course, because that's almost exclusively what I speak through. Analogies, metaphors, and similes really should be considered their own language. In that case, I'm bilingual... *with enough very basic German, Italian, and Spanish to ask someone how they are and tell them how to get to the bathroom.* This is what I shared with her:

"I have a big, gaping hole of a wound right now. I'm not sure what caused it, and I don't understand how it got this bad and this infected, but I've reflected on a few ideas—a few of which are my *own* doing. I've ignored this wound for so long that I feel like it has officially bled *dry*, and I have no answers for how to fix it. I need your help to clean out this wound, stitch it back up, and figure out how to heal from the pain I've experienced. I can't even think about what it looks like to live with the scars *after* it's patched up, so for right now, I just need *triage*."

Somehow, she got it. Because her questions always seemed to be the ones I needed, and my responses felt like an out-of-body experience. When you're a private person *(or used to be!)*, there's a lot of shit that goes on in your head that you never tell anyone. And I mean *anyone*. Because you have the fear that if they heard this crazy shit come out of your mouth, they'd either *commit* you to the psych ward or, worse, give you that pitiful look like you were an injured puppy. *(I have to imagine there are three meals a day and good meds provided in a psych ward, though...)* But when you meet with a therapist, you're keenly aware that you are paying her, *a distant third party*, to hear all of the shit in your head, and she will never tell your *family*! It's brilliant. And it's incredibly cathartic. And worth every damn penny, because if your mental health isn't worth the investment, then what the hell *is*?

I would attend several more visits with this therapist. She kept listening, and I used up all of her Kleenex. I would have sent her some for Christmas, but damn, with the hourly rate she was getting from me, I figured she could buy a truckload at Costco. I joke about the cost of therapy, but I also need to clarify that it's *priceless* and worth the cost to go to whomever, wherever you need to. Because quality therapy doesn't last *long* in my experience. Sure, I've taken up with other therapists since—*you have to play them off of each other so they know you're a hot commodity*—but it's always when I feel out of sorts and need a "tune-up." I know this isn't the reality for everyone, but for those who've never given it a go, I promise it's worth the short-term cost because of the incredible long-term gains.

Each visit, I listened to sappy songs on my drive up and inspirational tunes on the way home. It was a cluster fuck of emotions, but I was sorting through some deep shit, and I was no longer pretending to myself that everything was *okay*. This was the time in my life when that five-worded tattoo came into existence. I dug out *The Giving Tree* from an early teaching bin of books, and I was reminded to just stay focused on my boys, and we would all not only survive, but somehow find joy in the outcome. God and Shel Silverstein helped me to keep the faith, and I learned that tattoos are the physical pain I crave when the emotional pain is just too big to comprehend.

In hindsight, I had a vision of the end result—how all the bullshit would just need a lot of time *(and vodka)* to get through, and then there would be *good* and *healthy* and *peace* for all of us. I firmly believe that that vision is what helped to keep us all on track, the kids protected from the madness, and led us to the positive co-parent reality we have today. I had work to do. He had work to do. And now we all kick ass as a blended, unique, *"unconditionally loving of our kids"* family. (More on Backward Planning and the moment I knew it was over in *Decision Permission*).

Divorce is not something you choose. It's a death—the death of the life you thought you could reach if only you "tried" hard enough. It's the death of a love that you thought could stand up to all of those words you innocently stated in your vows. The death of your ignorant belief that either of you was in control all along. And just as etiquette at a funeral suggests that we don't ask a million questions about *how* the person died and *what* led to their death, as vulnerable as I've been, that's one story that needs to rest in complicated peace.

Asking someone what led to their divorce and why it happened, though often out of curiosity because of the questioner's *own* unstable relationship, is simply too emotionally complicated for words. Of course, there are the BIG factors that stand out to those who experience it, but so often, it's the small factors that kept drip, drip, dripping. The factors that kept coming, no matter how hard you worked to tighten up that leaky faucet—the droplets kept falling until you found yourself standing in water up to your eyelids, unable to breathe.

Divorce is a paradox in that it is a legally *public* event that is *personally* private. When your life-altering heartbreak is *legally* mandated to be published in local news, the LAST thing you want to talk about is "what happened"—especially someone in my case who didn't have a single, direct cause. Neither of us was physically abusive. Neither of us had a second family or someone we were leaving the marriage for. Neither of us secretly stole or spent money. But I know from conversations with women and men who *did* leave for these and other reasons, that having a direct "cause" *still* doesn't make the decision an easy nor obvious choice.

I left for my *sons*, and I left for *me*. I left because I finally believed that the pain of staying outweighed the pain of leaving—even though I doubted that truth for so long. I left because I lost myself a long time ago, and though I had visions of who I *could* be, I somehow knew that I couldn't reach her if I stayed. I left knowing that it wasn't *his* fault nor *mine*, because blaming one person would mean denying the reality that a relationship can't exist without the involvement of *two* peoples' words, actions, and inactions.

I left, but not before I checked every box on *my* figurative "gave it everything I had" checklist, because leaving couldn't just be about *me*. For the first time in my life, I didn't fall back on "When my mind is made up, my mind is made up." Because *nothing* encourages you to tell your mind to get the fuck out of the way like being a mom.

A New Adventure

When divorce was inevitable, the logistics became the next nightmare. How the hell would we be able to support separate households for our boys, each on a *teacher's* income? By the grace of God, supportive families, and my willingness to avoid lawyers by learning about and completing the insurmountable shit-ton of divorce documentation required by the state of Wisconsin, two separate homes became a reality. So I moved to a townhouse a few miles north, and I set myself on making this new home, just for the three of us. I wanted it to feel as authentically inviting as this decision felt to me. I wanted my boys to have a space where they could feel how they needed to feel while surrounded in a loving place where their mom could fully show up for them.

I did my best not to sugarcoat the transition for my nearly five-year-old Jonah and three-year-old Andrew. We talked about big feelings, and at the same time, at their age, I did my best to make a game of things—helping them realize that change *doesn't* have to equal discomfort. My proudest game, primarily because I was struggling so much with the initial transition, was "same or different." I had spent long nights at the townhouse. I would get them off to school and daycare from the "original" house, work a full day, pick them up, awkwardly eat dinner as a *soon-to-be-former* family in our *soon-to-be-former* shared home, get them to bed, and then head to my townhouse for the evening. I worked through the night, preparing their bedrooms first, then the kitchen, and finally the living room so that the boys had an inviting space to live within in the near future. At this uniquely transitional time, I was still *returning* to that *soon-to-be-former* home to sleep, wake up to prepare the boys for the day, and do it all over again.

In hindsight, I would *not* recommend this approach, but I genuinely didn't see any other option at the time. I didn't have the energy to fully evaluate or overthink each decision; I just needed to keep moving, persevering so that the weight of reality never sunk too deeply.

"Same or different" was played the first time the boys came to the townhouse with me. We walked the small but cozy, two-story townhouse, carefully inspecting this future home, pointing out what was the "same" as their current home (*now known only as their "dad's house"*) and what was "different." I made efforts to replicate some of their creature comforts—character-themed blankets on their beds, a Lego space that occupied half of the tiny living room, and shadow box silhouettes of their profiles that I made (*a second time*) so that they would see them at both homes. Their little voices would ring out, "Same!" Jonah, always with attention to detail, "Mama, that's the same character on the blanket, but it has a different feeling; it's not as soft." Thank you, my matter-of-fact, sensory-aware child; you are correct.

They pointed out "different" elements too—artwork on the walls, the fact that they now *shared* the master bedroom in this home, and that we had a Jack-and-Jill bathroom that would later make for fun adventures sneaking up on each other when we played hide-and-seek. Those double doors that led into their bedroom also made for a memorable nighttime routine that the boys still remember to this day. I would sing that goofy song "John Jacob Jingleheimer Schmidt" while gradually closing one door, and when I got to the part where "...the people always shout...," I would run over to surprise them out the *other* door and finish the tune, "...There goes John Jacob Jingleheimer Schmidt da, da, da, da, da, da, da!!" They would erupt in laughter, and in that way, we made so many "differents," *so many changes*, an opportunity for new, exciting, and memorable adventures.

Eventually, we settled into our new home with what they noticed were the *same* sliding glass doors with a patio and the *same* attached garage setup that allowed us to safely tuck the car into the garage and walk directly into our home. We learned that Mama was *different* in this home—engaged, present, full of crafting ideas, turning a closet into a clubhouse, and implementing mandatory Saturday snowman pancake breakfasts on the patio with coconut snow and chocolate chip coals. I was 100% mom when they were with me, and I collapsed to my knees each time they left. It was the most extreme cluster fuck of emotions that I've ever felt in my life. How could a life exist that gives me more fulfillment than I had ever known and *at the same time* equally break my heart knowing that it would never offer a wholly fulfilled feeling?

It takes time. Everything takes time. I now see time as such a gift. I see now that everything either requires *more* time that we have to patiently allow to pass, or we find ourselves challenged to acknowledge that we have *less* time than we thought, so we need to pay attention, decrease our pace, and be present. Those are the only strategies I've found that offer the *illusion* that time has slowed down.

Our time in that townhouse was so memorable—*in hindsight*. In the moment, I was just trying to put one foot in front of the other, make memories, and focus on positive outlets like writing and yoga to keep me from all of the negative vices that turning your life upside down can encourage. The boys, on the other hand, reminisce like those were the best years of their lives! Andrew will tell me how much he loved sledding down that hill in our backyard and how he wishes we could go back there. His memory warms my heart, because I accurately remember that the "hill" was *actually* a berm to block the construction company behind us, and the bottom of that "hill" was a cyclone *fence* boundary. The boys were small enough that they would sled down the berm and laugh so contagiously hard when they ran into the fence at the bottom.

    Jonah will tell me how much he loved making crafts and homemade treats at our kitchen table. His memory also warms my heart, because I remember purchasing that porcelain top table at an antique mall. I learned how to strip the paint from the legs, borrowed Uncle Jim's orbital sander, and figured out how to sand it so that it had more of an intentionally weathered look rather than an appearance that said, "I'm the tiny, crappy table replacing your large, family table in your other home." I recall purchasing the bench and three seats for that intimate kitchen table, because I knew it would have to serve as our kitchen, activity, and *everything else* table in our downsized new home.

    There is nothing more humbling than hearing your kids reminisce about the *lowest* part of *your* life as though it was the *highlight* of *theirs*. It tells me that I did something right. That I put my ego and needs second while they were so young, and I made them and their needs the priority. I showed up for them in that unfortunate transition, and in turn, they have fond memories with the mom who was the phoenix rising from the ashes instead of the mom who was a shell of her former self. Our time together in that house will always hold a special place for me, and when I begin to doubt my strength, as we all do from time to time in life, I recall that journey that we took together. I remember how I was able to bring us through by staying focused on what I innately *knew* our future had in store for us, even though I had no idea what it would look like.

When the World Shut Down

I refuse to give COVID more energy than it already took from me (and all of us), so let's get to the point:

The Top Five Things I Hated During COVID:

1. The threat of death like a 2020 version of Biblical plagues in the Book of Exodus. I came close to searching for a local farm to provide me with lamb's blood for my doorway... *just in case.*

2. Wondering if going to the grocery store would kill me or someone I loved. That shit really made you reconsider your priorities—*guacamole or Grandma?*

3. Working from home *suuuuuucked.* Don't get me wrong—I still value a work-from-home day here and there, because I'll get a ton of shit done from the comfort of my home, but that focus deteriorates

when it's *all* day, *every single day*. I missed going to work, connecting with my professional purpose, my colleagues, and our students.

4. Sending my kids to their dad's. To be fair, that adjustment post-divorce sucks anyway, pandemic or not. But especially during COVID, my kids were the only people I interacted with—even keeping my parents at bay for fear of both my kids' and my parents' health risks. We did enjoy some "hellos" through windows, sitting outside (*10 feet apart*) in bag chairs in the driveway, and not one but *two* birthday parades for each of the boys' spring birthdays. We made the best of it, but no matter how fun it was when I had the boys with me, when they were gone, it was just me... *and my thoughts.*

5. I was single. In a pandemic. You do the math.

The Top Five Things I Focused on During the Wrath of COVID:

1. Yoga all the time. I played so many Yoga with Adriene videos on YouTube that we might as well have been in an exclusive relationship—I knew her dog's name, we always did what *she* wanted to do, and we spent most mornings in "something comfy" to begin our day together.

2. My boys. We basically went into preschool and first-grade homeschool mode. Because while school districts did their best, education was still very far removed from the current days of Zoom, Google Meet, and the now overwhelming amount of platforms for learning. Holy crap did the techies come out of the woodwork during COVID—they gave birth to too many "COVID baby" programs that all do the *exact same thing*. The multitude of programs and our confusion still remain—"Your microphone is muted!"

3. Writing and reflecting and writing and reflecting.

4. The world. Slowed. Down.

5. A man re-entered my life—a lot less painful than COVID, and thankfully a lot longer lasting. (*Get your mind out of the gutter!*)

Blending

I've had the great fortune of working with many amazing educators throughout my career. I've experienced a vast variety of leadership styles, colleagues, and committees. I've now worked in five different schools in three separate school districts, and each has left its mark, helping me grow into the professional and person I am today.

There was one leader, though, whose collaborative, seemingly spontaneous and witty demeanor always resonated with me. He was the best at brainstorming great ideas based on what was genuinely best for students, and my linear, big-picture brain could always filter those ideas into a draft that we would take to fellow teammates in leadership so that they could "poke holes" and share feedback. It was the most natural partnership I'd ever had—personally or professionally. So when my former assistant principal, Mike, reconnected late into COVID, I was curious to say the least.

It started with swapping divorce stories, strains of living somewhere new, and helping our kids adapt—he had two like me, but his were a girl in first grade and a baby boy still in diapers. We talked about the struggles of single parenting, but even more, we talked about the *joys* of single parenting. And we both struggled like hell when our kids weren't with us. It's funny to capture this time in our lives, because I used to say that we would "watch Netflix and chill" on separate couches during the pandemic—making sure we kept our distance while still feeling some sense of company when our kids were away. THEN someone took that phrase and *completely* distorted it, so I will clarify here—always six feet apart, just watching movies, and *especially* after giving birth to two nearly ten-pound babies, I was still haunted by the fear of my matriarchy's fierce fertility!

From the beginning, we changed *all* of the rules. And why the fuck not?! We played by everyone else's rules all of our lives, and look where it left each of us—in our 30s and 40s, divorced, living in rental homes, single-parenting with two kids each, and investing in individual therapy to figure out where the hell we went wrong.

Mike's known for his one-liners, but the one we both live by the most is, "Better to ask forgiveness than permission." And that's exactly what we've done ever since we got together. The beauty of finishing my first book, *Decision Permission*, just as we were starting our lives together is that we were both at a place in life where we didn't feel the need to get *anyone's* permission to live life and raise our kids the way *we* knew best. Sure, we second-guessed that gut instinct from time to time, but when we did, we always found comfort and reassurance in *each other*, knowing that everything we did was for our kids and that maybe, just maybe, we had finally found the person we would walk through life *with*, not *for*.

To this day, when we resolve to follow our instincts and challenge each other to trust that voice, life always turns out in the most unexpectedly beautiful way. And the added bonus? Everyone else is usually left confused, questioning, or just plain frustrated by our lack of stress levels—*a sure sign that we've set a boundary that is uniquely our own!* Like when we began dating and gradually allowed the kids to hang out as COVID seemed to be ebbing. We had backyard water fights, explored every local hiking path to find Geocaches, and learned board games we never made time to learn in the past. We enjoyed each other, and we were coming to realize that the *six* of us made quite the team.

All of these experiences together and apart assured Michael and me that it was time to grow this crew into a family, under one roof. And we embarked on this new chapter just as uniquely as we had everything else. Like the way Mike came up with the idea that we buy a house *together*, but only the boys and I would move in—initially. The way that we agreed that we would use the last three months of his lease to intentionally spend time together—*just the six of us*—to see if this was really going to work. We would later learn that our family never asks, "Does it make *sense*?" We only ask, "Does it *feel* right based on what *we* know?"

We didn't need the three months but having them reassured us that not only was this going to *work*, but it was going to be a lot of fun along the way! So Mike's three moved in with my three into the home that had always belonged to *both of us* from the beginning. Except now the three-bedroom and one-and-a-half-bath house was filled to the brim. We weren't married—*we weren't even engaged*. We were redefining what "family" would mean to us and our kids, and it felt absolutely right for the first time in both of our lives.

Before I knew it, I had *three* sons and a *daughter*—the daughter I never thought I would have. In 2014, when I learned that I was having another boy, people chimed in about how, "You just have to keep boys alive until they're about 10 years old—then it's just about getting them to keep it in their pants. But with *girls?* They're so sweet until they're teenagers—then you don't stand a chance." I was told they're needier, more emotional, and will come to *hate* their mothers, so I dodged a bullet on that one. But, as fate would have it, now that I am blessed to have Ella in my life, I understand why many people make these generalizations, especially when the nature of girls is, more often than not, *very* different than the nature of boys. And when you see them grow up next to each other, you can see how those stereotypes are born.

However, I am learning very quickly that *how* we engage

with our daughters is a direct reflection of the way we *recreate* or tear down and *rebuild* the relationship we, as moms, had with our *own* mothers. Fortunately, my mom and I have prioritized engaging in a LOT of independent and shared mental health work to better understand each other and ourselves. I'm blessed that our boys and our girl are surrounded by positive female *and* male role models on all sides of their families—role models who are authentic, rough around the edges, and unconditionally loving. Because when you blend two adults and four kids, you're also blending two families who are just trying to figure out how to support and love you while also wondering what in God's name you're going to do next.

Not long after we moved in together, the pandemic was nearing its "end," and by the time it arrived, we had *four* kids under *one* roof attending *two* virtual schools in *three* different grade levels, a *three*-year-old still in Pampers, and *two* full-time careers that were gradually returning to in-person learning. We had a house we were making into a home, finances we planned to figure out... *one day*, and a *lot* of fun making and eating tasty food together, creating our own definition of "family."

And then, on April 1st, 2022, Michael and I dug up a couple of rings in our dresser drawer, requested the presence of two of our many wonderful neighbors as witnesses, and we were married at the courthouse. Sending those photos to our family was the best non-April Fool's prank ever, or at least *we* thought it was hilarious! And we continue to prove that our perspective—*on raising our kids, loving each other, and living life*—is *all* that matters.

My Boundaries

Kristy Jean

Dear Diary

If you haven't noticed by now, my brain is hardwired to focus on the *big* picture. Without a doubt, I am a "zoomed out" thinker, so I often struggle with staying focused on smaller details for too long. Inevitably, when I reflect on my life so far, I can't help but take this same bird's-eye view approach, looking for patterns and trends rather than honing in on individual experiences. To be honest, what appears to many people as my resilience, empathy, and strength can often be chalked up to my natural tendency to, put simply, not give many *fucks*. It's just not in my wiring to care too deeply about all of the *things*, because in the scope of my entire life, what does it matter? (If you caught that *Walk Two Moons* reference, we are soulmates.)

I'm grateful for this self-awareness now, but I also know that this level of awareness came to me, as it does for many of us, in gradual stages. When I reflect on the course my life has taken on the road to uncovering and defining my own boundaries, a generalized big picture of my interactions with society would look something like this:

Please Excuse My Boundaries

Ages 0-8: Hello, world! I *LOVE* the color blue! It's the best color out there, and I'm not going to entertain your opinion, because I'm not even *thinking* about what you have to say about it. Blue is the best because *I* know it's best. Duh.

Ages 9-12: So... I still like the color blue, but you say that YOU *don't* like blue? Oh. Well, that changes things. If you don't like blue, then actually, I'm not the biggest fan of it either. What color do YOU think is the best? Yes, me too! I *meant* to say green—I agree.

Ages 12-16: You think green is the *worst* color? I was beginning to think that too—how funny! (*laughter*) ...Oh. You say you don't like my *laugh*? Oh, sorry about that—I'll work on being quieter. Yeah, no problem! Whatever it takes to please you so that you'll like *me* and I can spend more time with *you*.

Ages 16-20: Do you think that situation is funny? Oh, great—me too! Now that I know *you* think that's funny, I'm going to laugh, but I'll still be sure to laugh quietly. Which, actually, is super easy for me because that's the *only* way I've laughed ever since I learned that it's important to you. This laugh is a part of my identity now—no problem!

Ages 20-30: *Nothing* is funny? Okay. Then I just won't laugh. But is there anything I can do to make *YOU* laugh? I mean, *you* deserve to laugh even if *I* can't, so what can I do? How can *I* fix this for *you*?

Ages 30-35: So, I've started spending time with people who are making this motion where they throw their heads back, mouths open, and this *noise* that seems joyful comes pouring out of their mouths. What *is* that? Deep down, I feel like I remember that action and sound... *what was it called*? Oh, I remember now! It's called "laughter"! They're *laughing*! And it looks like they're enjoying themselves—without worrying about making excuses for their behavior... I used to laugh, *didn't I?* I wonder if I still have it in me to laugh too... Oh, wow, here it comes—I can't hold back anymore. The laughs are climbing, and I'm scared. They're going to judge me... *but it feels so natural.* (*BIG LAUGHTER released*) Wait, they're laughing... *with* me. Everyone is smiling. They say they've missed my laugh and how wonderful it is to see me laughing once again. Why did I ever stop doing this? How did I lose my way? I think it's just taken me a little longer to understand how essential laughing is in my life, no matter what anyone else thinks. I can see now that I'm not responsible for making *them* laugh either; they're bringing their own smiles, and I'm bringing mine—*this is what love looks like.* I have to keep exploring what this means for *me.* Is that *selfish?*

Ages 35+: Oh, wait... Did *you* just look at *me* like I shouldn't be laughing or that I'm laughing too loudly? Oh, honey... I'm sorry, but you have me confused with someone who *wanted* your opinion. It's okay—you just have your *own* work to do. I've done mine, and I'm continuing to do mine. Bless your heart; I hope you learn how freeing it is to have your *own* definition of laughing and to know *who* deserves to hear you laugh. Do you want to talk?

I wonder how many women (*and men, for that matter*) would define the trajectory of their lives in a similar way. In the conversations I've had with people over the years, it seems that though the age ranges might differ, the pattern is consistent—there *was* a time when we knew who we were. Then, we lost that person because of people, events, trauma, or a mix of all of the above. And for many of us, a life-altering moment, realization, or person came into our lives and made us remember who we were before the world got in the way. We remember that we are deserving of love, free to set our own boundaries, embracing and defining an authentic life that *we* define.

Recently, I made the time to write down all of the roles I embody at this stage in my life. Sure, I was mentally aware of them, but I've found there's a magic in writing down my thoughts. Especially in a world that is obsessed with making everything digital, physically writing down the thoughts that your mind is cycling through can feel so empowering. There's something about making the invisible *visible* that inspires me to engage in this practice. And, once again, this ritual did not disappoint.

For the first time since my divorce, creating a new life for our family of three, making career shifts, blending our families, and getting married again, I could see *why* my life had moments of imbalance—I wear a *LOT* of hats. I'm a proud wife, mom, educator, author, speaker, daughter, Christian, and friend. As soon as I listed all of these "hats" on paper, giving each its own row with space for its own goals and planned "to-dos," I still felt like something was missing. And then I remembered. It's the one hat that is often the most forgotten—the one we keep tucked in the back corner of the closet because we'll get to it *one day*. It's the role that I once had to remind myself to wear, but is now the coziest one that I never go without—the hat of *"self."*

With so many roles to think about, plan for, and execute upon, no wonder my brain often finds itself swirling with an inevitable touch of guilt creeping in. I'm very grateful to have these blessings in my life, and in order to *continue* viewing them as blessings (*instead of burdens*), I really had to examine each to understand what I was prioritizing and what I was missing out on. Just because we *say* they're our priorities doesn't mean that our actions *reflect* that they truly are our priorities.

I could see how my "friend" row was quite empty of plans in the week, and that truth made me reflect on who I could reach out to if even only for a phone call to catch up on each other's lives. I could see how the "wife" row offered me the opportunity to plan for intentional conversation with my husband about more than our shared tasks and kids' needs. Taking those few small moments to reflect challenged me to come prepared to our dinner out that weekend, ready to ask quirky questions so that we could learn even more about each other's pet peeves, joys, and wonders. And then there was the "self" row. That row inspired me to stretch beyond the stereotypical self-care that often boxes women in. What could it look like to go beyond pedicures and shopping? To dig beneath the surface and truly connect with my own inner voice and needs? That row encouraged walks in nature, quiet moments awake before the rest of my family rose in the morning, and mindful tea selection rather than tossing a random sachet into my steaming hot water.

This self-work has become part "mindful agenda" for the week and part diary. My black-and-white, often linear, brain could breathe a little easier seeing all of this on paper. My logistics were suddenly balancing with my emotions much better, and I felt affirmed and reconnected with my boundaries. It's been some time since I've reflected in a *true* diary, and maybe that's because traditional entries often feel like I'm talking *to* a piece of paper. When I write as an author, I have my audience in mind. At the present moment, it helps me to picture all of you lovely readers who are making time to reflect on your own past and your own boundaries (*or lack thereof*) as you've read through stories of my own. I envision you connecting at different stages of life even though our journeys might be strikingly different. I imagine some of you cringing at the inclusion of colorful language but reading on to see where it goes and many of you thinking (*or audibly saying*) "Fuck yes!" because you too are bilingual in both politically *correct* English and authentic "what my mind is *actually* thinking," *guttural* English.

But when it comes to diary writing, I guess it doesn't feel as authentic—no matter how many "dammits" I include. But then it hit me—once again, I was allowing someone else's definition of diary writing to restrict how *I* could interpret and use it. When it comes down to it, diaries are meant to capture your present moment, feelings, and thoughts. They're meant to empower you and guide self-reflection in a way that speaking with others simply can't. So then why the hell would I address my thoughts *to* paper? (*dead trees, if you will...*) And then thinking of a dead tree leads me to imagine our friend, *The Giving Tree*. Could you imagine if after sitting his bony, shriveled ass on her stump at the end of his life he suddenly decided he wanted to write in a diary? In all her martyrdom, she'd reply, "If you want to write, you will need paper. Go ahead, boy. Grind up my remaining stump to make it into a pulp for your paper." And the tree was *an enabler*... not happy. Damn you, Tree—we'll rewrite your ending yet.

So what does it look like to write *in* a diary without writing *to* a diary? I guess it's time to stop directing my thoughts *to* the paper itself (RIP T.G.T.). What could it look like, instead, to write *to* the one person who needs to hear my words the most? What could it look like to honor that final "hat" that often gets kicked to the back corner? What would it look like to address my diary entries *to* myself, *from* myself?

Like any diary, writing to myself would help me capture the present moment with the awareness that it is *only* the present moment. It's not a *manifesto* that will determine the rest of my life... (*Unless you publish your diary in an actual book that will live on long after you—then, maybe your vulnerability is a little more permanent.*) Instead, it can act like a "pulse check" on where I am in life right *now*. I can intentionally process each of the "hats" I wear, able to honor them individually and reflect on the boundaries that have evolved in each one.

Alright—now, I can envision my audience for these diary entries! I see you, *dearest gentle reader*, finding connections to your *own* life, and I see *myself*, years down the road, revisiting these entries anytime I travel the road of giving too many fucks. Surely, I will smirk at my former ignorance, revise a few boundaries that have evolved with time and experience, and reconnect with my most authentic self—no matter how she's showing up at that point in life.

I've lived to please others. I've excused their shit and made excuses for my own. It's time to step into *my* boundaries—time to make the invisible *visible*, clearly articulating who I am, what I need, and what I don't give two fucks about.

Dear Christian,

You've had some jacked-up experiences with *religion*. You've seen the dark side when there's way too much human influence and far too little God influence, but you've also seen the beautiful side when humans keep God at the center and stay humbly aware that no one has it all figured out. Faith for you is now defined as a *knowing*, a *connection* that doesn't require words; in fact, it speaks its own language that we can't begin to put into simplified, human-created terms. You hear without hearing, and you see without seeing. In this way, it is a deaf and blind trust that you put into faith, but the *visceral* peace that it gives you makes the not knowing a small sacrifice to bear. Faith provides such a constant challenge that it leads you to believe that even if you *could* hear and even if you *could* see, you wouldn't be able to comprehend what you were experiencing anyway.

Your current church has gained your trust, and that's why you've gradually engaged your family into the congregation, volunteering as you're all able, and attending when it fits within the needs of your blended family. Keep following that knowing, because it *isn't* the church itself that keeps you coming back—it's the *people* and the way they *live* the truth that Jesus died for *all* of us, and we don't need to overthink much beyond that. It's the way the people live to serve and know that their purpose in this life isn't to condemn those "doing it wrong." Their purpose is to invite *everyone* to find faith and then define it by their own terms. Jesus didn't say "Teach everyone how to be faithful in the only way *you* know how to be faithful"; He said (*and I'm paraphrasing here*), "I hung out with lepers, whores, and thieves—you really think I want you texting Janice every time her ass isn't in the same seat every Sunday (*or Saturday at 4 p.m.*)? Quit being a Karen, and check yourself before you wreck yourself." (*I believe that last part was Ice Cube, but Bible verses and late 80s hip hop lyrics are just so challenging to differentiate...*)

When you start doubting or begin pretending like *you* are in complete control, get quiet, jot down some thoughts, and send up a prayer to remember what it truly means to be *Christian*. And when you've had the quiet solace that you need, remind yourself that faith was never meant to be a solely independent experience. You're meant to practice fellowship with others—*your husband, your family, your friends*—in a way that embraces each other's flaws, leading with empathy. Key takeaways? Jesus died for your sins. Get quiet to hear God. And if anyone asks if you'd like to attend a Pentecostal church, turn and *run* the fuck away and never speak to that person again. *Hard* boundary.

Dear Professional,

You work *for* no one. Sure, you will have supervisors, bosses, and colleagues who *think* they're your boss, but none of them are your "why" for showing up day in and day out. You work *with, alongside,* and *adjacent to* others, but you work *for* no one. You work to fulfill *your* purpose and follow *your* passion.

It's easy to forget that when you're a rule-following perfectionist and recovering people-pleaser. You have a knack for reading the room and responding accordingly, and that's a great skill to have when you're coaching and supporting others. But when it comes to the *influence* of others, you need to remember that no one could ever demand that you work harder than you're already working. No one knows your big-picture brain and the fact that while they're running around like chickens with their heads cut off, wondering why the hell *you* look so calm, remember that this level of contentment is the gift of *experience*.

Experience with kids in the inner city who tell you to "fuck off" and apologize an hour later, bursting into tears before sharing their deepest fears with you—a twenty-two-year-old who had gained their trust simply by showing up every day when most of their family members wouldn't. (Like the eleven-year-old who threatened to blow up your house and then, an hour later, apologized and told you that she might be pregnant and wasn't sure if either party used protection. True story. Turned out she *wasn't* pregnant, and as to her threat, joke was on her—you were living in an apartment, *not a house.*)

Experience with autistic, ADHD, ODD, and every other acronym of special education student who spit in your face one day and turn around the very next day to ask if you would come to their special event or birthday, because they liked you. Always "yes", never surprised.

Experience with parents who use their words and body language to threaten you, posturing until they realize that you *will* bark back and *no*, you won't take their shit on an entry-level salary. Parents who, once you set that boundary, similarly to the ones you set with their *children*, were surprised to hear the next words out of your mouth:

"Help me understand what you're afraid of, because I want to work as a team to help your child succeed, but I wonder if it would help to start with *your fears* before we can focus on *your child's* success here at school."

You have experience in spades, and you've grown so incredibly much since those days, decades ago, when you realized how much you *didn't* know. Holy shit were you ignorant—pissing families off because of the tone in your emails or teaching classes for an entire day, realizing that nothing you did "stuck" with your students. You faced *genuine* feedback from mentors who saw your potential and *shit* feedback from higher-ups trying to prove that their jobs were necessary.

There are many broken people in this world; if you get cut by them, it's not you—you're just standing too close. Take a step back and see their jagged edges for what they are— *their* trauma that only *they* can smooth out. If they (*and we*) can find healthy ways to smooth out those edges, then a hell of a lot less people get cut, and suddenly, everyone has the safe space to feel better about themselves.

You're always going to reflect and learn, but please savor the hard-earned truth that you *know* your shit, and you don't deserve to *take* anyone's shit. You've faced adversity, and you'll face it again. Your school closing in 2024—*its 100th year in existence that you made sure everyone in the community knew about, acknowledged, and celebrated*—hit deep. So many amazing people pouring their hearts into a broken school community, rebuilding it *with* the families and students... just to be shut down. That fucking sucked, and it felt personal.

You resented, and maybe still do, the profession that was supposed to fulfill and sustain you until retirement. Sure, you reached the point of acceptance in regards to that *situation* around *that* building closing, but you struggled even more to accept your professional "status" within your district in the *face* of that closing. You've never been good with waiting, so when the district told you, understandably, to wait and see how your fate would be determined, where they would place you in the archaic (*albeit necessary*) system of seniority and sucker punches, your instinct told you that this wasn't going to fit *you*. You knew this about yourself, and yet, like a good little public servant, you were sucked back into the conditioning of the profession—go where they tell you, work hard, don't worry about the pay, and you'll have a special place in Heaven waiting for you, and remember... you do this for the *kids*.

Except *your* Jesus clarified time and time again that you just have to *believe* in Him and His dad to get into Heaven, so screw that nonsense. It was time for you to push past the system you became way too comfortable settling within. Not to mention, that system always encouraged you to show up and stand out (but not *too* much), and you *did*, but that *still* landed you in a career waiting room. All of the times you requested feedback meetings. All of the times you dressed *business*, not business *casual*, when a senior administrator visited your building. All of the times you ran committees, led teams, got there early, stayed late, and *asked* for more. All of it, and you were still... just.... waiting.

Sure, it was a logistical struggle across the country (*declining birth rates, increased virtual learning, etc*), and it will likely continue, but it *felt* personal and what was being offered plainly and simply didn't fit *you*. But would you set that boundary or stay in the "comfort" of letting someone else determine your fate?

Girl, you wrote a book titled *Decision Permission*—and though you never claimed to be "the" expert, because none of us has or will ever encounter every possibly decision we will have to make in life, you did give a pretty damn good set of five states that even *you* reference frequently in your own life. Also, you're impatient by nature, and all of your self-work taught you that when you get sick of waiting, it's usually for one of two reasons:

1. You have road rage. (*Undeniable no matter how hard you try*)

2. You weren't built to follow the crowd, and your waiting "timer" was up.

Now, #1 is incredibly specific—*that's another batch of stories for a completely different time*. But #2 is a truth that will rear its head in the small moments and big moments in your life. #2 starts by speaking quietly, "This doesn't feel right... Why are we doing this?" and then eventually she roars—"Why are we putting up with this shit?!! We're so far beyond this that we should have moved on a long time ago!"

Remember how much you *love* that inner voice. You've spent years meditating, crying on your yoga mat, and sitting silently in church, learning how to *listen* to her. She's the "you" that you're often guilty of suppressing, but the longer she has to wait, the *louder* she gets. Your relationship with her is so strong now that you can hear her in even the noisiest coffee shops, telling you to "just write, dammit" when you're procrastinating by obsessing over which coffee to order and which seat will be the most "inspiring" to sit in.

And she's loud as ever right now. She's pretty pissed off that you worked so incredibly hard in that new building—

honoring the culture of the community and strengthening the supports offered to students and staff—only to watch it *close*. You tell her that it's okay, to take pride in her efforts and to remember that nothing is promised, *but* she has some pretty inappropriate things to say back, so just remind her that the language in this book is *colorful* enough without her two cents.

When you finally did listen to her, she had a lot of evidence to prove that this season of your professional life was coming to an end. You made time to weigh the logistics of your current career compared to others that were grabbing your interest. You even sat back down with *Decision Permission* to make all of your lists in State 2: Prepare. You'd been quiet enough to know that it was time to do the work, but even *you* forget *how* when there's so much emotion tied to the decision you're going to have to make. "No choice is still a choice." *God, she's annoying!*

Reading, journaling, and talking with your people has always been a huge help when you're spiraling, but you should be proud that you've learned how to *sit* in the shit instead of settling or rushing to find a solution right away.

After all of that work and a card-reading session with your kickass, intuitive healer friend, Jessie V., remember that you discovered two similar "threads," if you will, that run through your current professional life.

Thread Number One:

You are at a place in your life where you are *thriving* in the presence of female energy—a reality that was *never* a truth in your past. Besides the matriarchy that raised you, you've mostly pushed women away in your life in one way or another. Maybe it was your obsessive focus on your relationship with bachelors or maybe it was the societal pressure to always, always compete with other women, but it's a stark contrast to the way you *now* love cheering on fellow women and learning from them. It's taken you a long time to see that it IS possible, *contrary to the patriarchy,* for women to bring their badass qualities together with fellow women, who possess similar *or* different badass qualities of their own, and proudly stand together, changing all of the things that don't make sense in this fucked up world. *Hey, Siri, remind me to send Taylor Swift and Lizzo "thank you" cards...*

On top of empowering each other, many of you are also running side-by-side with your partners in life, caring for the family you've both decided to build *when* and *how* it made sense in your lives—not because your family was pressuring you or because male doctors pushed the agenda that your "clock is ticking." You've arrived at a time in your life when women refuel you, inspire you, and make you want to challenge your limits. It took you four decades, but you've finally stepped into your most authentic, feminine energy.

Thread Number Two:

You are tightly wound at this time in your life, trying to give your energy to everything and everyone. And though that's a positive quality that is received gratefully, it's time to slow down (*again*) and reflect on *how* you're using your time and *where* you're giving your time. You've been through a lot of change you didn't choose in the past few years, and that always requires getting quiet so that you can mend your heartbreak, heal, and step into the next phase of life. It's also a solid reminder to revisit that "self" hat that you wear so proudly—make sure you're taking care of her by authentically communicating what she needs so that she can confidently shift between her hats.

When Jessie V. reached to pull your final, future-oriented card, though you were curious what it would show, deep down, you knew all along. She drew the card for her own viewing, smiled a knowing smile, and placed it down in front of you. It was the "Queen of Wands" card—a grinning, powerful, and fierce bitch who looked like she was taking control of her own path *(and hovering, because why would a queen walk?)*. And suddenly, you realized that the tears welling in your eyes were the external release of your internal self-doubt. Let go of the patriarchy telling you to stay small and quiet, living to please others while excusing away your own voice and the life you know you're meant to live. You are a badass—grow a vagina, and go take the world by storm. *Tits up!*

Dear Friend,

Thank you for the work you've done to understand your friendships better. For a while there, you were inviting everyone and their mother (*literally*) into your life, and that shit was exhausting. Sharing your time with too many people often drains your energy—an introverted reality that you have come to honor. I think you were trying to make up for lost time. As soon as you dialed in with the awareness that your female friendships weren't a priority in the past, you doubled down on that epiphany and began overscheduling, over planning, and overexerting yourself. *(Moi?! Never...)*

Friendship is like a fine wine; you can't rush the process, and you have to let it *breathe* to find out what it's truly capable of. You, on the other hand, chose to go cold turkey on time with friends during the complex and confusing end of your marriage and then swung the pendulum over to *chugging* bottles of new friendships through your divorce—*often without even reading the labels.*

Gradually, though, you realized that you needed to "quietly quit" the people and energies that did not align with *your* needs at that time in your life. (*Shout out to my friend, Jeanette, for that brilliant little phrase—AA should really consider adopting that gem...*) Though your black-and-white brain struggles to live in the gray, you realized that the best option was to approach each friendship with intention, understanding that some are meant for a *moment*, some are meant for a *season*, and very few are meant for a *lifetime*.

You're never going to be the grudge-holding type, so it's not that you're kicking people out of your life forever, it's just a newfound acceptance of *reality*. Our lives are *supposed to* evolve; we're not meant to stay in a suspended state of existence where nothing changes around us. We're meant to take the God-given challenge to *feel* all the *feels* in life, and doing so will always require us to face and embrace change in our friendships and every other corner of existence. Sure it's painful as hell at moments, and self-doubt is a pretty consistent enemy, but you know what's on the *other side* of all of those challenging and uncomfortably shitty parts? YOU get to stand on "me mountain," proudly looking down on the river of untruths that you once believed to be *your* comfort zone.

You've had to learn that true friendships don't require an "end," but sometimes they need a "pause" button. The hard truth that many people don't want to accept is that even those rare friendships that last a lifetime can benefit from hitting the pause button. This isn't a deliberate end, separation, or angered response to a situation—it's an intentional response when you've gathered enough evidence to prove that it's just not working *right now* and you aren't willing to lie to yourself any longer. In an ode to Jeff Foxworthy's "You Might be a Redneck if..." list, here are a few reminders to assure you that "You Might Be Ready for the Pause Button..." in friendships throughout your life:

- When you continuously schedule plans that end up needing to be rescheduled, predictably resulting in one or both of being unable to even make *those* dates. Before you know it, you've gone *months* without seeing each other.

- When you feel *resentment* in choosing a gift that they picked out for themselves, their kids, or their dog on an Amazon wish list—only to send it to the party that you "aren't going to be able to make," even though, *technically*, you could have been there.

- When you walk away from quality time together feeling absolutely *drained*. Because when you process the experience later, you realize that your exhaustion is a direct response to the fact that there was never space in the conversation for you to decompress from any of your *own* stressors, but you definitely have a shit-ton of *theirs* on your plate now...

- When you force a *present* friendship solely because you had one in the *past*. If you are continuously trying to "get back to normal" in a friendship that was born in a time when you had a tight ass, perky boobs, fewer kids, less work, and/or fewer needs, it's time to swallow a fuck-ton of reality and hit the "pause" button. Or, in rare circumstances, maybe now is the right time to hit the "*stop*" button if you've each grown to embrace very different values and interests. Go ahead and genuinely honor and appreciate that past time in your life with them, but for the love of God, stop trying to play *Back to the Future* with everyone's feelings

- When you finally *do* get together with that person, impatience kicks in because one hour feels like *four* and you're checking your watch, thinking about what you have to "do" next. This is often paired with the fact that you've found yourself *solely* requesting speed-dating type outings like "a quick coffee" or a "brief walk at the park on my way to pick up groceries before I pick up the kids before..." If you're giving "quality time" a million parameters, it's no longer *quality* time. You're forcing it, and more likely than not, your hats feel like they're about to topple. Hit pause. Take a step back. Reassess. And try again when/if you're ready.

Be sure to swallow a bit of humble pie in all of these situations, because though you will find yourself on the button-*pushing* side of friendships, there will also come times when friends have the need to push the button on *you*. Feels a little shittier on that side of the tracks, eh? Remember, though, that if it *is* personal, hopefully you and the friend can both grow vaginas and have a courageous conversation to admit that it's over (*or minimally ghost each other like that one guy who couldn't take a hint*). But when it's *not* about the friendship itself and, instead, about all that you or the other person is carrying right now, suck it up and be patient. Don't be *that* friend who can't read the room—take the feedback and move on with life until your friend is ready to hit "play" once again. It might be a month; it might be a year, but like any solid relationship, if it's not built on a foundation of respecting each other's boundaries *without judgment*, you've got to wonder—can you even call it a *relationship*?

While all of these scenarios have existed as a truth in your friendships, they should also act as a lie detector for *quality* friendships at various stages in your life. For instance, if you start a new friendship and you're *already* running to the pause button, "quietly quit" that shit ASAP. We don't need to let everyone's three-ring circus into our small tent, you get me? Pump the brakes (*as Michael would say*), and check the space in your tent before you start making promises to the lion tamer, acrobats, and fire jugglers. Actually, *always* welcome the lion tamer, because she's a badass. Be wary of the acrobats—never know where they're going to come from. And only let one or two fire jugglers into your life at a time—they're fun as hell, but their penchant for taking things to the next level can end up getting both of you burned.

Also use these scenarios as you reflect on your current friendships. Use these "Pause Parameters" to confirm which are most authentic—sure, you need a "pause" once in a while, but you couldn't imagine a "pause" for too long. That's how you know that you're aligning with the right *person* at the right *time* in each other's lives. Give your limited time and energy to those relationships, because those are the friendships where you're truly fueling one another.

Remind yourself again—some friendships are meant for a *moment*, some are meant for a *season*, and very few are meant for a *lifetime*. Honor all of these—each serves a greater purpose for both of you. Just be careful not to hold onto a "moment" for a "season" or a "season" like it's a civil union—that type of enabling will fuck with your life. And, let's be honest, the same is true about *you*. If you're vibing that someone is feeling this way about what *you're* bringing or *not* bringing to the relationship, then honor *their* truth as well, and encourage them to embrace the stage in life that they're experiencing—no harm, no foul.

The older you get, the more you've gained clarity in articulating for yourself: "friend" versus "acquaintance." Your truth at this time in your life is that you're in your second marriage, you share four kids, two full-time jobs, a home, and a cabin. You love your life, and you have zero complaints. You chose this life understanding that there will be sacrifices, but the sacrifices you have to make shouldn't seem like *sacrifices* at all. Setting boundaries around time with your husband, responding to the revolving door schedule of your children, and spending time in a career you love often means that anyone outside of your family doesn't see you very often. And while you love people, and you're surrounded by *many* wonderful people, you need to remember that it's literally impossible to spend quality time with all of the people who would like time with you (*and vice versa when you want time with them within your schedule*).

You used to feel guilty about this. You used to take phone calls, make plans, grab coffee or lunch even when you knew it wouldn't be an experience that would fulfill you *or* them. You felt that it was so kind of them to want to spend time with you, and your boundaries would crumble. They needed someone to talk with even though you didn't have the mental or emotional capacity, and your boundaries would crumble. In those moments, let's get crystal-fucking-clear: Making time for things and people that don't fulfill you or worse, *drain* you, is the *opposite* of setting boundaries. It's people-pleasing.

And it leaves you absolutely depleted, voluntarily taking your focus off of your priorities.

So for those in your circle of friends, acquaintances, or a future one of these, continue to clearly communicate that you genuinely care and appreciate that they are a part of your life. Help them see that your boundaries aren't about *them;* your boundaries are the grounding you require in order to balance the aspects of life that are most precious to *you.* Your boundaries allow you to keep living a life that you are proud of, supporting your family and your dreams, and most crucially, your own wellness. Maybe, then, they too will feel empowered to press that "pause" button on you and anyone else in *their* lives when their hats are toppled over. Women setting and supporting each other's friendship boundaries? Damn. That sounds like one of the most genuine forms of love that I can imagine. That shit can change the world.

Dear Daughter,

Being an "only child" has been a cornerstone of your identity for the majority of your life. In every group icebreaker that asks members to share something that other people might not know about them, your response has always come down to one of two choices:

"I'm an only child."

Or

"I'm left-handed."

It's actually quite interesting to see the way that society has evolved around the idea of having an "only" child. First off, who the fuck decided on *that* label? It had to be the same idiot who came up with the "Baby Blues" phrase. No other amount of children has a reference like this. When you have four children, you don't say they are "1/4 children" or "quarter kids"—you just say that they have *siblings*.

The word "only" carries a bit of a negative connotation—as though Tammie and Fred *only* had one daughter, or they could *only* experience life with a *single* child, how unfortunate. Some ignorant people even asked my parents why they didn't have more *just in case.* Just in case... what? Because one human can easily replace another? WTF? Your mom says she stopped at *perfection,* thank you very much. Okay, okay—even though you're *far* from perfection, like *very* far, why would anyone believe that having *one* child should come with a doomsday label of having an *"only"* child?

If you dial it back a few generations, you can see that during the 17th century (*and prior*), having an "only" child was an unfortunate circumstance. Though the mother gave birth to six or more so that they could manage the homestead and fill a church pew, *only* one was likely to survive due to the plague, cholera, or tuberculosis, rendering them unable to ford the river on that Oregon Trail.

You're sure the majority of the stigma is born right out of the church. I mean, there had to be a point in time when Mormons, Catholics, and the like either pitied parents with "only" children or cast them out of society, fearful that they too could "catch" this apparent disease of being left with only one child to raise. (*Everything* spread like disease back then) But—*can you blame them?* Few children does not a religion build.

Fast-forward to the 20th century, and it was a status symbol that every kid in elementary school was jealous of. "Wait, you have your *own* room? And you don't have to share *any* of your toys?! Luckyyyyy!!" Friends loved coming to your house, because there was no little brother or sister annoying the piss out of you and your friends while you played. By your teenage years, there was no older brother or sister for friends to swoon over, and your birthdays were epic, because there was no other child to throw a party for. *And,* all this time, you had your cousins as your pseudo-siblings to hang out with every week and play with at family holidays. You were living your best *hybrid* life—enjoying the idea of siblings without any of the stresses that your friends complained about. You had it made.

It wasn't until your twenties and beyond that you began considering what it must have been like from your *parents'* perspective. Each came from a family of four—three girls, one boy. Your mom was the eldest, and your dad was the baby. These were birth orders that you never had to even consider because it was always just *you*. Each came from parents that, you later learned, they resented and could never fully understand. Both of them wanted unconditional love but never felt it was given (*with the partial exception of your mom's father*). Both of them wanted to be "seen" by their families but always felt misunderstood. And so they both approached parenthood ready to raise their child in the exact *opposite* rearing approach as their parents.

Even before your mom's serious bout of toxemia during her pregnancy with you, your parents had already rested in the contentment of having *one* child—hopeful it would be a baby girl. Each of their childhood experiences led them to believe that a home with multiple children equates with a home where the children are never seen as *individuals. They* never felt seen as individuals.

And so they raised you with this mentality and approach. They loved (*and still love*) you, each in their own, unconditional way. Your dad's never-ending collection of VHS home-recordings is proof that he felt absolutely blessed to be given the gift of his baby girl, and he was going to do everything in his power to be there for her in every possible way—*zero* exceptions. Your mom's love was definitely *less* than video camera's distance away, as she took more of the Mama Bear approach—always present, always fixing a hair or checking a bruise, always checking in and usually asking, "What's wrong?"

So, sure, your parents have always believed that you shit glitter and have the magical ability to turn any day into a sunny one, but they've also made intentional efforts to challenge you, exposing you to opportunities based on *your* interests. They were a far cry from the "lawn mower" parents of today—they let you feel some pains, and they made you face natural consequences for your actions, no matter how badly Mom wanted to fix the problem and take the pain away from you. You've been through the relationship rollercoaster that exists between all kids and their parents, if they're fortunate enough to *have* a relationship. The highs are high, the lows are low, and there's a lot of in-between moments where you're wondering how your relationship will continue to unfold and evolve.

Because you were raised an "only child," you had the luxury of being included in a lot of decision-making, very much like a mini adult in the family. Your voice was given space and time to be heard, but that did not mean your opinion would drive the decision-making. You were keenly aware of this, and it's what continues to make you a great parent today—you want your children to be heard, but you also need them to know for damn sure who pays the bills and who has the final say.

No story captures this awareness better than the "Green Dining Room" experience that is still a cornerstone of your relationship with your parents to this day. Remember back when your mom chose that *unique* shade of "baby poop green" paint color for the dining room walls? And how after your dad painted it, all three of you secretly wondered how the *fuck* you were going to survive dinner in that putridly blinding, green dining room?

Not one of you spoke up. Not Mom who felt bad because Dad worked so hard. Not Dad who assumed that Mom really liked it. And not you because you didn't know what the fuck was going on, and you were lucky to have a roof over your head that you weren't paying for.

It wasn't until *months* later, that the cat finally came out of the bag somehow. None of you could believe that you had kept quiet all along, just to preserve the feelings of each other. It was a very laughable moment that led to a quick errand to Menard's for a far-more-subtle paint color.

Now, when one of you *(always you or Mom)* sets a boundary or says "no" to an event, the first response is always, "*Green Dining Room?*"

As in,

"Thanks for the invite to meet you out for dinner, but we're going to lay low with the kids tonight—*Green Dining Room?*"

Or

"Dad and I are going to head out of the party to get on the road before the traffic really hits—*Green Dining Room?*"

It's your shared way of checking in with each other, confirming that you want the *honest* truth rather than a *sugar-coated, false* response that, in all actuality, leaves *everyone* without their needs met.

It's a funny but deeply beautiful sentiment that ensures boundaries are respected while consciously acknowledging that feelings might get hurt. It's a happy medium between the obligatory "Yes" and the resentful "No." In three small words, you and your parents are able to communicate, "I see you" while also ensuring that you see *yourselves.*

So when Mom spoils the shit out of your kids or is triggered by the firm *boundaries* that you give your children, even though they are very different than the unexplained *barriers* that were placed on her by *her* mother, have patience while she continues to heal her trauma. And when Mom wants to buy you everything and give you the adorable boots right off of her feet (*Thank God we wear the same size.*) just because you complimented them, smile, say, "No thank you," and remember that she shows love in ways that she could have only dreamed of receiving from her parents.

And when Dad... um... well, when Dad... ugh... offers to do *everything*... for you? Um... when Dad... never does *anything* for himself... When Dad sucks at practicing self-care—that's it—remind him to place a delivery order for a well-done pizza, throw on a war movie at the highest volume the TV can take, and tell him how much you appreciate his support but *also* want him to enjoy the retirement that he earned after a lifetime spent serving his country and his community.

Sure, their "quarter-child" experiences will always cause some confusion when they try to understand how the "only" child in you and their "half-child" son-in-law, Michael, continue to raise your children and carve your own unique path together in life, but the beauty of the safe space they've always raised you in is that you can come right out and say,

"I understand that it's not how you would do it, but this is what works for *us*. We are forming this family the best way we know how, and it's going to look strikingly different from anything *any of us* were raised with. But that's the beauty in our relationship and our approach to parenting. We're not going to make every extended family event, and we're not going to invite every family member to every one of our kids' events, but that doesn't change the face that we love *all* of you.

...Green Dining Room?"

Please Excuse My Boundaries

Dear Mama/KJ/ Kristy Jean,

I know that just saying the phrase "corn maze" will trigger a flight response inside of you, but hear me out—there's a lot of mom wisdom to gain from that hilariously unfortunate experience in this Midwestern tradition of torture.

Your parents, husband, all four kids, and you embarked on that intricately detailed corn maze at Yogi Bear campground. Apparently, from a drone's-eye-view, it was cut into the image of Yogi and Boo Boo running away from the ranger, but all you could see from the map posted out front was that you *definitely* did not pack enough snacks to keep everyone from getting hangry halfway through—damn you, Yogi, and your picnic basket of Hell. But you're a "let's just go for it and see what happens" kind of mom, so you did. And your predictions were spot on.

Everyone laughed until it just wasn't funny to traipse past Yogi's balls for the fifteenth time. At that point, you modeled for your kids that when you've given it your all and you still can't find a solution, sometimes you have to say, "Bend (*fuck*) the rules" and *break* one or two, because your sanity is more important than following someone else's directions. That's when you began *trampling* through cornstalks in a northern direction, because according to that map, you were only a few rows of Boo Boo's ass away from the exit. Sure, the map and posted signs urged you to "follow" the path, but you'd had enough of four hangry kids in Yogi's maze of torture, so you were *done*.

Sometimes, boundaries only become crystal clear at the very moment when you are physically, emotionally, and mentally *drained*. So you chose the path *never* traveled by any prior maze explorer as you communicated with your family, "For anyone who wants to get out of here, I'm cutting through. We're done." Your family could have easily refused your shortcut, but as a mom, you've realized that you tend to "feel" for everyone, so when you articulate a boundary, it's often what everyone was thinking but not saying. They're usually just grateful that Mom made the official call, because where *you* lead, *they* will follow.

After trampling a few yards, everyone successfully exited Boo Boo's ass—which in all hilarity should have been the official exit *anyway*. You weren't sure what the course looked like now that your family of eight called an audible, but you were safe, you listened to your instinct, and it felt like a victory. *Who's up for apple cider?!*

Getting to this point of speaking up for yourself and, at times, your family, has been a bumpy road filled with shame, guilt, doubt, and disappointment. That's the crux of boundaries—it takes FOREVER to finally figure out who *you* are and what *you* need as a person because there are so many external forces telling you who *they* think you are and what *they* think you need. So when you finally muster up the vagina to speak your truth, your mind instantly fills with guilt-drenched fear that your boundaries are selfish impositions that you are placing upon others based on your own best interest. Let's not believe that bullshit anymore, *deal?*

When the *opportunities* of the choice that you're leaning toward pale in comparison to the *negative* impact they will have on your family *(i.e. booking a speaking engagement on the same weekend when your kids have special performances or celebrations)*, then request a separate date for the speaking engagement, and don't give that decision a second thought. But when the *opportunities* of the choice that you're leaning toward have *little to no* negative impact on your family *(i.e. trampling through Boo Boo's ass)*, then go for it without giving that decision a second thought either.

Establishing boundaries as a mom/parent are the most difficult to confidently communicate, though, because at the moment when you *do* finally muster up the self-assurance to enforce a boundary that you instinctively know to be best and *not* give it a second thought, *other* parents and society are simultaneously judging your intuition, making you feel like a bad parent. You are inundated with messages about what *to* do and what *not* to do when raising your children. Raising kids is the equivalent of the egg dilemma in the health world; the one that flip-flops every few years:

Eat eggs: They're heart-healthy!
Don't eat eggs: They're terrible for your cholesterol!

You're a *good* parent: You're setting healthy expectations!
You're a *bad* parent: You're being too demanding!

Keep seeking your *own* family balance, Mama. You'll know when you're in the "sweet spot" simply by watching and listening to your family and your own inner voice. You've already discovered examples of this; keep leaning into those experiences rather than filtering your actions through the perception of the *outside* world:

It's okay to sit and enjoy listening to Jonah play piano, *and* to eventually walk out of the room to give yourself a manicure while he continues to proudly practice on his own.

It's okay to engage in stories with Ella while painting her room in a shade of teal that she herself picked out, *and* to eventually walk out of the room to take alone time in the garden while giving her space to enjoy her new surroundings.

It's okay to rest on the couch and soak in some peaceful snuggle time with Andrew, *and* to eventually leave for the kitchen to begin making dinner with your husband, catching up on the day while Andrew determines for himself if he wants to continue to relax or run off any play before dinner.

It's okay to get creative while building Legos with Logan, *and* to eventually shift to the couch to read your book while he explores and problem-solves without an adult there to fix everything for him.

And then absorb the confusing reality that parenting is a *paradox*, because just as your seesaw of methods finally finds balance in giving them (*and yourself*) independence, you have to be careful that it doesn't shift *too* far in that direction—leaving everyone doing their own thing and forgetting to come together.

You've had to work at this, because your mom-brain is hard-wired to stay "productive"—complete one task and then seek another to take on. While this is an admirable quality because of how much shit you get done for your family, it can be your demise when you let *tasks* take priority over *people*. Like when your kids are talking to you, but you've still got your eyes on your computer screen. Or when your kids want to play, but you just *have* to fold that last load of laundry. Like when your kids want to tell you about *their* day, but you're so exhausted from pushing too hard through your *own* that you can't focus on what they're talking about.

Days like this will rear their ugly heads, but that's why it's crucial that you anchor yourself back to the self-work you've done—you *know* better, and you are actually *doing* better. You are finding a balance that you didn't believe was possible before as you focus on the truth that each of your children has his/her own love language and an equally unique way that they want *you* to "see" *them*.

Of course, they love the way that you find (*and invent*) so many opportunities for your family—homemade meals, homemade Halloween costumes, local adventures, etc. Just be mindful that you are doing *with* your kids nearly as often as you are doing *for* your kids. Because while your kiddos appreciate your wacky ideas like the annual bake sale fundraiser that you let them plan at the end of every summer, they also just love being *with* you throughout the process.

So when it comes to your grand ideas, *no matter how fun they are*, check in to be sure you're not:

A. Going too big for your own sanity and theirs. (*Don't worry—Michael will continue to throw challenging questions your way when you start brainstorming.*)

Or

B. Giving too much energy to the "what" and the "how" and not enough to the *why*.

The *why* is building their independence, resilience, teamwork, and self-confidence—proving to themselves that they are more capable than they realize. Stay focused on those goals, and you'll give your mom-energy to all the right places.

Now that I've walked you through all the ways that I need you to step out of self-doubt and into confidence, I hope I've built up your self-esteem enough to challenge you in a blind spot that many moms miss. Blame it on society as much as you want, but *you* have control of how *your household* interprets what it means to be a *mother*.

Being a parent is an incredibly rewarding role to have in life, *and* it's hard as Hell. Don't let anyone try to persuade you otherwise—raising good human beings in a fucked-up world has been, and will continue to be, the biggest challenge of your lives. And they're worth it—they're so incredibly worth it, and you're lucky to be their parents. But when life gets extra challenging—I'm talking those mornings where all six of you are involved in some level of packing lunch, eating breakfast, brushing teeth, packing an instrument, packing for sports after school, and/or dressing for another goddamn spirit day at one of the *three* schools that your *four* children go to—be careful that you don't begin erecting a twenty-foot statue in *your* honor, *Mother Teresa*.

As a mom, especially, it's hard not to *feel* like the sacrificial martyr. You're doing so fucking much for so many fucking people that you naturally trample on your own fucking boundaries on your own road to sainthood. Knock that shit off. Just because scheduling, organizing, straightening, and doing "all the things" come *naturally (i.e. control freak)*, that does NOT mean that *you* must engage in (*and control*) all of them. Remember, someone wise once said, "No choice is still a choice." So if you're going to run around like a chicken with your head cut off, hoping someone (*i.e. husband or children*) is going to notice and step in to take tasks off of your plate that you never communicated that you wanted *taken* from your plate, I'm sorry to say, but you are the cause of your own decapitation.

Yes, in a perfect world, those aren't *your* tasks and they aren't *your* expectations that should be removed from *your* plate, but *would* that be a perfect world for you? I 100% doubt it. The truth is that YOU made the decision to be a mom. You made the decision to get married a second time and double the size of your family (*with Michael—it's his fault too. Wisconsin is a 50/50 state, after all*). Your mom status was a choice, and it *wasn't* placed upon you.

You are entitled to have your off moments, hours, or even days when things just don't line up or you're bleeding as much from your monthly cycle as you are from that decapitated chicken head. But the moment you start feeling bad for yourself as though *you're* the sacrificial lamb who *no one* understands (*Jesus Christ...*) that's when it's time to step the fuck up and put on your big girl panties and *communicate*. Communicate with your supportive husband. Communicate with friends or family who can relate and offer empathy. Communicate your expectations and needs with your kids, because they are not only capable, but they gain a sense of pride and responsibility when they can help you (*and others*).

It can be so easy to fall down that rabbit hole of feeling sorry for yourself, but remember that society celebrates the self-righteous victim; that's why it feels so *good* when people feel so *bad* for you. But never forget that you genuinely thrive off staying busy—for yourself and your family—and you like to make even life's smallest events extra special. So if there are aspects of making those events special that are no longer (*or never were*) enjoyable for you, then it's on *you* to communicate this with your family. In gratitude, your family always has and always will step up and step into the needs you lovingly express to them. Share the efforts, and watch as your family is able to take shared pride in the results.

You are not *The Giving Tree*. Break the cycle of teaching our children that "happy" kids come from *deprived* moms. Don't model for your daughter that a "mom" is someone who never takes care of herself. Show her a badass stepmom who is following her dreams and loving her family all at the same time. Someone who confidently says "No" to some things and "Yes" to others, proving that even when the *answer* changes, the *values* and *priorities* never will.

And show your sons that they should NEVER expect their significant other to sell their own mental and physical wellness short just so that *their partner* can live *their* best lives. Break the trend that the requirements for being a mom are self-sacrifice, exhaustion, and resentment. Be the mom who proves that balance is very possible when you communicate and define balance for *yourself.*

Be the mom who doesn't *tell* them what's wrong, but the mom who asks them what *they* see as the challenge. And then ask them how *they* are going to solve *their* problem. Help them continue to build their toolkits of strategies, and when they dig down deep and still can't find that damn tool for this situation, offer one of yours. Share how yoga, journaling, deep breathing, and therapy have been fan-freaking-tastic tools that you and Michael have both used to evolve into the people you are today. Share your tools, but for the love of all that is holy, *do NOT fix it for them!* Share your strategies, not your enabling. Watch as they take the tools you share with them and make them their own. Watch as they *use* those tools in different ways than you ever would. Watch (*and cheer them on*) as they develop their *own* tools, empowered to be exactly who they were meant to be.

The world is never *not* going to be fucked up in its perception and misperception of child rearing. I mean, we live in a country where women are expected to traumatize their bodies (*and minds*) by pushing a big head out of a tiny hole and then, *almost immediately after*, return to work only to uncomfortably have to *ask* for a space to pump their boobs so that their babies can *eat*. And that's just the fucked-up expectation for moms *before* you have a chance to jack up your kids. Remember to ignore the "experts" who speak as though they are all-knowing but stay curious about those who propose a new way of thinking about how we approach our children. Ultimately, the two of you will never go wrong if you stick to the only two truths about parenting that you're *sure* of. The only truths that research, experience, and observation have all aligned to confirm:

Parenting Truth #1:
Parents must continue to work on their *own* childhood shit so that they don't ignorantly dump that trauma on their *kids*.

Parenting Truth #2:
Parents have to *see* their children as they *are*, not whom the parents believe their children *should* be.

If you can continue to work at those two things in life, it doesn't matter how many camps, classes, or playgroups you *did* or did *not* bring them to. You will be able to bank on telling all four kids that you focused intently on these two truths and made time to have fun with them all along the way.

Every parent is going to make mistakes—push too hard, coddle a little too much—but if you can provide an environment where they know that they can tell you *anything*, and you will genuinely listen to *understand*, that's a safe space they will take with them wherever they go.

If you take anything away at this moment in your life, please let it be that your children need you simply because you are *you*. There's nothing a mom can do to earn that instinctual *need* that her children have for her, but she can continue to reflect and grow to show up for them in the way *they* need her to show up for *them*. No matter what life throws at you, the beautiful truth is that you will always need *your* mom, and your children will always need *you*.

Kristy Jean

Dear Wife,

You are *now* a firm believer that two people in any type of relationship need to *challenge* one another—to pause, to question, to reflect, to grow. You've never wanted to be lived *for*, and you realized too late into your first marriage that you were blindly seeking to live *for* someone else. You've learned through many struggles that marriage has to be about living "*with*"—each person approaching the relationship with the expectation that "I am me, and you are you, and *each* of us needs to bring our *own* best selves to this partnership."

At the beginning of your current marriage, though, you were like Donkey Kong, throwing barrels at his head every time he spoke your own truth back to you. Remember those days? Defensive as hell and unwilling to reflect on those truths because you were so used to playing the *victim* in the past. You've had to unlearn and re-learn how to use your words to communicate and clarify, without jumping to rash conclusions. You've had to pause and set your ego aside, prioritizing the "*us*" over the "*me*."

Beyond that, you've also had to learn how to communicate even the slightest twinge of resentment, frustration, jealousy, or anger. You learned that the people-pleasing façade you once wore was, in all actuality, a straight-up denial of the feelings that stirred up inside. You used to carry a deck of toxic relationship emotions that was totally rigged for a jacked-up version of "Go Fish":

Got any "Grin and bear it" cards? *Got one!*

Got any "Smile and nod until you can leave the room to cry" cards? *Got two of those!*

Got any "Apologize even though you did nothing wrong so that you can make this icky feeling go away and fix things so that they're back to normal" cards? *Got a Royal Flush of those!*

Got any "Create a small moment to share your small feelings before they become an avalanche of emotion and inaudible crying" cards? *I wish! Go Fish...*

In this marriage, though, the two of you have built a new deck from the very beginning. Your emotions were so raw, and you both felt such overwhelming grief over the failure of your first marriages that you simply had to build a new deck, because the only remaining cards in your deck were two jokers, attempting to help each other laugh through the tears.
You were straightforward with each other from the very beginning, clarifying your boundaries up front—something that was very new for both of you. Actually, you each had more *barriers* than boundaries back then, because each of you was too afraid to fuck up another monumental relationship, especially now that there were more important people to consider—*your kids.*
Gradually, each of you stopped comparing past relationships to current relationships. You realized that trusting God, your instincts, and your shared ADHD-nature got you this far, and that was no accident. If you kept fighting the same fights and expecting the same expectations that you

had in your first marriages, then you damn well couldn't be surprised when you got the same devastating result. Neither of you were (*or are*) "fit in the box" type people, so it was time to step beyond the false comfort of those walls to create something new that fit only the two of you and this new family you were blending. I mean, even on paper, everything about your family screamed for a *custom* approach—two divorces, four kids, two rental properties, and a global pandemic apparently *weren't* complicated enough for the two of you!

Every guru out there will tell you that "communication is key" in a marriage, but no one spells that out. What kind of communication? How often? What if my timing is shit? Where should we talk about these things—away from the kids, away from the pets, and away from *life* happening around us? And *when* do we have time for that?

You used to feel like it was *your* job to figure all of this out in your relationships, which is *ironic*, because how can *one* person handle an experience that, by nature, has to occur between *two or more* people?

Thankfully, you now have a partner who wants to figure this shit out *with* you, so the two of you have learned quite a bit on the road to clarifying the anomaly that is "communication" in a marriage:

1. No matter how "small" the concern or need seems, that shit will snowball quickly in your mind if you don't get it out. Share while it's a snowflake.

2. Never *wait* to share your feelings. Don't wait until the kids go to bed, the morning, a project is over, etc. If you're feeling it, share it ASAP with some situational awareness...

3. When you have hopes that something will happen (*for your birthday, anniversary, this weekend*) tell your spouse what it looks like, sounds like, and feels like! Stop the self-fulfilling letdown that comes from the belief that if you have to *tell* your partner what you want, then

getting what you want is somehow *less* special. Knock that shit off. If getting what you want isn't enough, then maybe that's not what you wanted all along. Would you hop on a boat expecting the captain to *intuit* where the hell you wanted to go? No, so don't do the same to your significant other—pick a freaking island, drink a piña colada, and enjoy paradise.

4. *How* we say things and *how* we listen are crucial. Listen with love; speak with love. Listen for information (*without* judgment); speak with information (*not* judgment).

That's why in your second marriages, you and Michael have drawn the same conclusions: when either of you is sucking at life, it's your partner's loving responsibility to let you know that living *with you* has been an unnecessary *struggle* lately, followed by asking two questions:

A. "Where in your day are you not taking care of yourself?"

and

B. "What in God's name are *we* (*and you*) going to do to help *you* get back on track?"

And when either of you is playing the victim, getting defensive, or being a grade-A asshole, you expect your significant other to stop you in your tracks, tell you to pump the freaking brakes, and take a look around before you say or do something you're going to regret. Because even if you *initially* react by taking asshole to another level, you will later apologize, communicate your appreciation for accountability in your relationship, and get back to the phrase of endearment that has come to define your marriage: *"I love the shit out of you."*

The biggest misconception about marriage is the crazy idea that you're meant to find *one* person to be *everything* for you. That's an excuse—a cop-out for not doing the work to figure your *own* shit out. You're supposed to find someone who you want to walk alongside, listening and sharing as you evolve independently *and* together. There's nothing sexier than a spouse who prioritizes him/herself, creates a hopeful and positive atmosphere just by *being* themselves, and then comes home to *you*. Hell. Yes.

Your husband genuinely and lovingly knows you, often better than you know yourself. He can read your mannerisms and instantly know that you're getting worked up about something that you didn't even realize you were bothered by. He will move things out of the way before you trip over them, because your lack of spatial awareness often inspires you to create problems that never had to exist. And when you have a spontaneous idea (*let's be real, those never end*) that you excitedly want to see to fruition in the next *12-24 hours*, he will ask you targeted questions. These are meant to help you fully absorb what you're planning *before* you put your time and energy into one of the millions of ideas you're going to have in that *single day*. Appreciate them.

Because of your relationship with your husband, you've learned that boundaries aren't just for keeping *yourself* intact. Learning about boundaries means that you then need to use that awareness to honor and promote your *husband's* boundaries as well.

Your husband is the most selfless man to friends, family, and especially you. It's your responsibility as his partner in crime to listen carefully, observe when he's putting himself last, and challenge him by offering opportunities and your complete support so that he does what he needs to do within *his* boundaries.

This is NOT the same as "fixing"—we're recovering from that condition, remember? Don't *tell* him what to do. Offer, suggest, and challenge, but Heaven help you if you try to surprise him, push him, or nag him—he's a grown-ass man; if he doesn't listen to his own intuition or take you up on your offer, then take a cue from Elsa and *"Let It Go!"*

Be extra mindful that you don't allow past trauma to

sneak back in, making you forget what your boundaries *aren't*. Your boundaries are no longer walls of armor to put up for protection in a defensive response to an impending attack. Instead, remember that Michael is your safe place. So when you have a knee-jerk reaction to a defensive thought in your head, let's set the record straight now that you can still control the *words* that come out of your *mouth*. (You already get more words out in a *morning* than there were in the script for an entire episode of *Gilmore Girls!*)

You are responsible for, and in control of, checking those feelings before they come out as defensive retorts. You are responsible for treating him the way he treats you and vice versa. You have both learned, personally and professionally, just how valuable and crucial it is to ask questions before you make assumptions. And that's where you must continue to begin when confusion, defensiveness, or worries arise—each other questions to understand better, remembering at the core of everything that you do is out of love for each other and your family.

You've *earned* so many lessons about what it means to be in a relationship, and that is why you were ready to step into *this* relationship, *this* marriage, so aware and ready when you finally found your partner in life. You found someone who was ready to walk *with* you through life's paths because *you* were finally walking in your *own*. You were telling and showing the universe who you were and what you needed, and so when this beautifully loving and sometimes stubborn-as-hell man came into your life, you already knew that you were ready to love him, and finally, you were ready to teach *him* how to love *you*.

He thinks you're the most intelligent, beautiful, and klutzy-to-a-fault woman he's ever met. And you think he's the most thoughtful, selfless, and least-organized man you've ever met. And together, you take the world by the vagina, raising your old-fashioneds to cheers in the face of every doubter, every societal expectation, and every false belief that this blended life you once could only *feel* could actually become a perfectly imperfect *reality*.

Kristy Jean

Dear Femininity,

It has taken you four decades to learn exactly what it means *to you* to be a woman. You have worn your femininity as one of two polar opposites—feeble proof that you require care and protection or a powerful source of internal pride that you've used to prove that you are equal to *or better than* men. The former showed up in many ways when you were a child—you always loved it when your dad doted on you, and your first reaction to trying new things was to shy away and refuse to try for fear that you weren't strong enough to surpass your comfort zones. The latter showed up primarily in the last two decades, as you have always been very intent, personally and professionally, to prove just how independent and capable you are.

Growing up in the 90s, there was definitely a shift toward messages of "girl power"—*thank you, Spice Girls*—but that was still contrasted with the fact that they were nearly naked on stage, shaking assets you definitely *didn't* possess for male attention that you definitely *didn't* want. On top of that, the most popular song on the radio and TRL *(if you know, you know)* was Dru Hill's "The Thong Song." You're still not sure if you believe that women dress for themselves, other women, men, or whichever sex they're attracted to. You do know for a fact that in your high school and college years, you were dressing to attract men, though your dick tease status was still very much intact. You didn't want to *do* anything with them; you just naïvely wanted them to *notice* you. But as you've grown older, you now know that if you *do* dress in a sexy way, it first and foremost provides a confident boost to yourself and *then* as a tease to your husband (though now you actually *do* want to do something with the attention you're seeking from *him*!).

But when you get past the surface distractions of gender—*clothes, jewelry, shoes, purses, makeup, and every other façade*—you've realized that the core of femininity isn't what you wear or how you act; the core of femininity is an inner knowing that needs *no one's* attention or approval.

Ironically, the North Woods have affirmed your understanding of what it means to be feminine. You've learned how to listen for God in the silence, take a step back as a parent as your children stretch their abilities, and you've finally uncovered a middle ground between those polar opposite definitions of femininity that you've always felt pulled between.

Let's start with your cabin in Northern Wisconsin. That statement alone continues to make you cringe a bit, doesn't it? You usually try to downplay this fact by adding synonyms for "small" before you say "cabin"—"tiny," "little," and "hunting" are your usual go-to words of choice. You're very aware that those intentional adjectives come out for fear that people will think you and Michael are some rich assholes with money to blow. But in all actuality, you're hard workers who have two smaller homes instead of one large one. Either way you slice it, you still feel like a privileged, white, middle-class asshole, but that's a different book for a different time. (*Please Excuse My Insecurities*—the prequel!) You still have more work to do on embracing your boss babe, empowered female identity, but until then, can you just take the baby step to *drop* the unnecessary adjectives already?

Being in the North Woods, *regardless of the scale of its grandeur*, has challenged you to come face-to-face with silence, stillness, and a lack of Wi-Fi. (*Though your DVD collection from the local thrift store is quite extensive—not bragging or anything.*) The North Woods has demanded, *not asked*, that you learn new skills and a new way of being, and you love the impact that you see that it has on your family. And you can directly attribute your newfound awareness of your contentment as a *woman* to the new skills that you are learning.

Remember the first time you settled in up north? You *asked* your husband if you could take *your* ATV for a ride... What the *fuck*?! First, let's clarify that your husband is the antithesis of an overtly masculine, ego-driven man. First, he has all faith in your abilities in most areas of life (*walking and chewing gum not being one of them*), and second, it's pretty obvious by now (*even to your readers*) that you tend to leap (*not step*) into new experiences in life. So this momentary glitch of asking your husband for *permission* to drive a vehicle that is your *shared* property was a very revealing experience that proved you're still on the journey to fully grabbing life by the vagina.

A similar occurrence took place one year later when the two of you purchased a used UTV. (*Notice how I added the adjective "used" before UTV just to make you a little more comfortable? I know, I know. I'm just as sick as you, but I'm your inner voice, so this issue is still on you.*) You and Michael were so jazzed to surprise the kids with that 6-seater vehicle that you could use year-round. By that time, you *had* grown a vagina when it came to driving all-terrain vehicles, so you jumped in, ready to take it for a spin. A UTV is pretty much a souped-up golf cart anyway, so it wasn't a far cry from what you've driven before at campgrounds—*because your ass has never played a single round of golf.*

A new lesson in femininity reared its head, though, when you invited your older kids to drive the UTV on your property for the first time. You turned to Jonah, 10 at the time, and he was chomping at the bit to get behind the wheel. He drove a little cautiously at first, but before you knew it, he was ripping through trails, carefree about the branches that were scratching away at the sides of the vehicle. He seemed to have an inner confidence *or* complete lack of giving a shit as he drove. He instantly demonstrated his awareness that this was an outdoor vehicle, it was meant for exploration, and if he made a mistake or shit went down, we (*Mike*) could just fix it (*everything*) like we (*Mike*) always do (*does*).

You obviously never planned to have a daughter, so when the two you started dating and Ella came into the picture, you didn't know what the hell to do with yourself. You had prided yourself on being a "boy mom." This was partially because you'd always felt wired in a more masculine-mindset (*by society's standards*) and partially because you thought you wanted, and ignorantly expected, a girl so badly in your first pregnancy that it was as though you needed to assert the "boy mom" identity for yourself in order to shift your mindset even more. And you genuinely did. You became more self-aware, realizing that you had always related more with your male middle school students than your female students (*i.e. sports and dumb humor vs. focusing on what other people were saying or doing and hair styling*). This reaffirmed for you that you were perfect for the boy-mom role God had planned for you.

But then came Ella, and you were scared shitless. What do *you* do with a *daughter*?! Like she was some alien being that you didn't know how to approach. Get a grip. You *were* a girl. She *is* a girl. The boys are *people*. She is a *person*. Just get to know *her* and chill the fuck out, all right? Old stereotypes, like bad habits, die hard.

Over the years, the two of you have learned how to better understand each of your kids and what their individual passions and needs are. Ella has taken a little longer because she tends toward the quiet side, but once you started dialing in with each other, you came to find how many things you have in common while uncovering and promoting that her voice among the many outspoken boys.

So on that day when Jonah was, as Michael would say, "Driving it like he stole it," your inner femininity spoke up and made it clear that Jonah had one more lap, then it was

Ella's turn to drive. Ella looked at you with her typical deer in the headlights look (*figurative in this moment, but also a very common occurrence up north*) when she's thrust into something new. Her eyes said, "What do you mean, my turn?! I didn't ask to drive this thing!" And then out of Ella's mouth came the standard, complacent, female response when any of you are faced with motor vehicles or power tools: "That's okay. I don't want to drive it."

Hell no. Not *your* daughter. The best part about your years getting to know Ella was that you knew she left two thoughts unsaid:

1. Ella was afraid of making a mistake and breaking the UTV,

And

2. Ella actually wanted to drive the *shit* out of that thing, but her fear of #1 was greater than her curiosity and excitement for #2.

This was the moment when you realized how much you learned to let go of *(and intentionally worked to contradict)* gender assumptions for your own kids. You decided that you would challenge yourself *(and them)* to see yourselves and others for who they *are*, not as a stereotype of their gender.

With this in mind, you didn't hesitate when you quickly replied to Ella directing, "You're going to drive it, and I'm going to teach you." In that moment, the *boys* learned a quick lesson about femininity, you embraced *your* femininity, and Ella was scared *shitless*. She knew she didn't have an out, but the fear on her face also reminded you to give her support and make sure the boys shut the hell up while she faced her fear.

In that moment, you posed a question that you learned the value of much later in life. You asked her, "What's the worst that can happen? You drive it at 1 MPH, and we're all patient while you figure it out. You're not going to drop your foot to the floor like your crazy brother, so let's give it a try."

And with a small twinkle in her eye, she hesitantly climbed into the driver's seat, you shifted into the passenger seat, and her three brothers sat befuddled in the back seats, wondering what was about to happen. She did drive at 1 MPH to begin, but as soon as she realized that her fears weren't as big as she imagined, she was in her *element!* Her anxious face dissolved, and it was replaced by a look of pride. Sure, you challenged her, but *she* did the damn thing, and she was rightfully proud of what she had accomplished. So proud, in fact, that she asked if she could take her dad for a ride to show him just how well she had mastered this new skill. And you had a tear in your eye as you proudly hopped out so that she could prove to her dad, but mostly *herself,* what a young woman was capable of when she stopped doubting herself and just went for it!

The awkward way that you asked permission to drive the ATV and the way Ella's fear nearly overrode her desire to try something new were two separate incidents that taught you the same lesson about being a woman—it is *fear,* not *ability,* that gets in women's way. Face the fear, and you will prove that you're capable of *anything.*

You've seen this truth play out within the 2:1 ratio of males to females in your own household. The males often go "full send" on everything, knowing that the thrill of the moment is *worth* any consequences (*Or, more likely, there was no forethought of the potential consequences*). Whereas, as females, you and Ella often check in with your head *first,* opening a door for your fears and thoughts which keep you from exploring what you're actually capable of accomplishing. You, as with most women, protect your perceived perfection in lieu of facing your fears and the potential for the result-that-shall-not-be-named—"Failure"—*Gasp! That* is what dooms women. It's never the woman herself; it's that women allow the impossible, self-imposed expectation of perfection to stop them before they start. They *(and you)* allow fear to tell the story of what *could* happen, avoiding living the story that you can *make* happen.

To embrace your femininity is to love *yourself* first before you pick and choose which societal definitions of femininity fit *you*. That's a big ask considering that society's pressures always get to women (*and men*) before you have the opportunity to know yourself. That's why you need to keep showing up, redefining what it means to think, talk, and act like a *woman*. You need to keep asking other women what it means to *them*, supporting *their* truths so that they, too, embrace stepping out of boxes intentionally constructed to keep them small and silent.

And you must always, always make time to get quiet and reconnect with your inner self, because those are the moments when the world and its bullshit slip away, and you can fully connect to that knowing of exactly who *you* are.

Dear Self,

As a woman who was consistently in a relationship or seeking the next one, it comes as no surprise that you skirted the process of figuring out who you were and what you needed. Sure people in your life would say, "Spend time alone" or "Give yourself time and space," but what the hell did *that* mean? To a teen or twenty-something who felt society screaming at you to hurry up and find someone to belong to, take care of, and settle down with ASAP because the *clock is ticking*, this was a severely contradicting message.

And what would that look like anyway? You used to think,

"Why do I need time on my own, apart from a relationship? So... *what*? I just go about life, giving myself an undetermined amount of time, avoiding getting serious with anyone I'm attracted to, and tell my instincts to shut up?"

Especially in this day and age, the idea is promoted that young people should stretch themselves, find new challenges, and explore who they are before they settle down. But be careful, ladies, that *you* don't wait too long—then you get extra scary phrases like "high risk pregnancy" and "cankles."

You have become so tired of these polarizing ends of the spectrum, and it kills you to hear young women still feeling that same strain that you did over two decades ago. It took going through your divorce and being on your own to realize what well-intentioned family and friends *meant* when they told you to take time for yourself. Walking through your divorce and shared custody meant that you were finally forced to face authentic alone time—not the cutesy "go for a pedicure" alone time, but the raw, stomach-churning emptiness of being alone when you don't want to be. Now, you had to face the fear that you had run from your entire life. Now you had to face the feeling of *not* belonging to someone. Now you had to face the feelings of guilt and regret for the journey your boys would face *paralleled with* the feelings of relief and hope that you were beginning to feel and envision for the three of you down the road. It was through those struggles that you finally understood what "alone time" was for all along.

While there isn't a universal amount of time to spend being single, you did find that there were key lessons to learn about yourself that you simply couldn't discover *in* a relationship. If you could go back to that teen or twenty-something, you would clarify the following with her:

"I get that everyone is telling you two very contradicting messages: 'Don't get into another relationship' and 'Trust your heart!' But what they don't understand is that you're already embracing the growth that comes from failure. You are following your heart, and you know that if it crashes and burns, you'll still have experiences and lessons to take with you into the next chapter of your life. They don't see it that way, though, so they will continue to talk out of both ends of their mouths. Confusing as fuck, right? Yeah, I hear you. So instead of completely disregarding the idea of being alone, and instead of dismissing everything they're recommending, take a *deep breath.*

Begin by simply recognizing that just because you are attracted to someone, that does not mean that you must enter a monogamous *relationship* with that person—that initial feeling *isn't* love. It's a cocktail of craving attention, seeking a sense of belonging from another person because you're still a hell of a way off from finding it within yourself, and, let's be real, your hormones are a clusterfuck right now. So don't let *lies* or *lust* blind you. Sure, you can learn a lot from romantic relationships, but they're going to blow up in your face every time until you finally gift yourself the time to figure out the following:

1. What do *you* think about when no one is around?

2. What gives *you* that burst of excitement and a fulfilling little smirk every time you do it?

3. If everyone you care about went POOF and vanished, where would *you* go and what would you do? Why?

4. What are *your* top three pet peeves? Even the ones you *pretend* aren't pet peeves because you are a people-pleaser.

5. When you're stressed, what do *you* gravitate toward to release that tension?

6. Are your talks with friends and family always surface-level positive, or are *you* practicing vulnerability to get to know them and let them help you find your own blind spots?

The answers to these questions are WHO YOU ARE and WHAT YOU NEED. Now, whether you wait ten minutes or ten years to get into another relationship, let these responses lead the way *before* you ever allow another person to take the lead *for* you. Only *you* have the power to decide what you say 'Yes' and 'No' to in this life—*no matter who guilt-trips you or advises you otherwise.* Fuck them. They have their own crap to figure out. Don't add their baggage to the carry-on you've already created for yourself. Pleasing others is *never* more important than meeting your *own* needs. The only way you're going to live a *fulfilled* life, meeting *your* purpose, is to trust your own voice above every other voice around you."

Well said! But you know *her*—she's stubborn as hell, so she won't give a shit what you have to say anyway. At least at this stage in your life, you're able to see these valid points, so keep reminding yourself, *even today*, to stand by this hindsight that you've processed into a gift of wisdom.

You've taken away many lessons about what it means to be yourself—which are non-negotiable *boundaries* for your overall well-being and which are more like *preferences* that just make you feel good. They will continue to evolve, but you've landed on a few really solid beliefs around boundaries that have come to define just what that word and its purpose means to *you*:

1. Conflict leads to boundaries.

You've never been one to *create* conflict, but you love the shit out of *fixing* conflict. Over time, though, you've learned that conflict is both a necessary and hopeful part of life. Conflict inspires, motivates and challenges the status quo. Conflicts in your profession have challenged you to muster up the self-confidence to ponder what's next and, eventually, produce a new path you never imagined before. Conflict with the people you love has challenged you *and them* to step back and reflect, digging deeper to understand and communicate better—a true sign of an authentic relationship that will grow with you throughout your life.

Conflict is a catalyst for a future that can't be seen. You don't shy away from it anymore because you know it has something to teach you about the boundaries you have and the boundaries you missed an opportunity to stand by—those missed "boundar-tunities," if you will, that you inevitably regret missing because you dismissed them in the face of adversity.

You love change, but that wasn't always true for you. It

comes as no surprise now that you're constantly reflecting and looking for room to grow. You used to self-reflect to a fault, and that burned you in the past because you held *no one* accountable but yourself. Since then, though, you've learned to curb that behavior so that you're not always assuming *you're* wrong or that *you* made a mistake; instead, you get curious, pay attention to how the choices of others support or contradict *your* boundaries, and you look for lessons to learn. Often, those lessons don't require you to change *anything*, and that is the hardest lesson you've *earned*—not to jump into forcing change when all you're supposed to do is listen and take in new information.

When the chips are down, though, this belief will waiver. Be careful not to settle for the illusion of peace in the moment; you're only prolonging the inevitable, and that shit is going to sting worse in the long-run. When conflict comes your way, you have two choices: suck it up or shake it up. The former continues to prove its inadequacy as a wolf in sheep's clothing, and the latter is becoming a more and more comfortable fit for you as you grow older.

"Suck it up" leads to resentment and ulcers because you're holding back your truth. And in all actuality, you're lying to the other person who isn't aware that they're getting a full dose of your complacency. "Shake it up," on the other hand, requires fear-facing, so you know you're speaking your truth when you have that inevitable, visceral, nauseating feeling of regret the very moment the words leave your mouth (*no matter what amount of preparation you put in so that you could speak your truth*). Then there is nothing, absolutely *nothing* that can prepare you for the resulting shock, surprise, and/or defensiveness that you receive from the person you just vomited your truth onto.

Ultimately, *thinking* your boundaries and *speaking* your boundaries are two monumentally different realities. I need you to trust, though, that choosing to "Shake it up," though it makes you feel like complete *shit* in the moment, proves that you are bravely living your most authentic life. When you're completely and vulnerably honest with someone in that moment, *and you don't sugarcoat the hell out of that truth with apologies and bullshit backtracking*, then you know you have done all that you can do. Remember that more often than not, embracing conflict means that both you and the other person/people in the conflict will all feel like crap in the moment. Continue to accept the short-term pain for long-term integrity. Sit in that shit; then grow from it.

2. Boundaries are not barriers.

That bears repeating. *Boundaries* are NOT *barriers*. Not communicating is a barrier. Getting defensive is a barrier. Getting angry over miscommunication is a barrier. Boundaries are not "No." Boundaries are "Yes" to your needs, your people, and your most authentic life. You used to believe that boundaries = bad and that boundaries were walls that kept things out, but over time, you've learned that boundaries (*more importantly*) keep the right things *in*. Boundaries say, "I love myself *and you* so much that I've done the work *on myself* so that I can confidently share who I am and what I need." Boundaries say, "Here is my truth; now, please, with all love and respect, share *yours* with *me.*"

You used to live unaware of your boundaries, which always left them uncommunicated. You left the doors open, inviting everyone *and their issues* in. The less you upheld your boundaries, the more *you* were the only one who felt pain. Your vice for people-pleasing was like a billboard, communicating that everyone could simply ignore the rules for engagement because *none* existed. Without boundaries, you never stood a chance to *assert* and *expect* respect for yourself and from others. You let everyone live in *their* comfort zones... at the expense of your *own*.

Boundaries are not barriers for you *nor* the people you care for. In strengthening your own understanding of boundaries, you must also consider the boundaries of those you love. How can your boundaries be about what's best for you *and* them? Is that possible? What would it look like for boundaries to be less about "barriers" and more like a *manual* for loving you, because *you* want *them* to be successful? Remember, you don't set boundaries to keep people *out*; you set boundaries to bring people closer, in hopes that they will trust you enough to share *their* boundaries with you.

Continue to work on stating your boundaries in a matter-of-fact, neutral way. Don't get defensive, and don't assume that the response will be negative—you show love to others by respecting their boundaries, and the people who are meant to be in your life will respect yours as well.

Oh, and could you please work on communicating these through direct delivery rather than nervous laughter? Sorry, not sorry if that was a blind spot you were denying. State your boundaries confidently, prepared to receive whatever response you get, fully aware that *their* response says more about *them* and the work *they've* done (*or not done*) than it does about you, your feelings, and your needs. Until you disclose your truth, your boundaries are like an invisible fence that you're expecting others to blindly perceive. Even if there is a gate of compromise or clarity that you know you've internally established, it's still *your* responsibility to lead others to it—*then* it is *their* responsibility to walk through it... or let it smack them on the ass on their way out.

3. You need boundaries *for* yourself and *from* yourself.

Sure, your boundaries tend to focus on you vs. the world, but that's not the end of the story. Your boundaries are also greatly about you vs. *you*. Just because you know something is right for yourself, that does not ensure that you will do what you need to do. This is why you need to pay close attention to your *apologies* and your *excuses*. These two offer polar opposite results—they will be your spiraling downfall or the guiding light that reminds you to reconnect with your healthy, *necessary* boundaries—no matter who doesn't like them. If you're over-apologizing, over-excusing, and over-giving-a-fuck, it's time to take a step back and reassess how you're presenting yourself to the world.

Boundaries are the rules you set to ensure your own wellness, clearly communicating with others what you are non-negotiable about. You're not exactly a high-maintenance person, and you've done your work, so your boundaries are few and specific—there's no wiggle room for compromise on the several that you have.

Example: Someone could tell you that they took the keys to your car, drove it off a bridge, and now it's at the bottom of Lake Michigan, and your response would likely be, "Oh no! How did you survive? Are you okay?!" shortly followed by, "You must be hurting to make a choice like that; what's going on?" Material possessions are *not* a boundary for you.

But find yourself in a room where someone is making direct or indirect comments that don't sit right with your boundaries, and a reaction is *assured*. Comments often include, but are not limited to: homophobic, racist, misogynistic, teacher-bashing, or other verbal vomit that assumes that their *lack* of humanity has a place in this world. While you've always had a clear sense of right and wrong in these situations, it took a long time for you to muster up the courage to actually *say* something about your views. This is why your boundary around *doing* something in those moments is truly *for* and *from* yourself. You used to feel like absolute shit when you didn't say something, and it ate away at you long after the incident. Now that you don't hide your head in the sand, your boundary and your self-respect both remain intact.

You've learned that boundaries aren't black-and-white lines in the sand, though. Boundaries aren't knee-jerk reactions; they are thoughtful parameters that you develop to protect *and* challenge yourself. They provide an opportunity to truly hear what is being asked of you *(by others or yourself)*, consider who you are and what you/ your family needs in that moment, and then, *only then*, provide a response. These three steps are what have now become lovingly known (*in your own head*) as the "Boundary Test." When you're faced with a situation that stirs your mind or your nauseous response:

1. Ask questions to understand.

2. Consider your priorities and needs.

3. Respond in a way that challenges you and honors your boundaries.

You use this test most often when it comes to the request for your *time*. For some (*only child*) reason, you have this (*only child*) knee-jerk reaction to reply with a (*only child*) "No" when strangers, colleagues, friends, or even family ask to spend time with you. It's a unique (*only child*) response that you have discussed at length with Michael, trying to understand why you (*only child*) have this seemingly *survival* instinct where your animal brain, lacking words, feels the need to *flee* in these situations. Okay, okay. The only child thing is a definite part of the equation, but ultimately, if you dig deeper, there has to be more. Run it through the Boundary Test.

1. You definitely don't have the whole picture. Find out *why*.

2. This is an area where you need to be challenged. Somehow your brain has associated the ideas of time with others, attending church, and going to the gym as all things to *avoid*. But give all of them even another moment's thought, and you remember that you absolutely love the feeling *after* experiencing these things. So what in God's name incites a "smoke alarm" response when these opportunities arise? Stop treating these experiences as isolated incidents—and maybe do a little research on the word "introvert"? You surely have a limited battery; it's not their fault that you have a tendency to run it dead.

3. Take a deep breath. Don't be an asshole. Embrace the *feeling* that those experiences offer instead of checking your approval against a "to-do" list of tasks on your plate that day. Learn from the challenge.

Keep these lessons in mind when it comes to other life experiences that tend to be a bit more complex for you, experiences when you need boundaries *from* yourself because they hit a little harder. Namely, moments when you feel left out for no apparent reason, moments when words sting more than if someone had just struck you, and moments when people midjudge you through the lens of people they've known. Like being punched in the nose emotionally, tears naturally come to your eyes and it seems like the pain is rippling outward to every part of your being. This is why these are the moments when you have to rely on your test, not your emotions.

Sharing struggles and failures like these requires quite a bit of vulnerability, something you've grappled with for a long time. However, you no longer see vulnerability as a releasing of every skeleton from your closet, sitting there bare-ass naked for the world to judge every flaw. Now, you see vulnerability as an opportunity to open up about who you are beneath the surface—a means for simultaneously strengthening your relationship with others *and* yourself.

So, while there are definite boundaries to help you protect yourself *from* yourself, remember that the most influential aspect of your boundaries is that they are *for* you. Your purpose is on the other side of your boundaries. "Yes" to consistent time with God, family, friends, nature, and yourself. "Yes" to connecting with fellow women, hearing their stories, learning with and from them. "Yes" to slowing down after honoring your nature to stay busy, productive, and fulfilled. "Yes" to writing, making time to write, and using your words to remind others that they're never alone.

4. You can't control the way people respond to your boundaries.

You are not responsible for someone else's reaction to your boundaries. You are not the default *offender* simply because *you* communicated *your* truth. If you're treated that way, it's because you just called someone out on their shit, and they don't know how to respond to that level of truth-telling.

But you *can* control how *you* respond to *their* response. This is what I was talking about when I told you not to add apologies, excuses, and bullshit. Enable and fix. Enable and fix. That's what you're hard-wired to do, but enabling and fixing are the exact OPPOSITE of boundaries.

Like Newton's Law of Motion, there's an assumption that when you finally find your voice and speak your boundary that you, by default, must be the initial force, right? And as the initial force, you'd better be prepared for the return force, because *you* are to blame for putting things in motion. Fuck Newton.

But now you're aware that asserting your boundaries is actually your *response* to someone doing (*or not doing*) something *first*. Just like Newton's clacking balls (*giggle*), suspended from fishing line quickly send force from the first ball to the last, too often you've seen yourself as the initiator of the force. Which means you've viewed the person you spoke your boundary to as the chain of balls (*Giggle. Last one, I promise...*)—you slam into the row and knock *them* into the air, and they *return* the contact, and now *you're* sent flying.

When you finally did muster up the vagina to express your needs, you always saw yourself as the first ball (*See, told you—I held it together this time...*), choosing to draw yourself back, "unprovoked," *forcing* an unnecessary conflict that didn't have to exist until *you* opened *your* mouth. But then, you began asking yourself—what if all along, you've actually been the one *absorbing* all of those initial forces? Contrary to the laws of Newton's balls (*Now that deserves a giggle—I'll have to look up the proper name, but "Newton's Balls" would be a far better branding name from a marketing standpoint*), you were consistently *absorbing* the impact of other people's forces for so long, never moving, that when you had finally taken enough and said something about it, your actions inevitably made it appear as though *you* were the initial force.

Or maybe you *were* flying into the air, but you simply never assumed that you had the right, nor the power, to swing back with the same force that was exerted upon you. You felt blow after blow, but you would always end up trying to decrease the speed of your return force so as not to disturb the *rest* of the chain. I mean, who were *you* to displace anyone else's comfort zone, right? *Enable and fix. Enable and fix...*

This is why boundaries are NOT expectations *for* other people. They are expectations for *yourself.* It's never about changing the behavior of others; it's about setting your own parameters and getting comfortable with the discomfort of speaking up with a "Yes" or "No" when people come into your life. You will never control the way people respond; for your boundaries to have the greatest impact, it's your job in life to *decrease* your expectations of *others* and *increase* expectations of *yourself.*

5. Do the work, and you'll gradually give less fucks about the impact of your boundaries.

You knew that you were tapping into your truth when your first instinct in any situation was no longer an obsessive curiosity about what *everyone* around you would find acceptable or entertaining. You knew you were onto something when your knee-jerk reaction shifted to asking yourself, "What do I want (*or need*) in this situation so that I am able to show up as my most authentic self?"

That's when you knew you were doing the right work on yourself, because it's not about ego, though it seems to be at first glance. The ego is all about me, me, me—this is *my* world, take it or leave it! No, the right "work" is all about making the time and effort to get your own shit figured out so that you can engage with the world in an honest, humble, and grateful way. Working on *yourself,* ironically, has *others* at the heart of it all along.

It's so easy to be strong in your convictions when you've done the work that leads you to less doubt, second-guessing, or regret. Those feelings only arise when you *haven't* done the work, because fear keeps you from facing those feelings to see what's on the other side. Fear is a sign that you're *onto something*; it's not the scary emotion that you've always believed it to be—or been told that it is. Fear is a signpost in the road that signals to you that you're on the right path, and you should keep moving forward. Sure, you might need to pick up a few resources along the way—*a baseball bat, a friend, a dose of Adderall*—but needing *help* has never meant that you need to *stop*. Needing help means that you have done enough work pondering and preparing on your own, that it's time for reinforcements to help you armor up for this next level of fear. Because holy shit is it worth it, every fucking time.

At this point in your life, you give very few fucks, because you know who you are and what you need. And that's not a statement of overconfidence or finality; it's a hard-earned self-awareness born from the trust you've built in looking for and noticing patterns in your life. It's the same quality that will keep you curious for the rest of your life.

You are still The Giving Tree, but you're not happy because you've given until it *hurts*. You've learned the difference between "sacrifice" and "giving"—a lesson the original tree never would. "Sacrifice" causes direct *pain* to the provider; whereas, "giving" provides *nourishment* to the provider *and* receiver. *You* give humbly and gratefully according to your own boundaries, so your version of giving never feels like a sacrifice. You never lose yourself in the giving, and so by giving, you actually gain the most.

You've come to realize that living your most authentic life has never, ever come from quitting something cold turkey or drastically removing someone or something from your life. It comes from small shifts—decreasing what's no longer serving you and increasing what you intuitively know is bringing the right energy to your life. You no longer look to the reactions of others, the booming voice of fear, nor your knee-jerk reaction to "fix and enable" as signs to follow, determining your next steps. Instead, you look within; you get quiet and reconnect with who and what is most important to you. Then, and only then, do you confidently take those next steps forward in alignment with your boundaries. You don't need to drown out the voices and the noise anymore, because you're no longer even *listening* for their approval.

    It's not that you know *best*. It's that you know *yourself* best. And that, my dear, is all that has ever mattered.

Acknowledgments

For those of you who absorbed my message in *Decision Permission*, you know that my first book was mostly logical self-help, sometimes humorous, and partially vulnerable. So to jump into a full-blown memoir filled with deep thoughts and language typically reserved for my *inner* monologues was likely startling for you too! Thank you for valuing *me* and my writing exactly as we are, and thank you for connecting so genuinely with me over these years. I hope to learn more about each person who reads and connects with this book and its message, encouraging you to be exactly who *you* are meant to be.

To Michael Braun and everyone at Orange Hat Publishing and Ten16 Press, and to fellow author Amy Sazama. My submission came from the glowing reviews I had heard of your people and your organization, and they were entirely accurate. Your expertise is only matched by your genuine love for the people behind the pen, and I thank you all for hearing my voice even before we had the opportunity to speak to one another. Also, thank you to my cover designer Dana Breunig for taking this journey with me to discover how PEMB could speak to readers even before they opened the cover.

To the past boyfriends and bachelors who were depicted *mostly* as they were, but with a bit of literary flair to account for my dramatic perspective at that age. Thank you for being a part of my journey and for helping me realize that it is possible to be a crucial part of someone's life and not end up with that person in the end.

To the lovely coffee shops and cozy spots that provided a temporary home where an author like me could get lost in writing her memoir. This book has traveled in my mind, in a Word document, and in my Notes app within all of your lovely businesses. PEMB was born within the welcoming walls of East View Coffee, Anna's on the Lake, Blak Coffee, The Buzz Café, Colectivo, The Coffee House, the Charleston Harbor Resort, The Captain's Quarter, and sunny spots in my home.

Thank you to *most* of the teachers who I anonymously shared about in this book. Some were captured verbatim, exactly as I remember them, and some were melded together—the blend of the best parts of caring educators who gave so much more than the job required. Whether you shared your gift with me in elementary, middle, high school, undergraduate, or graduate school, your impact continues to last a lifetime. You have inspired me, and your words continue to encourage me to this day. You have made, and you continue to make, a difference.

To every badass woman who lives her life the best way she knows how. Thank you for the inspiration you provide simply by being in your presence—especially my dear family friend, Jane, who passed during the writing of this book. You set boundaries others only dream of, and you imparted that same wisdom to your children. I can only "Wish Upon a Star" to be as much of a badass as you were. To the women who made the time to support this book through your genuine reflections—Molly, Kimberly, Candace, Brooke, Willow, Amy, and my mom—thank you for caring so deeply and supporting me so unconditionally. And to every woman who is *seeking* the badass from within, trust your journey and stay open to what the universe has in store—"She" does some amazing shit when you're ready for Her gifts.

To the friends mentioned in this book and those whose presence is found between the lines—Amanda, Aimee, Haley, Matthew, Janette, Keri, Evelyn, Jessie V., and so many more beautiful people I have been blessed to share this life with. Thank you for the way you have shown up in my life just when I needed you. I only hope that I can continue to learn how to be a similar presence in your lives, supporting you as you have supported me.

To Jeanette and Mick for sharing your cozy and inspiring AirBnB/ writing studio with me. Your "Captain's Quarters" provided the perfect, quiet location where I could pour myself into this memoir. You are beautiful people, thoughtful friends, and you are going to make fantastic parents (*ARE fantastic parents, since baby will be here by publishing!*).

To my family who have to deal with a *very* open wife, mom, daughter, daughter-in-law, sister-in-law, niece, and cousin. Thank you for always staying curious about my evolution as a person and as a mom. Thank you for understanding that my intentions are always good. And thank you for inviting me to show up just as I need to. Your unconditional love is a rare thing in this world, and I can only hope to encourage you, as you have encouraged me, to bring your truest self to our family and the world, knowing that we will always be there for one another.

To my mom for being the first to read this book and for responding to my idea in true Lorelai Gilmore fashion: "No. Absolutely not." ...And then for rescinding that demand, just as Lorelai did when Rory was adamant about writing a book about their lives. Thank you, Mom, for understanding that I have stories inside of me that *have* to come out, not only for my own mental health, but so that others can learn from the extraordinary relationship that you and I continue to journey through together. And to my dad for the unapologetic way that you always support my adventures in life. You never ask "Why?"; you only ask, "What do you need?" Your life has been a master class in teaching me what it means to love and be loved.

To my children—Jonah, Ella, Andrew, and Logan. Thank you for your patience with my *impatience* and your support and celebration of this adventure I call writing. I hope (*when you're older*) that reading this book reminds you that I love each of you exactly as you choose to show up in this world. Your potential knows no limits—may you always feel free to fully discover what life holds for you.

To my husband, Michael. For every time you told me, "Go write." For every time you listened and provided your brilliant insight. For every time you honor my boundaries and vulnerably share your own. Thank you for bringing your best self to our marriage and supporting me to do the same. You are my favorite person. I love the shit out of you.

And finally, to God, Jesus, Mary, and *all* the saints. I may not be Catholic with a capital "C" anymore, but my Christian faith is unwavering, and that's because of the foundation you gave me way back in Catholic school. Please forgive me for my crass remarks, my foul language, and my belief that you gave me both as gifts to unpretentiously connect with your people to help them define or redefine a faith of their own. *This little light of mine, I'm gonna let it shine...*

About the Author

Kristy Jean is a blended mom of four, wife, educational leader, speaker, and author whose mission is to help all of us redefine and live our most authentic lives. She values blending the expertise of education, business, and wellness professionals for a more holistic perspective in her personal and professional lives. Kristy lives in Wisconsin with her husband and four kids, where they explore the outdoors and compete in every card game imaginable.

Learn more: KJKristyJean.com
Social Media: @KJKristyJean

Author photograph: Tricia Rose Photography

www.ingramcontent.com/pod-product-compliance
Lightning Source LLC
Chambersburg PA
CBHW070527090426
42735CB00013B/2891